Ossa poetices:
A Cyclopedia of Early, Medieval and Renaissance Poetic Forms, Devices and Genres

STONEBUNNY PRESS

Ossa poetices: A Cyclopedia of Early, Medieval
and Renaissance Poetic Forms, Devices and Genres
Copyright © 2017 Todd H. C. Fischer

Published by Stonebunny Press
195 Drew Street, Oshawa, ON, L1H 5A4, Canada

Book design by Todd H. C. Fischer
Cover created by Mealnie E. Fischer.
Title font is Easy Lombardic.
Interior title font is Book Antiqua
Interior font is Book Antiqua

Visit our website at
www.stonebunnypress.ca

ISBN: 978-0-9947556-8-1

10 9 8 7 6 5 4 3 2 1

Published in Canada

Ossa poetices:
A Cyclopedia of Early, Medieval and Renaissance Poetic Forms, Devices and Genres

Todd H. C. Fischer

Other Books by Stonebunny Press

Poetry

Blue City by Dale Percy

Medieval Recreation

The Book of Chivalry of Sir Nigel MacFarlane by Todd H. C. Fischer

A Knight on Vigil by Finnvarr de Taahe

The Dialogue of Chivalry of Duke Finnvarr de Taahe by Finnvarr de Taahe

Fifty Years of Recreating the Middle Ages: A History of the Society for Creative Anachronism by Steven Muhlberger / Finnvarr de Taahe

Medieval History

On the Road in the Hundred Year War: Tales from Froissart Volume 1 by Steven Muhlberger

Folklore

A Canadian Bestiary by Todd H. C. Fischer

Horror

Deadstock by Ian Rogers

Fiction

The Other Voice by K. D. Miller

Ossa poetices:
A Cyclopedia of Early, Medieval and Renaissance Poetic Forms, Devices and Genres

Dedication

To Melanie: my muse and inspiration.
The sun rises in her eyes.

Acknowledgements

Thank you to the following academics who took the time to send me leads to pursue: Catherine McKenna, the Margaret Brooks Robinson Professor and Chair of Celtic Languages and Literatures at Harvard University; David Klausner, Professor emeritus of English and Medieval Studies, University of Toronto; and Damian Mc Manus, Chair of Early Irish, Head of Department (Irish), Chair of Early Irish, Head of Department (Centre for Irish-Scottish Studies), Trinity College Dublin (The University of Dublin).

Also thank you to the following for their unwavering support over the years: Gabrielle Underwood, Karina Bates, Marie l'Englois, Susan Carroll-Clark and—as always—Melanie Fischer.

Introduction

This book is called *Ossa poetices* (which is Latin for "the bones of poetry") as it is dedicated to the "bones" that made up medieval poetry (the genres, the poetic devices, and the stanzaic forms). As the words chosen by the poet's gave their work its flesh, that flesh was built around these bones.

It should be noted that the purpose of this volume is not to study in-depth the history of poetry and poetic structure or technique, but rather to look at the actual construction of medieval[1] poetry, with a particular eye to then writing modern poems in a medieval style. We are more interested in learning how to construct a poem in (say) a 14th century German style than in knowing who invented the stanza form we're using (though sometimes that information will also be noted).

This book was originally developed as a tool for my own use as no other book like it seemed to exist. I belong to a medieval recreation association, and as part of my participation in that group I have dedicated myself to the art of poetry. This book was originally intended to be a short work that I could print off and carry with me for easy reference so that, when at an event, if the muse struck, I would have this information on hand. However, when other people in my association saw my

---

[1] Please note that when I use the term Medieval in this volume I am referring to Europe from approximately 600 BCE to 1600 BCE.

initial draft they encouraged me to expand the scope of my manuscript and what you see now is the end result.

That said, even though this volume is now larger than I had originally intended, it is by no means exhaustive. There are likely dozens of forms, devices and genres I still need to gather information on. You will notice also that I have focused only on Medieval Europe (as this is my geographic area of focus) but other areas also had rich poetic traditions. As well, I have so far declined to include the poetic forms of Greece (such as odes) as I think information on those forms and genres is fairly easy to find already. There are also unfortunately holes in the information contained herein, especially in concern to the time certain forms developed and sometimes even where it developed. It seems that in scholarly works older than the past 40 or 50 years it was enough to simply say that something was medieval and to not document the date any further than that. Hopefully such holes will be filled in future editions.

With each entry's you will find a list cultures that made use of the entry, as well as a note as to whether the entry is a form, genre or device, the country of origin (if known) and the century in which the entry appeared (if known).

Within the context of this volume I have used the following definitions:

Form: A form is the structure of the poem, which may, depending on the style, include specific meters, rhyme schemes and use of other literacy devices (such as alliteration, assonance, and so on). Forms evolved over time and therefore many poems you may encounter while studying and reading medieval poetry will not seem to fit their form's commonly accepted construction. Within the entry for a form

- An unstressed syllable is shown as an x
- A stressed syllable is shown as a forward slash /
- An optional unstressed syllable is shown as an x within parentheses (x)
- Bolded syllables belong to the same word

Genre: A genre is a division of literary composition based on aspects such as the form used for the composition, the subject matter included, the tone used, and so forth. Genres are often fluid and evolving, and many have several sub-genres (related but slightly different groupings).

Device: A poetic device is a technique used in the composition of a poem (such as tail rhyme, repetition, and so forth). Sometimes certain devices must be used when composing in certain forms (or genres). Included at the end of this volume is a glossary for easy reference of details of many devices and terms commonly used in medieval poetry.

You may wonder why, as part of my participation in my medieval association, I chose to study poetry. The easy answer is that I am a writer and poet in my everyday life, so I find the study of past forms of literature of interest. The more expansive answer is as follows.

Within my association there are essentially three "paths" one can follow: service (helping the association operate), martial (we study forms of medieval martial arts), and what we call arts and sciences (recreating medieval artistic and scientific practices). I had never thought of myself as especially creative within the context of my association (most people involved with arts and sciences create physical goods like clothing, weaving, furniture, food and the like). I have never been very good with my hands. I therefore happily threw myself into service and fighting. However, I developed some health conditions which impacted my participation on those fronts, and for a time I felt that I no longer had a place — a function — within our society.

Then a good friend, who knew that I wrote outside the association, asked me why I did not pursue recreating medieval forms of literature. In my early years of membership I had written some poems and stories regarding the club but I had not endeavored to do so in a medieval style. With the encouragement of several people I therefore began to study diplomatics (which is the field of study of documents which looks at punctuation, language, structure, materials, seals, handwriting and all other aspects of the document, both physical (like the kind of material the document is written on) to the stylistic (what hand was it written in). I began to write texts for use within the club based on what I learned, and in doing so, found myself drawn to medieval poetry.

In many medieval societies (especially early ones such as the Norse, Anglo-Saxon and early Irish) poets were very important people. Not only did they sing songs, recite poems and tell stories, but they also recorded genealogies, kept records of history and spread important information. They praised the worthy and they publicly chastised those who deserved it.

As time went on, rules were developed to formalize how these bards, scops and skalds plied their craft. In Ireland the bardic tradition was entwined with that of the Druidic. Religion and poetry went hand-in-hand.

As the centuries rolled by and new kingdoms arose, the role of poet remained strong, with many artists vying to hold a position at some noble court. There was prestige in being a Meistersinger in Germany, a makar in Scotland or a troubadour in Occitania. The poet occupied a very important place in their society.

This then allowed me to find a space within my association. I began to keep genealogies of our members, chronicles of our own histories, written to emulate medieval styles. Likewise I began to write poetry in medieval styles.

This book then is for other modern day poets striving to recreate the medieval world through poetry. For my fellow modern trouvères, skalds, scops and versifiers--I hope you find this volume of some use.

FORMS, GENRES AND DEVICES

A

Ae freslighe

Form
Country of Origin: Ireland
Distribution: Irish
Century: examples dated from 5th century and beyond

Ae freslighe (pronounced ay fresh lee) were quatrains consisting of 7-syllable lines. Lines one and three had a triple rhyme (three syllables) while lines two and four had a double rhyme (two syllables). The poem should end with the first syllable or repeat the first line (*dunadh*). Each line should have two alliterated words. According to one source, a poem written in **ae freslighe** should not exceed four stanzas.[2]

x x x x **x x a**
x x x x x **x b**
x x x x **x x a**
x x x x x **x b**

Aicill

Device
Country of Origin: Ireland
Distribution: Irish
Century: examples dated from 12th century to possibly as late as 19th century[3]

---

[2] Poets World-wide: 12.

[3] The date the *aicill* fell out of use is currently unknown.

Aicill is a rhyme scheme where the final word of one line rhymes with either the beginning word or an internal word in the next line.

For instance:

> He was a man both strong and **tall**,
> Who, come the **fall**, would travel *round*
> To hallowed *ground*, and there kneel down
> etc.[4]

Below is an example in Irish:

> Cnoc lánmhar longhair **líonmhar**
> Paeon **fhíonmhar** fhonnmhar ághmar.[5]

Airdrinn
Device
Country of Origin: Ireland
Distribution: Irish
Century: unknown

In *deibide* meters, **airdrinn** (meaning 'high end') is a term that indicates a word with an unstressed syllable (or syllables) that thymes with the whole of another word.

Aiste
Device
Country of Origin: Ireland

---

[4] By the author.

[5]

http://www.scoilgaeilge.org/academics/mairead/EarlyIrishLiterature/TheLanguageof
Poetry.htm, February 22, 2016

Distribution: Irish
Century: unknown

A blanket term used to describe any meter.

Alba
Genre
Country of Origin: Occitania (southern France, Monaco, Italy, Spain)
Distribution: Occitan
Century: 12th to early 14th centuries

A genre of Old Occitan lyric poetry which depicts a pair of lovers who are lamenting the fact that they must part as the sun is rising. These lovers are usually afraid of being discovered by their respective spouses. **Alba**, in fact, means "sunrise". They often contain stock character such as the guard (*gualta*) who is the one that alerts the lovers that they must part, and the jealous rival (*lauzengiers*).

The German minnesingers developed a similar style known as the *tagelied*.

Albas tend to have no fixed metrical rate. They are broken into stanzas, with each stanza usually ending with the word dawn (*alba*).

Below is the first stanza of *Reis glorios, verais lums e clartatz* by Guiraut de Bornelh (1138-1215), in Old Occitan:

> Gaita be, gaiteta del chastel,
> Quan la re que plus m'es bon e bel
> Ai a me trosqu'a l'alba.
> E.l jornz ve e non l'apel!
> Joc novel

Mi tol l'alba,
L'alba, oi l'alba.[6]

[Ward well, little warden of the castle,
since the thing that is to me the best and fairest
is mine until dawn.
And the day comes, uncalled for!
The dawn
takes a new embrace away from me,
the dawn, alas, the dawn!][7]

Alejandrino
(Form, Catalan)

See *cuaderna via*.

Alexandrine
Form
Country of Origin: France
Distribution: French
Century: 12th – 19th centuries

An **alexandrine** is a line of poetry with 12-syllables. They were commonly used in Baroque German and early modern French poetry.

In French, the line is commonly divided into two equal parts by a caesura. Sometimes they may be divided into three 4-syllable sections.

6

http://www.trobar.org/troubadours/raimbaut_de_vaqueiras/raimbaut_de_vaqueiras_25.php, February 22, 2016

[7] Ibid.

x x x x x x | x x x x x x

x x x x | x x x x | x x x x

In English it is usually iambic.

x / x / x / x /

For instance here is an English **alexandrine**:

> I *want* to *go* to *bed* and *sleep* the *deep*est *sleep*[8]

Amas
Device
Country of Origin: Ireland
Distribution: Irish
Century: examples found by 12th century to as late as the 19th century[9]

Amas is a rhyme scheme relying on assonance. However, it would appear that the consonants that follow the vowel sounds do not need to be similar. In regular assonance rhyming words tend to be similar in construction (eye, my, pry) where as in **amas** the word "neck" assonates with "met". This is conjecture on my part as I have only found one definition of **amas** so far, and it was not very clear.

Amarouse
(Form, French)

See *chant royal*.

---

[8] By the author.

[9] The date that *amas* fell out of use is currently unknown.

Amra

Genre
Country of Origin: Ireland
Distribution: Irish
Century: examples from at least the 7th century

An **amra** is an elegiac verse usually written about a local saint. An example of an **amra** is the *Amra Cholium Chille* by Dalán Forgaill (c. 530-598), which appears to be using the *amas* rhyme scheme in certain sections.

> Fil suil nglais
> fégbas Erinn dara hais.
> noco n-acébá íarmothá
> firu Érend nách a mmna.[10]

> [There is a grey eye
> That will view Eriu backwards :
> By no means will it see afterwards
> The men of Eriu or its women.] [11]

Ard

Device
Country of Origin: Ireland
Distribution: Irish
Century: unknown

The final connsonating or rhymed foot in *rinnard* is called an **ard**.

---

[10] http://www.ucc.ie/celt/online/G301900/text003.html, February 24, 2016

[11] https://archive.org/stream/cu31924029424797/cu31924029424797_djvu.txt, February 24, 2016

Arte mayor
Form
Country of Origin: Castile (Spain)
Distribution: Castilian
Century: 14th – 16th centuries

Arte mayor is a line of nine or more syllables, though it is also the name of a strophe made up of such lines. The basic pattern was of an 8, 10 or 12-beat line divided into two hemistiches of four, five or six beats each and employing triple rhyme (so an *a*, a *b* and a *c* rhyme). The primary and secondary stress beats of each hemistich are supplied by accented syllables while the unstressed beats between them are supplied by two unaccented syllables. The remaining unstressed beats may each be supplied by one or two unaccented syllables or a rest beat. However, this pattern was not always strictly followed. This can be represented thusly:

(x) x x x / (x) | (x) x x x / (x)[12]

Two other arrangements (with the last being rare) are:

(x) x x x / x x | x x x / (x)
(x) x x x / | x x x x x / (x)[13]

They were normally collected into groups of 8 lines (called *copla de arte mayor*) and rhymed abbaacca. A less common rhyme scheme was ababbcb while other even less common rhyme schemes occurred.

12

http://search.proquest.com/openview/012684fa8883d070c9ef23de11eabfd1/1?pq-origsite=gscholar, February 24, 2016

13 Ibid.

Arte menor

Form
Country of Origin: Castile (Spain)
Distribution: Castilian
Century: 14th – 16th centuries

Arte menor is a short line of poetry, numbering two to eight syllables (though usually octosyllabic). The line usually only has one accent, which is on the penultimate syllable. The **arte menor** is a shortened version of *arte mayor* and literally means "lesser art".

(x) (x) (x) (x) (x) (x) / x

Atchiu fer find

Device
Country of Origin: Ireland
Distribution: Irish
Century: Unknown

According to my only source for this term[14], this is used to describe when an accented rhyme word could appear in the first or second of a pair of rhyme words or when verse ends were not regulated by syllables.

However, I have not been able to verify this with any other source. What I have found is that "Atchiu fer find" is actually the opening line of a lay addressed to Medb in *Táin Bó Cúailgne* (a pre-12th century Old Irish epic).[15]

---

[14] suburbanbanshee.net/irishptr/drchpoem/debhide.html, February 25, 2016

[15] http://adminstaff.vassar.edu/sttaylor/Cooley/Foretelling.html, February 25, 2016

Aubade

Genre
Country of Origin: Occitania (southern France, Monaco, Italy, Spain)
Distribution: Occitan
Century: 12th - 19th centuries

An **aubade** is a morning love song, or a song or poem about lovers separating at dawn. Strictly speaking, to be a true **aubade**, the poem should be directed towards a sleeping woman from a door or window. An *alba* is one type of **aubade**.

An example of an **aubade** is a poem named after the style by William Shakespeare:

> HARK! Hark! The lark at heaven's gate sing,
>   And Phoebus 'gins arise,
> His steeds to water at those springs
>   On chaliced flowers that lies;
> And winking Mary-buds begin
>   To ope their golden eyes:
> With everything that pretty bin,
>   My lady sweet, arise!
>   Arise, arise![16]

Awdl

Form
Country of Origin: Wales
Distribution: Welsh
Century: 6th – 15th centuries

---

[16] http://www.poemhunter.com/poem/aubade-2/, May 9, 2016

An **awdl** (pronounced ow'-dul; plural *awdiau*) is a long poem (*awdiau* could feature thousands of lines) that featured a single end-rhyme, and used one of the **awdl** meters. (**Awdl**, like *odl*, means rhyme.) During the 11th to 13th century the royal court poets developed the art to a highly sophisticated level with twenty-four strict meters codified in 1282 (see *cerdd dafod*). There were two **awdl** line forms, and eight **awdl** stanza forms.

Rhupunt (pronounced ree'-pihnt): *Rhupunt* were lines consisting of three to five sections with four syllables per section. The last two sections of the line feature cross alliteration. The next line uses c rhymes in place of a rhymes. These internal rhymes remain within the line while the end b rhyme connects not internally but with the next line's end rhyme.

x x x a x x x a (x x x a x x x a) x x x b
x x x c x x x c (x x x c x x x c) x x x b

Cyhydedd hir (pronounced cuh-hih'deth here): These were two lines comprised of three 5- syllable sections that shared an end rhyme, followed by a four syllable section with a new end rhyme. The next line uses c rhymes in place of a rhymes. These internal rhymes remain within the line while the end b rhyme connects not internally but with the next line's end rhyme. Alternatively, the lines can be displayed as two quatrains.

Version 1
x x x x a x x x x a x x x x a x x x b
x x x x c x x x x c x x x x c x x x b

OR

Version 2

x x x x a
x x x x a
x x x x a
x x x b

x x x x c
x x x x c
x x x x c
x x x b

Cyhydedd fer (pronounced cuh-hih'deth ver): Consisted of two 8-syllable lines with end rhyme.

x x x x x x x a
x x x x x x x a

The concluding lines of the anonymous Welsh poem "Huntsong for a Small Son" (here translated into English) are written in *cyhydedd fer*:

> This is no boast, this is no lie —
> If it escapes, then it can fly.[17]

Byr a thoddaid (pronounced bir ah thoth'-ayd): Consisted of either an 8-syllable line (with a *gair cyrch*), followed by a 6-syllable line, and then two 8-syllable lines, or two 8-syllables lines followed by an 8-syllable line (with a *gair cyrch*) and 6-syllable line. (Though some state it is either three 8-syllable lines — the last with a *gair cyrch* — and a 5-syllable line, or an 8-syllable line with *gair cyrch*, a 6-syllable line, and two more 8-syllable lines.[18]) In all versions the *gair cyrch* alliterates,

---

[17] Lines 17-18. Lewis Turco: 276.

[18] http://www.poetrymagnumopus.com/index.php?/topic/973-15-byr-a-thoddaid/, April 6, 2016

assonates or shares secondary rhyme with the beginning of the next line. The *caesura* before the *gair cyrch* could be shown as a dash.

I have seen scholars and poets give this form two different rhyme schemes. Lewis Turco and others give the following:

Version 1

x x x x x x a x b   OR

b x x x x a

x x x x x x x c

x x x x x x x c

Version 2

x x x x x x x a

x x x x x x x a

x x x x x x x b x c

x c x x x b[19]

Others show:

Version 3

x x x x x x a x b   OR

x x b x x a

x x x x x x x a

x x x x x x x a

Version 4

x x x x x x x a

x x x x x x x a

x x x x x x x a x b

x b x x x a[20]

You will note that structurally the examples are the same, but they have different rhyme schemes. Since **awdls** were supposed to be monorhymed, the second example is probably more correct.

Clogyrnach (pronounced clog-ir'-nach): Consisted of two 8-syllable lines, followed by two 5 syllable lines and two 3-syllable lines. The last four lines could also be written in one like similar to a *rhupunt*.

---

[19] Lewis Turco: 139.

[20]   http://www.poetrymagnumopus.com/index.php?/topic/973-15-byr-a-thoddaid/, April 6, 2016; http://www.poetrybase.info/forms/000/26.shtml, April 6, 2016

Version 1		*Version 2*
x x x x x x x a	OR	x x x x x x x a
x x x x x x x a		x x x x x x x a
x x x x b		x x x x b x x x x b x x b x x a
x x x x b		
x x b		
x x a		

Cynddelw Brydedd Mawr (fl. c. 1155 – 1200) wrote a poem called "In Summer" using **clogyrnach**. An English translation is below, where the two 3-syllable lines have been collapsed into one line.

> Summer I love, stallions abroad,
> Knights courageous before their lord,
> The comer booming,
> Apple tree blooming,
> Shield shining, war-shouldered.
>
> Longing, I went craving, alack —
> The bowing of the slim hemlock,
> In bright noon, dawn's sleight;
> Fair frail smooth, white,
> Her step light on the stalk.
>
> Silent is the small deer's footfall,
> Scarcely older than she is tall,
> Comely, beautiful
> And bred bountiful,
> Passion will heed her call.
>
> But no vile word will pass her lips.
> I pace, I plead — when shall we tryst?
> When will you meet me?
> Love drowns me deeply —

Christ keep me! He knows best![21]

Cyhydedd naw ban (pronounced cuh-hih'-deth): Consisted of two 9-syllable rhyming lines. This form would often use the same end rhyme for several lines in a row.

x x x x x x x x a
x x x x x x x x a

Toddaid (pronounced todd-eyed): Consisted of a 10-syllable line ending in a gair cyrch followed by a 9-syllable line. The end of the first line rhymed with the end of the second line, while the end of the *gair cyrch* rhymed with one of the middle syllables in the second line. The *caesura* before the *gair cyrch* could be shown as a dash. Sometimes this form was used in combination with a cyhydedd hir or a 9-line couplet.

x x x x x x a x x b
x x x b x x x x a *

* (The b rhyme could be any of the middle syllables.)

The following is an excerpt from an English translation of "Huntsong for a Small Son", an anonymous Welsh poem written mostly in *toddaid*:

> Dinogad's coat is specked with spots —
> I made it out of pelts of stoats.
> Flingabout, fling! Flingabout, flingabout!
> Eight times the song we'll sing.[22]

---

[21] Lewis Turco: 153.

[22] Lines 1-4. Lewis Turco: 276.

Gwawdodyn (pronounced gwaw-dod'-in): There are two versions of the *gwawdodyn*. The first consisted of two 9-syllable lines, followed by a *toddaid* (a 10-syllable line that ended in a gair cyrch, and another 9-syllable line). The *caesura* before the *gair cyrch* could be shown as a dash. All four lines share end rhyme, while the *gair cyrch* rhymed with one of the middle syllables in the second line. The second form consisted of two 9-syllable lines followed by *cyhydedd hir* broken into two lines (a 10-syllable line with internal rhyme that also shares internal rhyme with the second 9-syllable line).

With toddaid

x x x x x x x x a
x x x x x x x x a
x x x x x x x a x b
x x x b x x x x a *

* (The b rhyme could be any of the middle syllables.)

OR

With cyhydedd hir

x x x x x x x x a
x x x x x x x x a
x x x x b x x x x b
x x x x b x x x a

Gwawdodyn hir (pronounced gwaw-dod'-in here): Consisted of four 9-syllable lines, followed by a 10-syllable line ending in a gair cyrch, followed by another 9-syllable line. The *gair cyrch* had to rhyme and not just alliterate with an internal rhyme in the following line. The *caesura* before the *gair cyrch* could be shown as a dash.

x x x x x x x x a

x x x x x x x x a
x x x x x x x x a
x x x x x x x x a
x x x x x x a x x b
x x x b x x x x a (the b rhyme could be any of the middle syllables)

Hir a toddaid (pronounced here ah thoth'-ayd): Consisted of five 10-syllable lines, with the last ending in a *gair cyrch*, followed by a 9-syllable line. The *gair cyrch* had to rhyme and not just alliterate with an internal rhyme in the following line. The *caesura* before the *gair cyrch* could be shown as a dash.

x x x x x x x x x a
x x x x x x x x x a
x x x x x x x x x a
x x x x x x x x x a
x x x x x x a x x b
x x x b x x x x x a

Cyrch a chwta (pronounced kirch ah choo'ta): Consisted of six 7-syllable lines followed by an *awdl gwydd*.

x x x x x x a
x x x x x x a
x x x x x x a
x x x x x x a
x x x x x x a
x x x x x x a
x x x x x x b
x x x b x x a

Tawddgyrch cadwynog (pronounced towth'-girch cahd-win'-og): Consisted of four 8-syllable lines of four sections each, utilizing internal rhyme.

Version 1		*Version 2*
x x x a x x x b	OR	x x x a x x x b
x x x b x x x c		x x x b x x x a
x x x a x x x b		x x x a x x x b
x x x b x x x c		x x x b x x x a

One of the most famous *awdiau* is by Gruffydd ab yr Ynad Coch, written as an elegy for Llywelyn ap Gruffydd, Prince of Wales, in the late 13th century. An excerpt (in Welsh) is below:

> Oer gallon dan vron o vraw allwynin
> am vrenhin derwin dor Aberffraw.
> Eur dilyf yn a elit oe law,
> eur daleith oed deilwng idaw.
> Eurgryn eur deyrn nym daw llewenyd
> Llywelyn, nyt ryd ym rwyd wisgaw.[23]

> [The heart is cold under a breast of pitiful fear
>   for a king, the oaken door of Abberfraw.
> Fine gold was paid to us from his hand
> and he deserved the golden chaplet.
> Golden horns of a golden king do not bring me the joy
>   of Llywelyn; I am not free to arm as I would.][24]

Awdl gywydd
(Form, Welsh)

See *cywydd*.

---

[23] https://cy.wikisource.org/wiki/Marwnad_Llywelyn_ap_Gruffudd, February 25, 2016

[24] Gwyn Williams.

B

Bádud
Device
Country of Origin: Ireland
Distribution: Irish
Century: unknown

The Irish term for elision.

Balada
Form
Country of Origin: Provence (France)
Distribution: Provençal
Century: unknown

A **balada** is a dance song with no fixed form; however it has a refrain which is repeated several times in a stanza. The **balada** is almost indistinguishable from the *dansa* and is also known as *balaresc*.

One form of the **balada** would divide each stanza into three parts. The first and second part are identical, each ending with the same rhyme as the first line of the poem. The stanza's third part is identical to the refrain (*refranh*) in form. The refrain, which begins the **balada**, is repeated after each stanza.

Balaresc
(Form, Provençal)

See *balada*.

Ballad
Form
Country of Origin: English?
Distribution: across Europe
Century: 13th - 19th century

A form of verse, often narrative and set to music and derived from the *ballade* (French dancing songs), **ballads** were popular from the later medieval period to the 19th century.

Ballads were often composed in couplets with refrains in alternate lines. Those refrains would have been sung by the dancers in time to the music. Most northern and western European **ballads** were written in ballad stanza or quatrains of alternating lines of iambic tetrameter and iambic trimeter (known as *ballad meter*). The rhyme scheme was usually abcb. However, there was considerable variety with length, number of lines and rhyming scheme. **Ballads** would often repeat the fourth lines of succeeding stanzas as a refrain, or the third and fourth lines of a stanza and sometimes even of entire stanzas.

The narratives of the **ballads** tend to deal with tragic, historical, romantic or comic themes and rely heavily on imagery. Ribald **ballads** featuring rural labourers and details of their sexuality are common.

Below are the first two stanzas of a ballad called "The Three Ravens" which is a traditional English folk ballad. It was included in a song book called *Melismata*, which was compiled by Thomas Ravenscroft and printed in 1611. This particular ballad consists of stanzas starting with a quatrain rhyming abab followed by a tercet rhyming aab. It also employs repetition as a refrain (though the lines are slightly different).

There were three rauens sat on a tree,
downe a downe, hay downe, hay downe,
There were three rauens sat on a tree,
with a downe,
There were three rauens sat on a tree,
They were as blacke as they might be.
With a downe, derrie, derrie, derrie, downe, downe.

The one of them said to his mate,
downe a downe, hay downe, hay downe,
The one of them said to his mate,
with a downe,
The one of them said to his mate,
Where shall we our breakfast take?
With a downe, derrie, derrie, derrie, downe, downe.[25]

Ballade
Form
Country of Origin: France
Distribution: French
Century: 13th - 15th centuries

Along with the *rondeau* and the *virelai*, the **ballade** is one of the *formes fixes*. Between the late 13th and the 15th centuries, **ballades** were often set to music.

The **ballade** is a verse form usually consisting of three 8-line stanzas, each with a consistent meter and a particular rhyme scheme. The last line in the stanza is a refrain. The stanzas are often followed by a 4-line *envoi* (concluding stanza), usually

---

[25]   http://www.springthyme.co.uk/ballads/balladtexts/26_ThreeRavens.html, February 26, 2016

addressed to a prince. The rhyme scheme is usually ababbcbC ababbcbC ababbcbC bcbC (the capital C being the refrain).

The musical form is a *bar form* (AAB) with a first repeated section (called a *stollen*) setting the two initial pairs of verses (rhyming ab-ab) and the second section (the *abgesang*) setting the remaining refrain verse (bcbC). The two statements of the A section have different endings (known as *ouvert* and *clos*), with the harmony on the *ouvert* and leading back to the beginning, while that of the *clos* ending leads forward into the B section. In many **ballades** the final part of the B section may reintroduce melodic material referring back to the end of the A part (which is known as "musical rhyme" or *rücklaufballade*). The *ballade duplex* or *balladelle* also has the B part divided into two repetitions, with the refrain line sung as part of the repetition.

A *ballade royal* is a 7-line ballade consisting of four stanzas of *rhyme royal*. All four stanzas employed the same three rhymes and ended in a refrain. There were no *envois*.

A *ballade supreme* consisted of 10-line stanzas rhyming ababbccdcD with the envoi rhyming ccdcD or ccdccD.

An example of the (regular) **ballade** is *Je puis trop bien ma dame comparer* by Guillaume de Machaut, written in the 14th century:

> Je puis trop bien ma dame comparer
> A l'image que fist Pymalion.
> D'ivoire fu estoit, tant belle et si sans per
> Que plus l'ama que Medée Jason.
> Li fols toudis la prioit,
> Mais l'image riens ne li respondoit.
> Einsi me fait celle qui mon cuer font,

Qu'adès la pri et riens ne me respont.

Pimalions qui moroit pour amer
Pria ses dieus par tele affection
Que la froideur de l'image tourner
Vit en chalour et sa dure fasson
Amolir, car vie avoit
Et char humeinne et doucement parloit.
Mais ma dame de ce trop m'i confont
Qu'adès la pri et riens ne me respont.

Or vueille Amours le dur en dous muer
De celle a qui j'ay fait de mong cuer don,
Et son franc cuer de m'amour aviver,
Si que de li puisse avoir guerredon.
Mais Amours en li conjoit
En fier desdaing, et le grand desir voit
Qui m'ocira; si croy que cil troiz font
Qu'adès la pri et riens ne me respont.[26]

Ballade duplex
(Form, French)

See *ballade*.

Ballade royal
(Form, French)

See *ballade*.

Ballade supreme
(Form, French)

---

[26] http://www.medieval.org/emfaq/composers/machaut/b28.html, February 26, 2016

See *ballade*.

Balladelle
(Form, French)

See *ballade*.

Ballata
Form
Country of Origin: Italy
Distribution: Italian
Century: late 13th – 15th centuries

This poetic and musical form was in use from the late 13th to the 15th century. It was one of the most prominent secular musical forms at the time. They were usually love poems, directed at the object of said love.

Its rhyme scheme is usually AbbaA, with the first and last stanzas having the same text. It is similar to the French *virelai* (not the *ballade*, as the name would suggest). The first and last A are called *aripresa* or *ripresa*, the b lines are *piedi* (feet), and the fourth line is a *volta*. Longer *ballate* (the plural of *ballata*) may be found with different rhyme schemes such as AbbaAbbaA. The two b lines usually have exactly the same music, though eventually they would have an open and close ending.

A **ballata** with a 1-line *ritornello* is called a *ballata piccolo*.

A **ballata** with a 2-line *ritornello* is called *ballata minore*.

A **ballata** with a 3-line *ritornello* is called *ballata mezzana*.

A **ballata** with a 4-line *ritornello* is called *ballata grande*.

A **ballata** with a 5-line *ritornello* is called *ballata stravagante*.

An example of longer single-stanza **ballata** (piccolo) by Francisco Petrarch (14th century) is *Ballata I*:

> Lassare il velo o per sole o per ombra.
> PERCEIVING HIS PASSION, LAURA'S SEVERITY INCREASES.
>
> Never thy veil, in sun or in the shade,
> Lady, a moment I have seen
> Quitted, since of my heart the queen
> Mine eyes confessing thee my heart betray'd
> While my enamour'd thoughts I kept conceal'd.
> Those fond vain hopes by which I die,
> In thy sweet features kindness beam'd:
> Changed was the gentle language of thine eye
> Soon as my foolish heart itself reveal'd;
> And all that mildness which I changeless deem'd—
> All, all withdrawn which most my soul esteem'd.
> Yet still the veil I must obey,
> Which, whatsoe'er the aspect of the day,
> Thine eyes' fair radiance hides, my life to overshade.
> [Capel Lofft.][27]

Ballata grande
(Form, Italian)

See *ballata*.

---

[27] http://www.gutenberg.org/files/17650/17650-h/17650-h.htm, February 26, 2016

Ballata mezanna
(Form, Italian)

See *ballata*.

Ballata minore
(Form, Italian)

See *ballata*.

Ballata piccolo
(Form, Italian)

See *ballata*.

Ballata stravagante
(Form, Italian)

See *ballata*.

Bar form
Form
Country of Origin: Germany
Distribution: Germany
Century: 12th – 18th centuries

The **bar form** was often used by the minnesingers of Germany. It was made up of a strophe (stanza) divided into two *stollen* (confusingly also referred to as stanzas, and collectively known as an *aufgesang*). They were followed by an *abesang* (the after-song). It was apparently not uncommon for the *stollen* to be of different lengths. Melodically, the *abesang* would mirror the end melody of the *aufgesang*. The **bar form** was usually represented as AAB (with the As being the two *stollen* and the B being the *abesang*).

An illustration of the bar form featuring a 14th century melody by Meistersinger Hans Folz.[28]

Below is a modern poem, written to be set to music using the bar form, and written to mimic the bar form's structure:

> From Eastern lands
> Glad tidings flow around the knowne worlde spann'd
> For Ysemay Sterlyng's deft and graceful hands
> Glad tidings flow around the knowne worlde spann'd
>
> For Eastern royals
> Will glad increase the standing of Their Laurels
> With Ysemay Sterlyng, both kind and loyal
> Will glad increase the standing of Their Laurels
>
> With Eastern grace
> She stands a Peer, forever in her place
> Bright Ysemay Sterlyng of the smiling face

---

[28] https://commons.wikimedia.org/wiki/File:Vielchenweise.svg, February 27, 2016

She stands a Peer, forever in her place[29]

Deconstructed, here is the first strophe of this poem:

Aufesang
[*Stollen 1*] From Eastern lands
[*Stollen 2*] Glad tidings flow around the knowne worlde
spann'd

Abesang
For Ysemay Sterlyng's deft and graceful hands
Glad tidings flow around the knowne worlde spann'd

Barzelleta
(Form, Italian)

See *frottola*.

Begging Poem
Genre
Country of Origin: across Europe
Distribution: across Europe
Century: 5th – 14th centuries

The begging poem existed in almost every culture with a poetic tradition, from the Anglo-Saxons to the 14th century. The begging poem, as the name would imply, is a poem where the writer is entreating a person to bestow money or goods upon them or another person. These poems could be written in any form.

---

[29] For Ysemay Sterlyng, on Becoming a Vigilant of the Order of the Laurel, by the author, 2015.

An example of an early English begging poem can be found in *Beowulf* (between 8th and 11th century), where Widsith addresses Hrothgar and reminds him that lords should be generous to guests. Widsith ends his poem by saying:

> Swa ic þæt symle onfand   on þære feringe,
> þæt se biþ leofast   londbuendum
> se þe him god syleð   gumena rice
> to gehealdenne,   þenden he her leofað.[30]

[So I always discovered in that wayfaring that the one most beloved to land-dwellers is he who gives them goods to maintain the kingdom of men while he lives here.][31]

A late period example of a begging poem is the following excerpt from a verse epistle written by Guillaume Crétin (c. 1460 – 30 November 1525):

> Quant a part moy je pense et me souvient
> Du temps passé, et de celluy qui vient,
> Que j'ay vescu, et qu'il fault que je vive,
> Et que le sort sur moy si mal advient,
> A peine scay que tout mon sens deviant,
> Craignant de veoir que paovreté s'ensuyve…[32]

[When I consider and remember times past and to come, that I have lied and yet must live through, and that fate treats me so poorly, I hardly know what will become of my sanity, fearing as I do to see poverty

---

[30] Dave Hendersen: 47.

[31] Ibid.

[32] Antony J. Hassler: 71.

follow...][33]

Bergerette
Form
Country of Origin: France
Distribution: French
Century: 14th – 18th centuries.

A **bergerette** was a *virelai* with only one stanza (or also possibly the only surviving stanza of a *virelai*). An 18th century example of a **bergerette** is *L'amour s'envole* (Ah, Love is but a Child):

> L'amour est un enfant, ti mi
> La sévérité lui fair peur.
> C'est la liberté qui le gui de
> Pour trouvert le chemin d'un couer.
> Tandis qu'il n'a rien à craindere,
> Les ris et les jeux sui vent ses pas;
> Mais dès qu'on le veut contraindre
> Il s'envole
> Et ne revient pas, et ne revient pas.
> L'amour est un enfant, ti mi
> La sévérité lui fair peur.
> C'est la liberté qui le gui de
> Pour trouvert le chemin d'un couer.[34]

> [Ah, love is but a child, don't chide him!
> Timid, at a harsh word he'll start.
> Freedom 'tis alone that may guide him
> On the highway of the heart.

---

[33] Ibid.

[34] J. B. Wekerlin: 4-6.

While his liberty enjoying,
Laughter gay and gladness swell his train;
If coercion you're employing
Off he'll fly
Nor return again, nor return again.
Ah, love is but a child, don't chide him!
Timid, at a harsh word he'll start.
Freedom 'tis alone that may guide him
On the highway of the heart.][35]

Johannes Ockeghem's famous "Ma maitresse" has been called both a *chanson*[36] and a **bergerette**[37], though it doesn't seem to conform exactly to either form. "Ma maitresse" consists of a refrain, followed by a stanza consisting of two tercets, a quintain (a stanza of five lines) and a repeat of a refrain. *Chansons* usually had five or six matching stanzas, and a **bergerette** (as mentioned above) was a single stanza. It is possible that the refrain is a **bergerette** with the following two stanzas added to it.

In the Old French, "Ma maitresse" reads:

Ma maistresse et ma plus grant amye
De mon desir la mortelle ennemye
Parfaite en biens s'onques mais le fut femme
Celle seule de qui court bruit et famme
D'estre sans per, ne vous veray je mye ?

Helas de vous bien plaindre me devroie

---

[35] Ibid.

[36] http://gloegeeg251.web.unc.edu/johannes-ockeghem/, February 29, 2016

[37] http://www.allmusic.com/composition/ma-maitresse-chanson-for-3-voices-mc0002410019, February 29, 2016

S'il ne vous plaist que briefment vous revoye
M'amour par qui d'aultre aimer n'ay puissance
Car sans vous voir en quelque part je soye
Tout ce que voys me desplaist et ennoye
Ne jusqu'alors je n'auray suffisance.

Incessament mon dolent cuer larmye
Doubtant qu'en vous pitie soit endormye
Qui ja ne soit ma tant amee dame
Mais s'aincy est si malheureux me clame
Que plus ne quiers vivre heure ne demye.

Ma maistresse et ma plus grant amye
De mon desir la mortelle ennemye
Parfaite en biens s'onques mais le fut femme
Celle seule de qui court bruit et famme
D'estre sans per ne vous veray je mye.[38]

[My mistress and my greatest love
Mortal enemy of my desire
Perfect in good things if ever woman was
She alone whom fame and reputation hold
To be peerless -- shall I never see you again?

Alas, I ought indeed to complain of you
If you aren't willing to see me again briefly,
My love, because of whom I have no power to love
        another;
For without seeing you, wherever I am
Everything I see displeases and irritates me.
Not till then [when I see you] will I be satisfied.

Unceasingly my grieving heart weeps,

[38] http://www.lieder.net/lieder/get_text.html?TextId=92560, February 29, 2016

Suspecting that in you pity has fallen asleep,
You who may never be my beloved lady;
But if it is so, I call myself so unfortunate
That I wish to live not an hour -- or half an hour –
    longer.

My mistress and my greatest love
Mortal enemy of my desire
Perfect in good things if ever woman was
She alone whom fame and reputation hold
To be peerless -- shall I never see you again?][39]

Bispel
Genre
Country of Origin: Germany
Distribution: German
Century: Unknown

A short narrative used to illustrate a moral point (a fable).

Blason
Genre
Country of Origin: France
Distribution: French
Century: 16th century

The **blason** is an ordered poem of praise, or blame, usually directed towards a woman and praised her physical features using metaphors. The genre takes its name from the heraldic term "blazon" which forms the root of the word "emblazon" which means to celebrate or adorn (with heraldic markings). Though the term is from the 16th century, similar poems were

---

[39] Ibid.

being written by at least the 13th century.

A famous example of a **blason** is the poem "There Is a Garden in Her Face" by Thomas Campion (1567-1620):

> There is a garden in her face
> Where roses and white lilies grow;
> A heav'nly paradise is that place
> Wherein all pleasant fruits do flow.
> There cherries grow which none may buy,
> Till "Cherry ripe" themselves do cry.
>
> Those cherries fairly do enclose
> Of orient pearl a double row,
> Which when her lovely laughter shows,
> They look like rose-buds fill'd with snow;
> Yet them nor peer nor prince can buy,
> Till "Cherry ripe" themselves do cry.
>
> Her eyes like angels watch them still,
> Her brows like bended bows do stand,
> Threat'ning with piercing frowns to kill
> All that attempt with eye or hand
> Those sacred cherries to come nigh,
> Till "Cherry ripe" themselves do cry.[40]

Blasonner
(Genre, French)

See *blazon*.

Blasonneur

---

[40] http://www.units.miamioh.edu/visualrhetoric/blason.html, February 27, 2016

See *blazon*.

Brag
Genre
Country of Origin: unknown
Distribution: across Europe
Century: unknown

A **brag** is a poem in which the speaker — unsurprising — boasts about something.

See also *rant*.

Breccbairdne
Form
Country of Origin: Ireland
Distribution: Irish
Century: unknown

Breccbairdne were quatrains consisting of one 5-syllable line followed by three 6-syllable lines. They rhymed xaxa xbxb (and so on, where the x lines do not rhyme). All end words have two syllables. The poem concludes with *dunadh*.

x x x **x x**
x x x x **x a**
x x x x **x x**
x x x x **x a**

Breton lai
(Genre, French)

See *Breton lay*.

Breton lay

Genre
Country of Origin: France
Distribution: French, English
Century: 12th – 14th centuries

Lays, popular in both French and English literature, were short rhymed tales of love and chivalry usually numbering between 600 and 1000 lines. They often involve motifs from the supernatural and Celtic mythology. Arthurian tales were popular.

The **Breton lay** is the term the English applied to the *lai* genre in the 14th century.

Breton musical lays are believed to be the precursor of this genre and were of Celtic origin. They are thought to have been more lyrical in style and to be introduced by a summary narrative (though none have survived).

An example of the **Breton lay** is the anonymous *Sir Orfeo* (c. 1330) which reads in part:

> Orfeo was a king,
> In Inglond an hei3 e lording,
> A stalworþ man & hardi bo,
> Large & curteys he was also.
> His fader was comen of king Pluto
> & his moder of king Juno
> Þat sum time were as godes yhold
> For auentours þat þai dede & told.[41]

---

[41] http://auchinleck.nls.uk/mss/orfeo.html, March 16, 2016

Breton musical lay
(Genre, French)

See *Breton lay*.

Breton Romance
Genre
Country of Origin: France
Distribution: French
Century: 12th – 14th centuries

The **Breton romance** was a metrical *romance*, emphasizing love and drawing on courtly love and legend such as King Arthur and Tristan. Likely another name for a *Breton lay*.

Brúilingeacht
(Form, Irish)

See *dán díreach*.

Büchlein
Form
Country: Germany
Distribution: German
Centuries: unknown

A **büchlein** was an epistolary poem (that is, a poem written as a missive or letter). Ulrich von Liechtenstein, a famous knight, is known to have written a **büchlein** for a princess whose heart he desired[42].

Bylina

---

[42] Loius Barbé: 754.

Form
Country of Origin: Russia, Ukraine
Distribution: Slavic
Century: 10th – 13th century

Byliny (which is the plural) are a traditional East Slavic form that contained 10-syllable lines and was broken into three sections (an Introduction, the Narrative and an Epilogue). The introduction usually introduces the hero being given some sort of a quest. The narrative details the tasks taken on by the hero to complete his mission and the epilogue shows the hero gaining his reward. Byliny were likely originally written by court minstrels. They tended to be loosely based on fact but were embellished with fantastical elements.

Most byliny were a few hundred lines in length, unrhymed and written in free verse. However, each line only had two or three stressed syllables, usually with the first stress on the third syllable and the last stress on the third from last syllable.

The term **bylina** is a 19th century creation. It seems that at the time they were written they were likely called *starina* or "songs of old times".

One famous **bylina** was called *Sadko* and begins:

> In Novgorod, in famous Novgorod,
> There lived Sadko the merchant, the rich guest.
> But formerly Sadko had no property,
> He only had his maple gusli.
> Sadko used to go and play at feasts.
> The first day they didn't invite Sadko to a feast of honor,
> The second they didn't invite him to a feast of honor,
> And the third they didn't invite him to a feast of honor.

Because of this Sadko grew sick at heart.[43]

Byr a thoddaid
(Form, Welsh)

See *awdl*.

---

[43] http://www.artrusse.ca/Byliny/sadko.htm, February 28, 2016

C

Cabeza
(Form, Spanish)

See *estribillo*.

Caccia
Form/genre
Country of Origin: Italy
Distribution: Italian
Century: 14th century

These poems were about aristocratic outdoor activities (such as hunting, fishing, dancing or even battle). Sometimes the hunting motive was used to depict sexual conquest. As a form they have short lines and include a final refrain. The body of the **caccia** was an undetermined series of uneven verses, a wide variety of meters, and could be written with or without rhymes or assonance. If set to music, it would employ two or more voices repeating the same melody and words at a distance of three or more beats. It is sometimes compared to the *frotolla*. Some early **caccia** were written as *madrigals*[44].

An example of a **caccia**, here translated into English, is by Franco Sacchetti (c. 1355 – c. 1400):

---

[44] Roland Greene: 173.

ONCE, deep in thought, I, passing 'neath some trees,
Beheld a troop of maidens gathering flowers;
One cried: 'Ah look'; another: 'Nay, see these,'
'What hast thou there? ' 'I doubt not lily-showers.'
'And here, I trow, are violets blue.'
A rose — woe's me, a thorn hath pricked my finger
through! '
'Alas, alas! '
What's that in the grass? '
'A cricket.' 'Make haste,
Here are salads to taste.'
'No, no! '
'But it's so.'
'Thee and thee I will show
Where the mushrooms do grow:
And this is the way
For the wild-thyme spray.'
'Come homewards, it darkeneth and soon it will rain,
It lightens, it thunders, hark! vespers again! '
'But it's early still! '
'Lend an ear if you will.'
'The nightingale, I'll be bound.'
'I hear a louder sound.'
' 'Tis strange to me.'
'O what can it be? '
'Where, where? '
'Out there? '
'In the bushes.' Tic, toc.
Ever nearer the knock,
Till a snake crept out:
Then they turned about
In a wild affright:
'Ah me, sorry plight! '
'Alack aday! '
'Flee away! '

Then the rain poured down forlorn,
One slipped, another fell,
One trod upon a thorn,
Bossoms were spilled pell-mell,
Some cast aside, some left to lie,
Most fortunate who could swiftest fly:
And while I watched what they would do
The rain-shower drenched me through and through. [45]

Canción
(Form, Spanish)

See *canción petrarquista*.

Canción libre
(Form, Spanish)

See *silva*.

Canción paralelística
Form
Country of Origin: Galicia (Spain)
Distribution: Galician, Portuguese
Century: 13th century

Often written in octosyllabic couplets, **canción paralelística** added an initial *estribillo* when it was adopted by Castilian poets.

Canción petrarquista
Form
Country of Origin: Spain

---

[45] http://www.poemhunter.com/poem/caccia/, February 29, 2016

Distribution: Spanish
Century: Unknown

Likely the Spanish version of a *Petrarchan Sonnet*. They made use of a *remate*.

Canso
Form
Country of Origin: Occitania (southern France, Monaco, Italy, Spain)
Distribution: Occitan
Century: 12th – 13th centuries

This song style was extremely popular with the troubadours and would not be challenged for poetic dominance until the end of the 13th century (losing out to the *coblas esparsas)*. The **canso** was known in Old French as the *grand chant*, and in Italian as the *canzone*.

Typically, a **canso** has three parts: the *exordium* (the first stanza where the composer explains his purpose), the main body of the text and then one to three *envois* or *tornadas* (which were not always present). Except for the *envois*, the stanzas all have the same sequence of verses (each verse has the same number of metrical syllables). The *envois* took the form of a shortened stanza, containing only a last part of the standard stanza used up to that point.

Each stanza has the same internal rhyme scheme (so if the first line rhymes with the third line in the first stanza, it will do so in each successive one). If the stanzas followed the same rhyming pattern but the actual sounds differed, they were called *coblas alternadas* (alternated stanzas). If the last rhyme sound of one *cobla* becomes the first of the next they are called *coblas capcaudadas* (head-tailed). If the rhyming scheme and rhyming sounds are the same in each stanza they were called *coblas capfinidas* (head-finished). If the rhyming scheme and rhyming sounds are the same in each stanza but the sounds of each stanza are different they were called *coblas unissonans* (unison). If the rhyming scheme never changed but the sound did every second stanza they were called *coblas doblas* (double). If the rhyming scheme never changed but the sounds did every third stanza they were called *coblas ternas*. If the rhyme changed position in accordance with an algorithm they were called *coblas retrogradadas* (retrograded).

An example of a **canso** is *Be m'an perdut lai enves Ventadorn*, written by Bernart de Ventadorn (c. 1130 – c. 1200):

> Be m'an perdut lai enves Ventadorn
> tuih mei amic, pois ma domna no m'ama;
> er es be dreihz que ja mais lai no torn,
> c'ades estai vas me salvatj'e grama.
> Ve us per que m fai semblan irat e morn:
> cal en s'amor me deleih e m sojorn
> ni de ren als no s rancura ni s clama.
>
> Aissi co l peis qui s'eslaiss'el cadorn
> e no n sap mot, tro que s'es pres en l'ama,
> m'eslaissei eu vas trop amar un jorn,
> c'anc no m gardei, tro fui en mei la flama,
> que m'art plus fort, no m feira focs de forn;
> e ges per so no m posc partir un dorn,
> aissi m te pres s'amors e m'aliama.
>
> Uo m meravilh si s'amors me te pres,
> que genser cors no crei qu'el mon se mire:
> bels e blancs es, e frescs e gais e les
> e totz aitals com eu volh e dezire.
> No posc dir mal de leis, que non i es;

qu'e ·l n'agra dih de ioi, s'eu li saube
mas no li sai, per so m'en lais de dire.

Totz tems volrai sa onor e sos bes
e ·lh serai om et amics e servire,
e l'amarai, be li plass'o be ·lh pes,
c'om no pot cor destrenher ses aucire.
No sai domna, volgues o no volgues,
si ·m volia, c'amar no la pogues.
Mas totas res pot om en mal escrire.

Alas autras sui aissi eschazutz;
la cals se vol, me pot vas se atraite,
per tal cove que no ·m sia vendutz
l'onors ni ·l bes que m'a en cor a faire;
qu'enoyos es preyars, pos er perdutz;
per me ·us odic, que mals m'en es vengutz,
car trait m'a la bela de mal aire.

J'en Proensa tramet jois e salutz
e mais de bes c'om no lor sap retraire;
e fatz esfortz, miracles e vertutz,
car eu lor man de so don non ai gaire,
qu'eu non ai joi, mas tan can m'en adutz
mos Bels Vezers e ·N Fachura, mos drutz,
e ·N Alvernhatz, lo senher de Belcaire.

Mos Bels Vezers, per vos fai Deus vertutz
tals c'om no ·us ve que no si'ereubutz
dels bels plazers que sabetz dir e faire.[46]

The first stanza and concluding envoi can be translated as:

---

[46] http://ducalucifero.altervista.org/tb_026.htm, February 29, 2016

[I am indeed lost from the region of Ventadorn
To all my friends, for my lady loves me not;
With reason I turn not back again,
For she is bitter and ill-disposed towards me.
She why she turns a dark and angry countenance to
        me:
Because I take joy and pleasure in loving her!
Nor has she ought else with which to charge me...

My beauteous vision, God works such wonder through
        you
That no one seeing you would not be enraptured
Who knew what to tell you and what to do.][47]

Canso de crozada
(Genre, Provençal)

See *sirventes*.

Canso-sirventes
(Genre, French)

See *sirventes*.

Canson
(Form, Occitan)

See *Canso*.

Cantiga
Genre
Country of Origin: Galicia (Spain), Iberian Peninsula (Spain,

---

[47] Carl Parrish: 29-30.

Portugal)
Distribution: Galician, Iberian
Century: 13th – 14th centuries

The **cantiga** is a genre of lyric poetry with four major divisions.

The *cantiga d'amigo* was erotic in nature with an emphasis on the female perspective. The earliest known examples are from the 1220s. The speaker in a *cantiga d'amigo* is almost always a girl, her mother, the girl's female friend or the girl's lover. They have simple strophic forms, using repetition, variation and parallelism, as well as a refrain.

The *cantiga de amor* differs in that the narrator of the poem is male, where the narrator laments the absence of his love.

The *cantiga de escarbo* was covert insult poetry. *Cantiga de mal dizer* is also insult poetry but it openly mocks its target.

Below is a **cantiga** (*de amor*) by Alfonso X El Sabio (23 November, 1221 – 4, April, 1284):

> LADY, for the love of God,
> Have some pity upon me!
> See my eyes, a river-flood
> Day and night, oh, see!
> Brothers, cousins, uncles, all,
> Have I lost for thee;
> If thou dost not me recall,
> Woe is me![48]

Cantiga d'amigo

---

[48] http://www.poemhunter.com/poem/cantiga/, March 1, 2016

(Form, Galician, Iberian)

See *cantiga*.

Cantiga de amor
(Form, Galician, Iberian)

See *cantiga*.

Cantiga de escarbo
(Form, Galician, Iberian)

See *cantiga*.

Cantiga de mal dizer
(Form, Galician, Iberian)

See *cantiga*.

Cantiga de refam
Form
Country of Origin: Galicia (Spain), Iberian Peninsula (Spain, Portugal)
Distribution: Galician, Iberian
Century: unknown

A refam is a refrain, so presumably the **cantiga de refam** was a version of the *cantiga* making use of refrains.

Canu brudd
(Genre, Welsh)

See *cywyddau brud*.

Canzone

Form
Country of Origin: Italy, Provence (France)
Distribution: Italian, Provençal
Century: 13th – 14th centuries

Meaning "song" the *canzoni* (which is the plural) were Italian or Provençal songs or *ballads*, or a type of lyric resembling a *madrigal*, originating during the 13th century. Derived from the Provençal *canso*, the **canzone** consists of five to seven stanzas usually set to music, with each stanza (usually hendecasyllabic) resounding in the first rhyme scheme and in the number of lines (between seven to twenty lines). It ends with a *congendo* or *commiato* as a *tornada* (the Provençal version of the *envoi*).

Stanzas in a **canzone** are divided into the fronte (or piedi) and the sirma (or volte). A fronte is metrically indivisible, whereas a piedi is divided into two metrically identical parts. The same is true of the sirma and volte. The most common division in a **canzone** is two piedi and a sirma, with the rhymes in the sirma different from the piedi, with the exception of the first rhyme which repeats the last rhyme of the piedi (which is called concatenatio or "chaining together"). The sirma often concludes with a juxtaposed rhyme (called rima baciata) though it was not always observed.

Francesco (Petrarch) Petrarcha (1304-1374) codified the canzone into the form described above. Below is an excerpt from his poem "Canzone 128":

> Italia mia, benché 'l parlar sia indarno
> canzone, n. 128 del canzoniere di Petrarca
> analisi del testo di Alissa Peron
> testo

Italia mia, benché 'l parlar sia indarno
a le piaghe mortali
che nel bel corpo tuo sí spesse veggio,
piacemi almen che ' miei sospir' sian quali
spera 'l Tevero et l'Arno,
e 'l Po, dove doglioso et grave or seggio.
Rettor del cielo, io cheggio
che la pietà che Ti condusse in terra
Ti volga al Tuo dilecto almo paese.
Vedi, Segnor cortese,
di che lievi cagion' che crudel guerra;
e i cor', che 'ndura et serra
Marte superbo et fero,
apri Tu, Padre, e 'ntenerisci et snoda;
ivi fa che 'l Tuo vero,
qual io mi sia, per la mia lingua s'oda.

Voi cui Fortuna à posto in mano il freno
de le belle contrade,
di che nulla pietà par che vi stringa,
che fan qui tante pellegrine spade?
perché 'l verde terreno
del barbarico sangue si depinga?
Vano error vi lusinga:
poco vedete, et parvi veder molto,
ché 'n cor venale amor cercate o fede.
Qual piú gente possede,
colui è piú da' suoi nemici avolto.
O diluvio raccolto
di che deserti strani
per inondar i nostri dolci campi!
Se da le proprie mani
questo n'avene, or chi fia che ne scampi?[49]

[49] http://www.atuttascuola.it/alissa/italiano/canzoniere/canzone_128.htm, March 1, 2016

[O my own Italy! Though words are vain
The mortal wounds to close,
Unnumbered, that thy beauteous bosom stain,
Yet may it soothe my pain
To sigh for Tyber's woes,
And Arno's wrongs, as on Po's saddened shore
Sorrowing I wander, and my numbers pour.
Ruler of heaven! By the all-pitying love
That could thy Godhead move
To dwell a lonely sojourner on earth,
Turn, Lord! On this thy chosen land thine eye:
See, God of Charity!
From what light cause this cruel war has birth;
And the hard hearts by savage discord steeled,
Thou, Father, from on high,
Touch by my humble voice, that stubborn wrath may
yield!

Ye, to whose sovereign hands the fates confide
Of this fair land the reins–
(This land for which no pity wrings your breast)–
Why does the stranger's sword her plains invest?
That her green fields be dyed,
Hope ye, with blood from the Barbarians' veins?
Beguiled by error weak,
Ye see not, though to pierce so deep ye boast,
Who love, or faith, in venal bosoms seek:
When thronged your standards most,
Ye are encompassed most by hostile bands.
O hideous deluge gathered in strange lands,
That rushing down amain
O'erwhelms our every native lovely plain!
Alas, if our own hands
Have thus our weal betrayed, who shall our cause

sustain?[50

Capitolo

Form
Country of Origin: Italy
Distribution: Italian
Century: 14th – 19th centuries

This form was originally a parody or imitation of the *terza rima* (whose characteristics it apes). Up to the 15th century its subject matter was political or didactic, but by the end of the century it was also being used to explore the topic of love. At the beginning of the 16th century it had also become used for humourous and satirical subjects.

There was apparently an alternative form called the *capitolo quadernario*, which was instead based off the Occitan *sirventes*.

An example is "Capitolo L'Occasïone" by Niccolò Machiavelli (1469-1527):

"CHI sei tu, che non par donna mortale,
   di tanta grazia il ciel t'adorna e dota?
 perchè non posi? e erchèa' piedi hai l' ale?"
      "Io son l' Occasïone, a pochi nota;
 e la cagion che sempre mi travagli
 è perchè io tengo un piè sopra una rota.
      Volar non è ch' al mio correr s' agguagli;
 e però l' ale a' piedi mi mantengo,
 acciò nel corso mio ciascuno abbagli.
      Gli sparsi miei capei dinanzi io tengo;
 con essi mi ricopro il pette e 'l volto,

---

50   http://www.webexhibits.org/poetry/explore_obscure_canzone_examples.html, March 1, 2016

perch' un non mi conosca quando io vengo.
    Dietro dal capo ogni capel m' è tolto,
onde in van si affatica un, se gli avviene
ch' io l' abbia trapassato, o s' io mi volto."
    "Dimmi: chi è colei che teco viene?"
"È Penitenza; e però nota e intendi:
chi non sa prender me, costei ritiene.
    E tu, mentre parlando il tempo spendi,
occupato da molti pensier vani,
già non t' avvedi, lasso! e non comprendi
    com' io ti son fuggita tra le mani!"[51]

["WHO art thou? Mortal woman were less sweet;
  The Heavens have richly decked and dowered thee!
Why
  So restless? Whence these wings upon thy feet?"
    "Few know me, Opportunity am I.
The reason that I never can be still
Is because on a wheel my foot doth lie;
    Unto my course no flight but matcheth ill,
Nathless, so all be dazzled as I run,
Wings on my feet I have maintained; I spill
    My tresses forwards that they flow as spun
Veil covering over face and bosom, so
In passing I be recognized by none;
    Behind my head no single hair doth grow,
Wherefore he gazeth vainly when maybe
I hasten by or look back as I go."
    "Tell me, who is it that accompanieth thee?"
"She is called Penitence: O take good care,
He keepeth her who cannot capture me!
    And thou who chattering wastest time so rare,
Immersed in matters vain and manifold,

---

[51] http://www.elfinspell.com/MachiavelliPoem.html, March 1, 2016

Alas, hast thou not seen, nor art aware
That I meanwhile have slipped out of thy hold!"][52]

Capitolo quadernario
(Form, Italian)

See *capitolo*.

Casbairdne
Form
Country of Origin: Ireland
Distribution: Irish
Century: unknown

Casbairdne (pronounced koss buyer-dne) were quatrains of 7-syllable lines. Lines two and four rhyme and lines one and three consonate with them. Each couplet had at least two cross-rhymes (though in the first couplet this is not necessarily adhered to). The final syllable of line four alliterates with the preceding stressed word. Two words per line alliterated. The poem ended with *dunadh*.

x x a x x x b
x x x b x x a
a x x x x x b
x b x x x **x a**

Ceathramhain
Device
Country of Origin: Ireland
Distribution: Irish
Century: 12th – 19th centuries

---

[52] Ibid.

Ceathramhain is the old Irish term for a line of verse.

See also *dán díreach*.

Cerdd dafod
Device
Country of Origin: Wales
Distribution: Welsh
Century: 6th – 15th centuries

Meaning literally "tongue craft", **cerdd dafod** is the tradition of creating verse or poetry to a strict meter in the Welsh language, indicating a mastery of *cynghanedd* (sound arrangement within poetic lines). The bard Einion Offeiriad (fl. c. 1320 - c. 1349) listed twenty-four canonical meters for writing **cerdd dafod**. Around 1450, Dafydd ap Edmwnd changed two of these meters for more complicated ones of his own devising which became preferred by the bardic community.

Meters used to write **cerdd dafod** are divided into three categories: *awdl, englyn* and *cywydd*. The *englyn* meters are: *englyn penfyr, englyn milwr, englyn unodl union, englyn unodl crwca, englyn cyrch, englyn proest dalgron, englyn lleddfbroest* and *englyn proest godwynog*. The *cywydd* meters are: *awdl gywydd, cywydd deuair hirion, cywydd deuair fyrion* and *cywydd llosgyrnag*. The *awdl* meters are split between line and stanza forms. The *awdl* line forms are: *rhupunt* and *cyhydedd hir*. The *awdl* stanza forms are: *cyhydedd fer, byr a thoddaid, clogyrnach, cyhydedd naw ban, toddaid, gwawdodyn, gwawdodyn hir, hir a toddaid, cyrch a chwta* and *tawddgyrch cadwynog*.

Cethramtu Rannaigheacht Mor
Form

Country of Origin: Ireland
Distribution: Irish
Century: unknown

Cethramtu rannaigheacht mor were quatrains consisting of 3-syllable lines. The lines rhymed xaxa xbxb (and so on, where the x lines were unrhymed). The poem ends with *dunadh*.

x x x
x x a
x x x
x x a

Chançon de la mal mariée
(Genre, French)

See *mal mariée*.

Chanso
(Form, Occitan)

See *canso*.

Chanson
Genre
Country of Origin: France
Distribution: French
Century: 11th – 15th centuries

A **chanson** was any lyric driven French song, usually polyphonic and secular; they were usually about courtly love and consisted of five or six matching stanzas with a concluding *envoi*. The name is derived from the Latin *cantio* and means "song". A singer specializing in **chansons** was known as a *chanteur* (if male) or a *chanteuse* (if female), while a collection of chansons was known as a *chansonnier*.

See also *chanson de geste* and *chanson de toile*.

The following poem by Charles d'Orléans (1394-1465) is classified as a **chanson**:

> Dieu, qu'il la fait bon regarder
> La gracieuse bonne et belle!
> Pour les grands biens qui son ten elle,
> Chacun est prêt de la louer.
>
> Qui se pourrait d'elle lasser?
> Toujours sa beauté renourelle.
> Dieu, qu'il la fait bon regarder
> La gracieuse, bonne et belle!
>
> Par deça, ai del à la mer,
> Ne sais Dame ni Demoiselle
> Qui soit en tous biens parfaits telle;
> C'est un songe que d'y penser.
> Dieu, qu'il le fait bon regarder![53]

Chanson d'histoir
(Genre, French)

See *Chanson de toile*.

Chanson de geste
Genre
Country of Origin: France
Distribution: French

---

[53] Alan Boase: 13-14.

Century: 11th – 15th centuries

Meaning a "song of heroic deeds" in Old French, the **chanson de geste** is an epic poem, dating from the late 11th and early 12th centuries. Composed in verse, they were usually around 4000 lines, and meant to be sung or (later) recited. The subject matter was legendary events in French history, including the times of Charles Martel, Charlemagne and Louis the Pious. Something that set the **chanson de geste** apart from the *romances* (which tended to explore the role of the individual) was their exploration of the role of the community. The epic French heroes were seen as figures of destiny, championing France and Christianity.

Over time themes other than great battles and historic prowess such as money, urban scenery, female characters and the role of love began to appear. Muslims, who were often the foes of the **chansons**, were now joined by mythological enemies such as giants, magic and monster. They also began to draw on the Crusades for inspiration. During the Hundred Years War the **chansons** experienced a resurgence in popularity due to nationalistic fervor.

The poems feature a set of stock characters, including: the valiant hero, the brave traitor, the cowardly traitor, the Saracen giant, the beautiful Saracen princess, and so on.

Early **chansons de geste** were usually composed in 10-syllable lines grouped in assonance stanzas (called *laisses*). They were of variable length. Later *chansons* were composed in monorhyme stanzas, in which the last syllable of each line rhymes fully throughout the stanza. They also tended to be composed in 12-syllable lines (*alexandrines*).

One of the most famous **chansons de geste** was *La chanson de*

Roland (The Song of Roland) written in the late 11th or early 12th century. The first *laisses* reads:

> Carles li reis, nostre emper[er]e magnes
> Set anz tuz pleins ad estet en Espaigne:
> Tresqu'en la mer cunquist la tere altaigne.
> N'i ad castel ki devant lui remaigne;
> Mur ne citet n'i est remes a fraindre,
> Fors Sarraguce, ki est en une muntaigne.
> Li reis Marsilie la tient, ki Deu nen aimet;
> Mahumet sert e Apollin recleimet:
> Nes poet guarder que mals ne l'i ateignet.[54]

> [Charles the King, our Lord and Sovereign,
> Full seven years hath sojourned in Spain,
> Conquered the land, and won the western main,
> Now no fortress against him doth remain,
> No city walls are left for him to gain,
> Save Sarraguce, that sits on high mountain.
> Marsile its King, who feareth not God's name,
> Mahumet's man, he invokes Apollin's aid,
> Nor wards off ills that shall to him attain.][55]

See also *gest*.

Chanson de mal mariée
(Genre, French)

See *mal mariée*.

---

[54] http://www.hs-augsburg.de/~harsch/gallica/Chronologie/11siecle/Roland/rol_ch01.html, March 2, 2016

[55] http://www.gutenberg.org/cache/epub/391/pg391-images.html, March 2, 2016

Chanson de toile

Genre
Country of Origin: France
Distribution: French
Century: 12th – 13th century

A late 12th and early 13th century Old French genre of narrative Old French lyric poetry. They are usually set to music and tell the tale of a young, often unmarried woman pining for her lover, with a happy ending. The poem's female narrator is usually singing as they relate their story, and the *chanson* itself was supposed to have been sung by women as they were weaving. The act of sewing was often present within the framework of the poem.

In most cases the song begins with a brief and sympathetic history of the female narrator who is either absent from her lover or unhappily married to an older nobleman while being in love with a knight. **Chansons de toile** sometimes appeared in *romances*, sung by the heroines.

An excerpt from *Bele Yolanz en ses chambres seoit* (Bele Yolanz was sitting in her chambers) reads:

> Bele Yolanz en ses chambres seoit.
> D'un boen samiz une robe cosoit:
> a son ami tramettre la voloit.
> En sospirant ceste chançon chantoit.[56]
>
> [Bele Yolanz was sitting in her chambers,
> Sewing a gown of beautiful silk
> Which she wanted to send to her lover.
> Sighing, she sang this song.][57]

---

[56] E, Jan Burns: 91.

Chanson royale
(Form, French)

See *chant royal*.

Chant royal
Form
Country of Origin: France
Distribution: French
Century: 13th – 16th centuries

A variation of the *ballad*, the **chant royal** was often used for stately or heroic topics. In the 14th century it consisted of five 11-line stanzas with a rhyme scheme of ababccddedE and a 5-line *envoi* rhyming ddedE or a 7-line *envoi* rhyming ccddedE. No rhyming word was used twice. In the 15th century the form acquired a refrain. The number of syllables in the refrain (between ten and twelve) were equal to the number of lines in each stanza with the *envoi* normally being half that number of lines.

The *envoi* was often directed towards a prince.

There were several different kinds of *chant royal*, including:

Serventois: A 13th century version which pontificated on the Virgin Mary.

Amoureuse: A love poem.

Sotte amoureuse: A playful love poem.

---

[57] Ibid.

Sotte chanson: A comic poem.

An example of a *chant royal* is *Chant royal de l'arbre de vie* by Guillaume Crétin (1460 – 1525):

Le maistre ouvrier en vraye agriculture
Planta jadis au terrestre verger
Arbres plusieurs, de fruict et floriture
Belles a veoir et doulces a manger ;
Dont ordonna une fructueuse ente
De ses clozier et cloziere estre exempte
Du fruict cueillir ; mais le serpent hideux
Si fort souffla qu'en mangerent tous deux,
Soulz fainct blazon de parole fardee ;
Pour ce fut veue a l'occasion d'eux
L'arbre de vie en tout temps bien gardee.

L'arbre touchee avoit telle nature
Qe la science aprenoit de leger
Du bien et mal, et par coup d'avanture
Faisoit la vie au mangeant abreger ;
Mais se l'homme eust en pensee innocente
Gardé justice originelle absente,
Au mesme instant qu'en desir convoiteux
Gousta le fruict deffendu, fort piteux,
N'eust sa fortune en tel point hazardee ;
Car il avoit pour repas non doubteux
L'Arbre de Vie en tout temps bien gardee.

Moult différente est l'arbre en nourriture
A celle ayant goust de mortel danger,
Elle preserve ung corps de pourriture,
Et vivifie en tout sans rien changer ;
Elle a vertu si grande et excellente,

Que ne l'actaint froidure violente
Grésil, frimas, gresle, vent despiteux,
Divers oraige estrange et hazardeux
N'ont la beauté de son tainct blasfardee ;
Mais fut et est pour humains souffreteux
L'Arbre de Vie en tout temps bien gardee.

Le cherubin du verger ayant cure
Garde tousjours celle arbre endommager ;
Glayve trenchant et ardente closture
Font de ce lieu tous perilz estranger.
Or entendons, Eve est l'arbre dolente,
Marie aussi celle très redolente* ;
L'une a porté germe deffectueux,
Et l'autre si très digne et vertueux
Que par luy fut paix au monde accordee ;
Dont bien se nomme, a tiltre sumptueux,
L'Arbre de Vie en tout temps bien gardee.

Le Createur voulant sa creature
Du fyer dragon plutonique venger,
L'arbre a gardee entiere sans fracture,
Et mal n'y sceut loy commune exiger ;
Corruption d'originelle sente
Onc n'encourut, et fault que d'elle on sente
Racyne, tyge et branches vers les cieux
Estre exaltez, sans ce qu'aer vicieux
Ayt la vertu de sa fleur retardee ;
Veu qu'a produit fruict sur tous précieux,
L'Arbre de Vie en tout temps bien gardee.

Prince du puy, ne soions soucieux,
Fors d'humble bouche et cueur devocieux
Tenir la Vierge, en concept regardee,
Estre en despit des faulx seditieux

L'Arbre de Vie en tous temps bien gardee.[58]

Clogyrnach
(Form, Welsh)

See *awdl*.

Cobla esparza
Form
Country of Origin: Occitania (southern France, Monaco, Italy, Spain)
Distribution: Occitan
Century: 12th – 13th centuries

The "scattered stanza" is a single stanza poem in troubadour poetry and was the dominant form for post 1220 authors. **Coblas esparzas** were usually presented in large groupings.

Sometimes two authors would write a **cobla esparza** in a form of dialogue or exchange (similar to the *tenso* or *partimen*).

Cobles d'acuyndamens concerned bonds of vassalage, love or fidelity, while *cobles de questions* posed dilemmas.

Cobla exchange
(Form, Occitan)

See *tenso*.

Coblas alternadas
(Form, Italian)

---

[58] Guillaume Crétin: 16-18.

See *Canso.*

Coblas capcaudadas
(Form, Italian)

See *Canso.*

Coblas capfinidas
(Form, Italian)

See *Canso.*

Coblas doblas
(Form, Italian)

See *Canso.*

Coblas retrogradadas
(Form, Italian)

See *Canso.*

Coblas ternas
(Form, Italian)

See *Canso.*

Coblas unissonans
(Form, Italian)

See *Canso.*

Cobles d'acuyndamens
(Form, Occitan)

See *cobla esparsa.*

Cobles de questions
(Form, Occitan)

See *cobla esparsa.*

Complaint
Genre
Country of Origin: England
Distribution: English
Century: at least 13th – 16th centuries

Complaints (also known as *plaints*) were poems of lament, often directed at an ill-fated love. They could also be satiric attacks concerning social injustice and immorality.

An example of the complaint is "Complaint of the Absence of Her Love Being Upon the Sea" by Henry Howard, Earl of Surrey (1516-1547)

> O happy dames, that may embrace
>   The fruit of your delight,
> Help to bewail the woeful case
>   And eke the heavy plight
> Of me, that wonted to rejoice
> The fortune of my pleasant choice;
> Good ladies, help to fill my mourning voice.
>
> In ship, freight with remembrance
>   Of thoughts and pleasures past,
> He sails that hath in governance
>   My life while it will last;
> With scalding sighs, for lack of gale,

Furthering his hope, that is his sail,
Toward me, the sweet port of his avail.

Alas! how oft in dreams I see
   Those eyes that were my food;
Which sometime so delighted me,
   That yet they do me good;
Wherewith I wake with his return,
Whose absent flame did make me burn:
But when I find the lack, Lord, how I mourn!

When other lovers in arms across
   Rejoice their chief delight.
Drowned in tears, to mourn my loss
   I stand the bitter night
In my window, where I may see
Before the winds how the clouds flee.
Lo! what a mariner love hath made of me!

And in green waves when the salt flood
   Doth rise by rage of wind,
A thousand fancies in that mood
   Assail my restless mind.
Alas! now drencheth my sweet foe,
That with the spoil of my heart did go,
And left me; but, alas! why did he so?

And when the seas wax calm again
   To chase fro me annoy,
My doubtful hope doth cause me pain;
   So dread cuts off my joy.
Thus is my wealth mingled with woe,
And of each thought a doubt doth grow;
"Now he comes! Will he come? Alas, no, no!"[59]

---

[59] http://www.poetryfoundation.org/poem/180630, March 4, 2016

See also *lament*.

Conachlonn
Form
Country of Origin: Ireland
Distribution: Irish
Century: 6th – 16th century

Conachloon (pronounced con-ach-lonn) was a type of poem using *dunadh* (chain rhyme). There were no set number of lines nor set line length. Also vulgarly known as *padairin* and *slabhradh*.

Angus the Culdee (8th century) wrote a **conachlonn** called *Féilré* written in a short meter. Translated into English, the opening stanzas read:

> Bless O Christ my speaking
> > King of heavens seven,
> Strength and wealth and power
> > In this hour be given;
>
> Given O thou brightest
> > Destined not to sever,
> King of angels glorious
> > And victorious ever,
>
> Ever o'er us shining
> > Light to mortals given,
> Beaming daily, nightly,
> > Brightly out of heaven...[60]

---

[60] Douglas Hyde: 157.

Conte dévot

Genre
Country of Origin: France
Distribution: French
Century: 13th – 14th centuries

A genre from the 13th to 14th century, the **conte dévot** were pious tales told in either prose or verse. Many of them are miracle tales, but not all of them are. The most famous **conte dévot** is *Tombeor Nostre Dame* (Jongleur de Notre Dame) in which a former juggler, now a monk, performs his tricks for the Virgin Mary who appears and wipes the sweat from his brow in appreciation.

Contenson

(Genre, Occitan)

See *tenso*.

Copla

Form
Country of Origin: Spain
Distribution: Spanish
Century: unknown

Copla were short stanzas of irregular length and with no fixed rhyme. They were frequently sung.

Copla de arte mayor

(Form, Castilian)

See *arte mayor*.

Copla de arte menor

(Form, Castilian)

See *arte menor*.

Copla de Juan Mena
(Form, Castilian)

See *arte mayor*.

Copla real
Form
Country of Origin: Spain
Distribution: Spanish
Century: 15th century

A **copla real** is made up of two *quintillas* using different rhyme schemes but with the scheme used for the first pair remains set throughout. This form was often used to express deep emotions.

Coq-à-lâne
Genre
Country of Origin: France
Distribution: French
Century: 16th century

Created in 1530, these poems were satires dealing with vices, faults and foibles of individuals, groups and even institutions. They were generally verse epistles of varying length, written in octosyllabic rhyming couplets.

Coronach
Genre
Country of Origin: Scotland
Distribution: Gaelic

Century: 17th century

A **coronach** ("wailing together") was a song of lamentation; a *dirge*. *The Bonnie Earl of Murray* (The Bonnie Earl O'Moray) is sometimes called a **coronach**. It begins:

> Ye Hielands an ye Lowlands
> O, whaur hae ye been
> They hae slain the Earl o' Moray
> And lain him on the green.[61]

Courtly Compliment
Genre
Country of Origin: France
Distribution: French
Century: 12th – 19th centuries

The courtly compliment poem is one in which the proper chivalric attitudes towards a lady was the paramount concern. The verse is lyrical, praising a lady, and can be considered a sub-genre of the *chanson*.

Alexander Montgomerie (1550? – 1598) write a courtly compliment that begins:

> Sweit hairt rejoiss in mynd
> With consorte day and nicht,
> Ye have ane luif as kynd
> As ever luifit weicht…[62]

Courtois

---

[61] https://projects.handsupfortrad.scot/scotlandsings/scots-songs/, March 4, 2016

[62] Carl Woodring: 96-97. Gonzalo de Berceo: 1-2.

(Genre, French)

See *grand chant*.

Cro cumaisc etir casbairdne ocus lethrannaigecht

Form
County of Origin: Ireland
Distribution: Irish
Century: unknown

Cro cumaisc etir casbairdne ocus lethrannaigecht were quatrains where the first and third lines consisted of five syllables, while the second and fourth lines had seven syllables. The line rhyme abab cdcd and so on. Line one and line three often ended on three syllable words. If line three ended with a two syllable word the next line would rhyme internally (aicill). The poem would end using dunadh.

Version 1
x x x x a   OR
x x x x x x b
x x x x a
x x x x x x b

Version 2
x x **x x** a   OR
x x x x x x b
x x **x x** a
x x x x x x b

Version 3
x x x x a
x x x x x x b
x x x **x a**
x x a x x x b

Cuaderna via
Form
Country of Origin: Catalonia (Spain)
Distribution: Catalan

Century: 13th – 15th centuries

Cuaderna via (four fold way) was a Spanish meter introduced in the 13th century by the clergy, and influenced by French poetry. It is very rigid in form, with lines made up of carefully counted syllables. Each line consisted of two hemistichs of 7-syllables each, with the lines grouped into stanzas of four monorhymed lines, with the rhymes being in consonance. Hiatus was apparently obligatory, whereas contraction, apocope, alpaersis, dialysis, synizesis and sometimes syncope might appear. There are a few examples of cuaderna via that deviate from the norm.

There is some speculation that **cuaderna via** were only written by clerics and men of learning, and not by minstrels. However, this does not appear to be the case.[63]

Also known as *alejandrino, mester de clerica* (craft of clerks/clerics) and *nueva maestria*.

The *Libro de Apolonia*, an anonymous work from the 13th century, begins:

1. En el nombre de Dios y de Santa María,
    si ellos me guiasen estudiar querría,
    componer un romance de nueva maestría
    del buen rey Apolonio y de su cortesía.

2. El rey Apolonio, de Tiro natural,
    que por las aventuras visco grant temporal.
    Cómo perdió la fija y la mujer capdal,
    cómo las cobró amas, ca les fue muy leyal.

---

[63] Germán Bleiberg: 1079

3. En el rey Antioco vos quiero comenzar,
    que pobló Antiocha en el puerto de la mar;
    del su nombre mismo fízola titolar.
    Si entonces fuese muerto nol' debiera pesar.[64]

[1. In God's and Holy Mary's name,
    If they will guide, it is my aim
    In a new style of poetry
    To tell of a king's courtesy.

2. King Apollonius of Tyre
    Lost queen and child through evils dire,
    But, through his long fidelity,
    He won them both back finally.

3. But now I will my tale begin
    With Antioch's first sovereign,
    Antiochus. After he built
    His great seaport, he turned to guilt.][65]

Cuarteto

Form
Country of Origin: Spain
Distribution: Spanish
Century: unknown

A **cuarteto** is a quatrain of four hendecasyllables rhyming abab or abba.

Version 1
x x x x x x x x x x a   OR

Version 2
x x x x x x x x x x a

---

[64]   http://www.cervantesvirtual.com/obra-visor/libro-de-apolonio--0/html/fedc1e46-82b1-11df-acc7-002185ce6064_1.html, March 5, 2016

[65] Richard L. Grismer: 1.

```
x x x x x x x x x x b          x x x x x x x x x x x b
x x x x x x x x x x x a         x x x x x x x x x x x b
x x x x x x x x x x x b         x x x x x x x x x x x a
```

Curse

Genre
Country of Origin: England
Distribution: Anglo-Saxon
Century: unknown

A curse, is, as the name suggests, a poetic malediction. Anglo-Saxon curses appear written in Old English and Middle English. The following curse called "The Blacksmiths" is translated from the original Middle English:

> Sooty, swart smiths,   Smattered with smoke,
> Drive me to death   With the din of their dents.
> Such noise at night   No men heard, never!
> What knavish cries   And clattering of knocks!
> The crooked cretins   Call out, "Coal, coal!"
> And blow their billows   Til their brains burst:
> "Huff, puff!" says that one,"Haff, paff!" that other.
> They spit and sprawl   And spill many spells;
> They gnaw and gnash,   They groan together
> And hold their heat   With their hard hammers,
> Of bullhide are made   Their broad aprons;
> Their shanks be shackled   For the fiery flinders;
> They've heavy hammers   That are hardhafted.
> Stark strokes   On a steely stump:
> LUS, BUS! LAS, DAS!   Rant the row —
> So doleful a dream,   The devil destroy it!
> The master lengthens little And labors less,
> Twines a two   And touches a trey:
> Tick, tack! hick, hack!   Ticket, tacket! tyke, take!
> LUS, BUS! LAS, DAS!   Such lives they lead,

These cobblemares: Christ give them grief!
May none of these waterburners   By night have his
rest![66]

Cyhydedd fir
(Form, Welsh)

Also spelt *cyhydedd fer*.
See *awdl*.

Cyhydedd hir
(Form, Welsh)

See *awdl*.

Cyhydedd naw ban
(Form, Welsh)

See *awdl*.

Cymeriad
Device
Country of Origin: Wales
Distribution: Welsh
Century: 6th – 15th centuries

Meaning "memory," **cymeriad** is the repetition of the first
consonant of the opening line at the beginning of the
successive lines.

Cymeriad geirol is when poets started successive stanzas (or
even the whole poem) with the same letter, syllable, word or

---

[66] Lewis Turco: 206.

line.

This is illustrated in the poem "Cân yr Henwr":

> **Kynn bun kein**-vaglawc bum kyffes-ciryawc.
> Keinmygyr uy eres.
> Gwyr Argoet eiryoet a'm porthes.

> **Kynn bun kein**-uaglawc bun hy.
> A'm kynnwyssit yg kyuyrdy
> Powys, paradwys Gymry.

> **Kynn bun kein**-vaglawc bum eiryan.
> Oed kynwaew vym par; oed kynwan.
> Wyf keuyngrwm, wyf trwm, wyf truan.[67]

Cymeriad geirol
(Device, Welsh)

See *cymeriad*.

Cynghanedd
Device
Country of Origin: Wales
Distribution: Welsh
Century: 6th – 15th centuries

Cynghanedd was the basic concept of sound arrangement within one line, using stress, alliteration and rhyme in Welsh language poetry. There are various forms of **cynhanedd**, which show up in all formal Welsh verse forms (such as the *awdl* and *englyn*).

---

[67] Jenny Rowland: 4.

Cynghanedd gros ("cross-harmony") is when all consonants surrounding the main stressed vowel before the caesura must be repeated after it in the same order. However, the final consonants of the final words of each half of the line must be different, as must the main stressed vowel of each half. There are no consonants in the second half of the line which are not part of the consonantal echoing. The vowels other than those under the stress may be of any kind.

Y mae i'm bron, mam y brad,   Crupl y cur, croyw epil cof.
   m   m br (n) | m m br (d)   cr pl (r) | cr   p l c(f)[68]

Cynghanedd draws (partial "cross-harmony") is the same as *cynghanedd gros* except there are consonants at the beginning of the second half of the line which are not present in the series of echoed consonants. There may be any number of unanswered consonants in this part of the line, as long as the initial sequence of consonants and accent is repeated.

Caru y bûm, cyd curiwyf,   Cadw a orwyf i'm ceudawd
 c r | (b m c d) c r (f)   c d | (r f m) c d (d)[69]

Cynghanedd sain ("sound-harmony") employs internal rhyme. If a line is divided into three sections by two caesuras, then the first and second sections must rhyme, and the third section must repeat the consonantal patterns of the second.

Corsen o blanbren blaenbraff.   Cariad, twyllwr, cnöwr cnawd.
   en | bl nbr<u>en</u> | bl nbr (ff)   <u>wr</u> | cn <u>wr</u> | cn (d)[70]

---

[68] Benjamin Burch.

[69] Ibid.

[70] Ibid.

Cynghanedd lusg ("drag-harmony") is when the final syllable before the caesura in the first half of the line makes full rhyme with the penultimate syllable of the main stressed syllable of the second half.

Cyfragod cariad tradof,　　　　Ceisio heiniar o garu
　　　　<u>ad</u> <u>ad</u>　　　　　　　　　　<u>ar</u>　　<u>ar</u>[71]

Cynghanedd draws
(Device, Welsh)

See *cynghanedd*.

Cynghanedd lusg
(Device, Welsh)

See *cynghanedd*.

Cynghanedd gros
(Device, Welsh)

See. *cynghanedd*.

Cynghanedd sain
(Device, Welsh)

See *cynghanedd*.

Cyrch a chwta
(Form, Welsh)

---

[71] Ibid.

See *awdl*.

Cyrch-gymeriad
Device
Country of Origin: Wales
Distribution: Welsh
Century: 6th – 15th centuries

This "link-taking" was when the poet repeated the last word or syllable of a stanza as the first word of the succeeding stanza.

The first few stanzas of "Ode in praise of Dafydd ap Tomas of Blaen-tren" by Guto'r Glyn (c. 1412 – c. 1493):

> Llawen wyf i'm plwyf a'm plas – diofal,
> Llys Dafydd ap Tomas,
> Llin Dafydd, y trydydd tras,
> A Llywelyn wayw lliw**las**.
>
> **Glas**fedd i'w gyfedd a gaf
> Gan hwn, llawer gwan a'i hyf.
> Gorau gŵr a gwraig araf,
> Gorau dau hyd ar *Gaerdyf*.
>
> O *Gaerdyf* y tyf hyd Deifi – ei glod
> Ac i wlad Bryderi,
> Ac i Fôn a Gefenni
> Egin fydd a ganwyf **i**.
>
> **Di**gri fu i mi fy myw – pan dyfodd
> Pendefig Mabeilfyw.
> Da am win hyd ym Mynyw,

Da am aur a phob dim yw.[72]

Cywydd

Form
Country of Origin: Wales
Distribution: Welsh
Century: 6th – 15th centuries

The cywydd (pronounced cuh'-with) is one of the three important metrical forms in Welsh traditional poetry. There are four forms of *cywyddau* (which is the plural), which are all part of the twenty-four codified meters in *cerdd dafod*

Awdl gywydd (pronounced aw'-dl guh'-with): Though called an *awdl* it is actually categorized as a **cywydd** (though it is art of the *awdl* form called *cyrch a chwta*). It consists of two lines of seven syllables. The rhyme at the end of the first line recurs in the middle of the second line, while the end rhyme of the second line recurs at the end of the next couplet.

x x x x x x a
x x x a x x b

Below is a modern version of an anonymous Welsh poem called "Spring Song":

> Earthspring, the sweetest season,
> Loud the birdsong, sprouts ripple,
> Plough in furrow, ox in yoke,
> Sea like smoke, fields in stipple.
>
> Yet when cuckoos call from trees
> I drink the lees of sorrow;

---

[72] http://www.gutorglyn.net/gutorglyn/poem/?poem-selection=012, March 5, 2016

Tongues bitter, I sleep with pain—
My kinsmen come not again.

On mountain, mead, seaborne land,
Wherever man wends his way,
What path he take boots not,
He shall not keep from Christ's eye.[73]

Cywydd deuair hirion (pronounced cuh'-with die'-ire here'-yon): It consists of 7-syllables lines in rhyming couplets, with all the lines written in *cynghanedd*. One of the lines must end with a stressed syllable (masculine), while the other must end with an unstressed syllable (feminine). (For example: sword/forward.) The rhyme may vary from couplet to couplet or it may remain the same. There is no rule as to how many couplets there must be. This was the most popular form of the **cywydd**.

x x x x x x a (masc.)
x x x x x x a (fem.)

Dafydd ap Gwilym (c. 1315/1320 – c. 1350/1370) wrote "Love in Exile" using *cywydd deuair hirion* (here presented in English):

Her grace has charmed away my
Heart—Morfudd, godchild of May,
Hail her, give her good morrow:
Hapless I lie the night through.
Her the wild swore has sown
Her seed to break my breastbone.
Hurt will bloom and heartwail blame
Hours trystless, bleak as henbane.

---

[73] Lewis Turco: 127.

Heavenly being of grace,
Haunting voice, face, enchantress —
How I plead, without avail,
Hunger inconsolable.

Haply, lore might find a way
Hope can win my fair lady;
However , into exile,
Hurled, I shun her domicile.
Heaped within my breast, yearning
Hurkles and writhes the night long;
Higher than waves on the shore
Hurtles the lust I bear her.
Heart to beauty has been chained,
Haft to fettering fastened.
Hard and bright as gold is she —
Hushed love creeps slow toward me.
Hale, long life is my wandream:
How can water flow upstream?
Heartchild of Ynr — lifer were
Harder than death without her![74]

Cywydd deuair fyrion (pronounced cuh'-with fie'-ire veer'-yon):
It consists of two 4-syllable lines, using rhyme or near rhyme.
This form was rarely used.

x x x a
x x x a

The following is a 12th century poem called "My Choice"
written by Hywel ab Owain Gwynedd (d. 1170) using *cywydd
deuair fyrion* (as translated into English):

---

[74] Lewis Turco: 50

I choose a fair
Maid so slender,
Tall and silver,
Her gown of heather
Hue — I choose her,
Nature's daughter,
For the kind word
Dropped, scarecely heard,
And for my part
Take her to heart
Fr gift, for grace,
For her embrace.[75]

Cywydd llosgyrnog (pronounced cu'-with clos-geer'-nog): This consisted of a pair of tercets (or a sestet) consisting of an 8-syllable rhymed couplet followed by a 7-syllable rhyme that has cross-rhyme to the couplet in the middle and rhymes with the sixth line of the couplet followed by another 8-syllable couplet and 7-syllable line with cross-rhyme to lines four and five. This form was rarely used.

x x x x x x x a
x x x x x x x a
x x a x x x b
x x x x x x x c
x x x x x x x c
x x c x x x b

Cywydd deuair hirion
(Form, Welsh)

See *cywydd*.

---

[75] Lewis Turco: 167-168.

Cywydd deuair hirion
(Form, Welsh)

See *cywydd*.

Cywydd llosgyrnog
(Form, Welsh)

See *cywydd*.

Cywyddau brud
Genre
Country of Origin: Wales
Distribution: Welsh
Century: 15th centuries

In the 15th century, **cywyddau brud** (also known as *canu brudd*) were prophetic poems concerning politics. The use of animals to refer to heroes was often employed so as not to name them directly. Indeed, the **cywyddau brud** were highly symbolic.

Dafydd Llwyd of Mathafarn wrote a **cywyddau brud** concerning Harri and Jaspar Tudor who he saw as future deliverers of the Welsh nation:

> Siasbar a fag in ddragwn,
> Gwaed Brutus hapus ywhwn.
> Gwers yr angel ni chelir,
> Hwyntau biau tyrau'r tir.
> Tarw o Fôn yn digoni, --
> Hwn yw gobaoth ein iaith ni.
> Mawr yw'r gras eni Sisaber,
> Hil Cadwaladr paladr pér.

[Jaspar will rear our dragon [i.e. Harri Tudor],
One of the blood of fortunate Brutus.
The angel's lesson will not be kept hidden,
And theirs will be the towers of the land.
The Bull of Anglesey [i.e. Jaspar] succedding —
This is the hope of our people [language].
Great is the grace of Jaspar's birth,
Of Cadwaladr's lineage, the sweet beam.][76]

---

[76] Philip Schwyzer: 16.

D

Dán Díreach

Form, device
Country of Origin: Ireland
Distribution: Irish
Century: 12th – 19th centuries

Dán díreach were poems written from the 12th to 19th century using complex forms and meant to be accompanied on the harp.

To be considered a true **dán díreach** the rules must be strictly adhered to. Otherwise it was considered to be a *brúilingeacht* (using the same form but simpler rhyme) or an *óglachas* (a less formal style used by amateurs).

The poem should begin and end on the same sound (the same letter, word or syllable) though sometimes, just to be confusing, this particular rule was not followed. (This device was called *dúnadh*, meaning "conclusion"). Also, when two or more words in a line rhyme with words in a line preceding or following it, no non-rhyming unstressed words should come between the rhymed words.

Modern scholars have divided up different forms of **dán díreach** into different categories (whose names I will not use here since they were not used at the time).

One form of **dán díreach** rhymed aabb where the rhyme

words on the a lines were one syllable shorter than the b lines. The a rhymes began on accented vowel, while the b rhymes were usually non-accented.

Another rhymes abab where each line can have anywhere between nine and thirteen syllables with every line ending in a 3-syllable word. Every stressed word must have rhyme, consonance and alliteration with a word in another line (though not always when it's the first word of odd lines). If writing a *brúilingeacht* or *óglachas* this was not so strict.

x x x x x x x x (x x x x) a
x x x x x x x x (x x x x) b
x x x x x x x x (x x x x) a
x x x x x x x x (x x x x) b

A third was an 8-line stanza with a consistent but unspecified meter rhyming aaab cccb.

A fourth was a *rann* (quatrain) where the first line has 3-syllables, and the remaining three have seven each. It rhymed aaba with a cross-rhyme between the third and fourth rhymes.

x x a
x x x x x x a
x x x x x x b
x x b x x x a

I've also seen the name used to describe a form of consonance where the vowels preceding the final consonants had to be different but of the same quantity.

See also *droighneach, lethrannaegecht morb, séadna, treochair,* and *trian rannaigechta moire.*

Dança
(Form, Occitan)

See *dansa*.

Dansa

Form
Country of Origin: Occitania (southern France, Monaco, Italy, Spain)
Distribution: Occitan
Century: 11th – 14th centuries

Also spelt *dança*, the **dansa** was an Old Occitan form of lyric poetry developed by the troubadours that peaked in the late 13th century. As the name would suggest, it was often accompanied by dancing. The *balada* is a related form with a more complex structure.

A **dansa** begins with a *respos* of one or two lines with a rhyme scheme that matches that of the first line or two of each following stanza. The *respos* itself may be repeated between stanzas as a refrain. There were usually three stanzas. The verses of a **dansa** were sung by a soloist with a choir singing the refrain. A **dansa** without a *vuelta* is called a *danseta*. The dominant Occitan meter was hexasyllabic (6-syllables) while the Italians preferred heptasyllabic (7-syllable lines) with the primary stress on the sixth syllable

Una danseta voil far by Uc de Saint Circ (fl. 1217-1253) is an example of a **dansa**:

> Una danseta voil far
> Jogan risen
> De Ma Vida, cui Deus gar
> Son gentil sen,

A qe-il farai alegrar
Son cor dolen.
Ab dous chan
En dansan
Voil que s'anes conortan,
Baratan
E trichan
La domnas e galian.

Sos bons sens li fai canjar
Alberg soven,
Car es venguz sai estar
E vai qeren
Autra que puesc' enganar
C'aia argen.
Ab dous chan
En dansan
Voil que s'anes conortan,
Baratan
E trichan
La domnas e galian.

Mantoana e Verones,
Perdut l'ai,
E Trevis' e Senedes
Atresi sai,
E se-l perc Visentines
O-l menerai
Ab dous chan
En dansan
Voil que s'anes conortan,
Baratan
E trichan
La domnas e galian.

En Alvergne et en Fores
Et en Veslai,
Lai on no sabon qi s'es
Ni-ls trag q'el trai!
Pueis me trai l'en Vianes,
A Anonai.
Ab dous chan
En dansan
Voil que s'anes conortan,
Baratan
E trichan
La domnas e galian.[77]

Danseta
(Form, Occitan)

See *dansa*.

Deachnadh cummaisc
Form
Country of Origin: Ireland
Distribution: Irish
Century: unknown

Deachnadh cummaisc were quatrains that consisted of four lines numbering eight, four, eight and four syllables, or consisting of an 8-syllable line, two 4-syllable lines and concluding with another 8-syllabe line. The lines rhyme abab cdcd and so forth. The lines usually ended on two syllable words. If the third line ended with a two syllable word then it rhymed internally with the next line (*aicill*). The poem concluded with *dunadh*.

---

[77] http://www.trobar.org/troubadours/st_circ/poem24.php, March 7, 2016

Version 1		Version 2
x x x x x x **x a**	OR	x x x x x x **x a**
x x **x b**		x x **x b**
x x x x x x **x a**		x x **x b**
x a **x b**		x x x b x x **x a**

Deachnadh mor
Form
Country of Origin: Ireland
Distribution: Irish
Century: unknown

Deachnadh mor (pronounced da-gnaw-moor) were quatrains that consisted of four lines numbering eight, six, eight and six syllables. The lines have di-syllabic endings (where the last two syllables are both involved in the consonation). The lines rhyme abab cdc and so forth and there are at least two cross rhymes in each couplet. The final word of line three rhymes has an internal rhyme with line four. The internal rhyme in the first couplet can consonate instead of true rhyme whereas in the second couplet must true rhyme. Two words should alliterate in each line. In the fourth line the final word alliterates with the previous stressed word. The poem concludes with *dunadh*.

x c x x x d **x a**
x d x c **x b**
x e x x x f **x a**
x f x e **x b**

Débat
Genre
Country of Origin: England, France
Distribution: English, French

Century: 12th – 13th centuries

A **débat** (or debate) is a poem (unaccompanied by music) in dialogue that takes the form of a debate on a topic between opposing personifications (such as fire and water, or love and hate). They were popular in the late medieval period, though they had antecedents in ancient poetry. Medieval **débat** can be divided into four broad categories: amatory, moral, religious and scholarly.[78]

One of the most famous **débat** is the Middle English poem *The Owl and the Nightengale* (c. 1210) in which the owl (the didactic/religious poet) debates with the nightingale (love poet)[79]. It begins:

> Ich was in onė sumere dale,
> in onė swithė diyhėle hale;
> Y-herde ich holdė gretė tale
> an hule and onė niyhtingale.
> That plait was stif and starc and strong,
> Sum whilė softe and lud among;
> And either ayein other swal
> And let that uvelė mod ut al;
> And either seide of othres custe
> That alrė-wurstė that hi wuste;
> And hure and hure of othres songe
> Hi holdė plaiding swithė stronge.
>   The nightėgale bigan tho speche,
> In one hurne of onė breche…[80]

---

[78] Emma Cayley: 31.

[79] Edward Hirsch: 149.

[80] Lines 1-14. Celia sisam: 6-7.

Debate
(Genre, English, French)

See *débat*.

Décima
Form
Country of Origin: Spain
Distribution: Spanish
Century: 14th – 15th century

The **décima** was a form consisting of 10-line stanzas dating from the 14th and 15th centuries. In the 16th century, Vencinente Espinela developed the modern version of the **décima** which is very popular to this day in Latin America.[81]

See also *espinela*.

Décima espanela
(Form, Spanish)

See *espinela*.

Decir
Form
Country of Origin: Castile (Spain)
Distribution: Castilian
Century: 14th - 16th century

Also known as the *dezir*, the **decir** was meant to be recited (as opposed to sung). They were often long narrative or didactic poems. A typical **decir** was constructed of octosyllabic stanzas

---

[81] Edward Hirsch: 154.

(*de arte menor*) but could also be sextillas with the third and sixth lines foreshortened in hexasyllables (*copla de pie quebrado* and *copla de arte mayor*). Many **decir** were written in octosyllabic stanzas of eight lines rhyming abbaacca, with the rhyme carrying through the first 4-line half stanzas to the second. The rhyme is assonantal and interlinked by repeating the lines of the first stanza in subsequent stanzas (*unisonancia plena*). This is done by repeating the rhymes of the first and last lines of the half stanzas (*unisonancia media*), by beginning all stanzas with the same line, and so forth. The form eventually developed a concluding stanza that was half the length of the other stanzas and whose rhyme was linked to the main stanza. This concluding stanza was known as a *finida*, *fin* or *cabo*.

Version 1		*Version 2*
x x x x x x x a	OR	x x x x x x x x
x x x x x x x b		x x x x x x x x
x x x x x x x b		x x x x x x
x x x x x x x a		x x x x x x x x
x x x x x x x a		x x x x x x x x
x x x x x x x c		x x x x x x
x x x x x x x c		
x x x x x x x a		
(x x x x x x x d		
x x x x x x x e		
x x x x x x x e		
x x x x x x x d)		

Decit
Genre
Country of Origin: Castile (Spain)
Distribution: Castilian
Century: 14th - 16th century

A late 14th to early 16th century poem of fixed form that is usually narrative, satiric, didactic or allegorical in nature. They sometimes attained great length. The *copla de arte mayor* was considered the appropriate meter for the **decit**, though *copla de arte menor* could also be used.

Deibhidhe
Form
Country of Origin: Ireland
Distribution: Irish
Centuries: unknown

Deibhidhe (pronounced jay-vée; "light rhyme") and its variations are *dán díreach*. All **deibhidhe** employed couplet rhymes that rhymed a stressed end syllable with an unstressed syllable (though when written in English the rhyme is usually between two stressed syllables). The poems concluded with *dunadh*.

Regular *deibhidhe* were quatrains consisting of 7-syllable lines with at least two alliterating words per line. The lines rhymed aabb ccdd and so forth. The final word of line four alliterates with the previous stressed word. There should be at least two cross-rhymes between line three and four.

x x x x x x a
x x x x x x a
x b x x x x b
x x x b x x b

Deibhidhe baise fri toin were quatrains consisting of a 3-sylable line, followed by two 7-syllable lines and ending on a 1-syllable line. Each line had at least two alliterated words. Lines one and three ended on two syllable words.

x **x** a
x x x x x **x** a
x x x x x x b
b

Deibhidhe guibnech were quatrains consisting of 7-syllable lines with each line having at least two alliterated words. They rhymed aabb ccdd and so on with all end rhymes stressed.

x x x x x x a
x x x x x x a
x x x x x x b
x x x x x x b

Deibhidhe guibnech dialtach were quatrains consisting of 7-syllable lines rhyming aabb ccdd and so on. At least two words per line should alliterate and all end words should consonate.

x x x x x x a
x x x x x x a
x x x x x x b
x x x x x x b

Desdança
(Form, Occitan)

See *desdansa*.

Desdansa
Form
Country of Origin: Occitania (southern France, Monaco, Italy, Spain)
Distribution: Occitan

Century: unknown

The **desdansa** or *desdança* has the same structure as a *dansa*, but instead of having joyful lyrics and joyful music, it was a lamentation with sorrowful music.

Descort
Genre
Country of Origin: Occitania (southern France, Monaco, Italy, Spain)
Distribution: Occitan
Century: examples dated from at least the 12th century

Descort (pronounced day-court; "discord" or "discordant") was lyric poetry written by the troubadours, which is very discordant in verse form and/or feeling, and was often used to express disagreement with something. This genre was likely invented by Raimbaut de Vaqueiras (fl. 1180 – 1207). The **descort** was made up of stanzas with a variable number of lines, with the lines having a variable number of syllables. The rhymes of the **descort** were usually used within a single stanza and then discarded, forcing the troubadour to write a new melody for each section of the song. In at least one example (*"Eras quan vie verdejar"*) each stanza is written in a different language.[82] Descort are often expressions of unrequited love.[83]

An example of the **descort** is *"S'a midons plazia"* by Aimeric de Belenoi (fl. 1215 – 1242) whose first three stanzas are below:

S'a midons plazia,

---

[82] Judith A. Peraino: 94.

[83] Darcy Butterworth Kitchin: 18.

Cui am ses bauzia,
Guay descort faria,
Que l'enviaria,
E si - lh retrazia
Cossi nueg e dia
S'amors m'aucizia --
E no - y truep guandia;
Quar ja no - m guerria
Nulh' autra que sia,
Mas vos, douss' amia;
Gensor no - n say mia.

Mal ay
Que - m fay
Tan gran erguelh dire
De lay
On ay
Mon major dezire.
Maltray
Mi play
Sol qu'il me denh rire.
Mal fay
Qui - l jay
No vol ni dezire
Donc mai
No say
Quom ieu la remire:
Querray
Retray
Quo - l sia jauzire.

Qu'a - l sieu pays
Estau aclis,
Mos mas jonhs ambedos;
Qu'anc pellegris

De paradis
No fon tan enveyos,
Quon ieu servis
Son belh cors lis,
E de gentas faissos,
E que auzis
So qu'ieu l'ai quis,
(qu'adoncx seria joyos)
E no - ns partis
Nulhs fals devis
Ni - ns lunhes ambedos:
Que anc Hyris
Jorn de Biblis
No fo tan enveyos...[84]

Dezir
(Form, Castillian)

See *decir*.

Dirge
Genre
Country of Origin: unknown
Distribution: across Europe
Century: unknown

A dirge is a song or poem sung to commemorate a death or deaths; a death march.

See also coronach.

The anonymous poem "A Lie-awake Dirge" has been

---

[84] http://www.trobar.org/troubadours/aimeric_de_belenoi/aibel11.php, March 10, 2016

translated from Middle English strictly following the form of the original:

This very night, this very night,
    Every night and all,
Fire and sleet and candle-light,
    And Christ receive your soul.

When you are passed away from here,
    Every night and all,
To thorny moor you come at last,
    And Christ receive your soul.

If ever you gave hose and shows,
    Every night and all,
Sit ye down, put them to use
    And Christ receive your soul.

If hose and shoes you gave to none,
    Every night and all,
The thorns shall prick you to the bare bone,
    And Christ receive your soul.

When from the Bridge of Death you pass,
    Every night and all,
To Purgatory's fire you come at last,
    And Christ receive your soul.

If ever you gave meat or drink,
    Every night and all,
The fire shall never make you shrink,
    And Christ receive your soul.

If meat or drink you gave to none,
    Every night and all,

The fire will burn you to the bare bone,
    And Christ receive your soul.

This very night, this very night,
    Every night and all,
Fire and sleet and candle-light
    And Christ receive your soul.[85]

Dizain
Form
Country of Origin: France
Distribution: French
Century: 15th – 16th centuries

A **dizain** is a French poetic form from the 15th and 16th century, employing a stanza of 10-lines, using eight or ten syllables to the line, and having a specific rhyming pattern (such as ababbccdcd). **Dizain** can also be used to refer to poems written using this kind of stanza.

x x x x x x x (x x) a
x x x x x x x (x x) b
x x x x x x x (x x) a
x x x x x x x (x x) b
x x x x x x x (x x) b
x x x x x x x (x x) c
x x x x x x x (x x) c
x x x x x x x (x x) d
x x x x x x x (x x) c
x x x x x x x (x x) d

The following poem by Maurice Scève (c. 1501 – c. 1564) is a **dizain**:

---

[85] Lewis Turco: 170-171.

L'Œil trop ardent en mes jeunes erreurs
Girouettoit, mal cault, a l'impourveue:
Voicy (ô paour d'agreables terreurs)
Mon Basilisque avec sa poingnant' veue
Perçant Corps, Cœur, et Raison despourveue
Vint penetrer en l'Ame de mon Ame.
    Grand fut le coup, qui sans tranchante lame
Fait, que vivant le Corps, l'Esprit desvie,
Piteuse hostie au conspect de toy, Dame,
Constituée Idole de ma vie.[86]

[My eye too ardent in my youthful errings
Was turning, misguided, unawares:
Whence suddenly (o fear of pleasurable terrors)
My Basilisk with her poignant gaze
Piercing Body, Heart, and Reason unarmed,
Came to penetrate the Soul of my Soul.
    Great was the blow, which using no cutting blade
Makes it so that, while my body lives, my Spirit
        dies/deviates,
Pitiful host upon beholding your image, Lady,
Constituted Idol of my life.[87]

Droighneach
Form
Country of Origin: Ireland
Distribution: Irish
Century: 12th – 19th centuries

Droighneach (pronounced dra'iy-nach) is an *oglachas* version

---

[86] Mary Lewis Shaw: 59-60.

[87] Ibid.

of *dán díreach* and were octaves (though sometimes quatrains). Lines numbered between nine and thirteen syllables, with each line ending on a word of three syllables. They used alternating rhymes (abab cdcd and so forth) as well as cross-rhyme and at least two alliterating words per line. The final word of the last line usually alliterates with the preceding stressed word. The poem ends with *dunadh*.

x x d b x x x x x **a**
x x x x **a** x x x **x b**
x x x x x b **x x a**
x x x x **a** x x x **x b**
x x x x x d x x **x x c**
x x x c x x x x x x **x x d**
x x d x x x x x x **x x c**
x x x x c x **d** x **d**

"A Blessing on Munster", attributed to Saint Patrick (c. 385 – 461) but likely written in the 7th century, uses *droighneach*. It is presented here in English.

> God's blessing be invoked upon Munster now,
> Upon its men and boys, its womenfolk;
> Blessing be upon the land, peak and down,
> That boons the flock fruit, root, stem and stalk.
>
> A blessing upon all kinds of fruitfulness
> That shall be bourne upon this meadowland,
> No neighbor going in want of helpfulness.
> God place over Munster his healing hand!
>
> A blessing be upon the high ridge,
> Upon their cottages' bare flagstones;
> A blessing upon heather, sedge, the sheer cliff edge;
> A blessing upon lea and ledge; their gloaming glens!

Like sands of oceans under vessels
Be the numbers of their dwellings' hearthstones
Upon their downlands and their sloping hills,
Upon their crags and fells, their misty mountains![88]

Dolce stil novo
(Genre, Italian)

See *dolce stil nuovo*.

Dolce stil nuovo
Genre
Country of Origin: Italy
Distribution: Italian
Century: 13th – 14th centuries

Also spelled *dolce stil novo* ("sweet newstyle"), this type of lyric poetry was introduced in the second half of the 13th century. They expressed sincere feelings (especially of love) and employed musicality of verse. This genre made great use of metaphor, symbolism and double meanings. The human form (especially the female human form) was praised and compared to creatures of paradise (such as angels). Poets who worked in this genre were called *stilnovisti*. Guido Guinizzeli (c. 1240 – 1276) is credited with creating the genre; Dante Alighieri (c. 1265 – 1321) was a major proponent. Common forms used to write **dolce stil nuovo** include the *sonnet*, *canzone* and *ballata*.

Below are the first two stanzas of Guinizelli's poem "*Al cor gentil rempaira sempre amore*":

---

[88] Lewis Turco: 174.

Al cor gentil rempaira sempre amore
come l'ausello in selva a la verdura;
né fe' amor anti che gentil core,
né gentil core anti ch'amor natura:
ch'adesso con' fu'l sole,
sì tosto lo splendore fu lucente,
né fu davanti 'l sole;
e prende amore in gentilezza loco
così proprïamente
come calore in clarità di foco.

Foco d'amore in gentil cor s'aprende
come vertute in petra prezïosa,
che da la stella valor no i discende
anti che 'l sol la faccia gentil cosa;
poi che n'ha tratto fòre
per sua forza lo sol ciò che li è vile,
stella li dà valore:
così lo cor ch'è fatto da natura
asletto, pur, gentile,
donna a guisa di stella 'lo nnamora.[89]

Drápa
Form
Country of Origin: Iceland
Distribution: Norse
Centuries: 10th – 13th centuries

Drápa is an elaborate skaldic poem form with a number of stanzas in the same metrical pattern (often *dróttkvætt*) with a refrain of two or more half lines at regular intervals. Shorter

[89]   http://www.oilproject.org/lezione/guido-guinizzelli-al-cor-gentil-analisi-del-testo-poesie-stilnovo-4991.html, March 10, 2016

court poems were known as *flokkr* and were regarded as inferior works.

The anonymous 13th century poem *Óláfsdrápa Tryggvasonar* (the drápa of Óláfr Tryggvason) is an example of a drápa. The first to stanzas are below:

> 1. Yfirhilding biðk aldar
> einn hróðtölu beina
> mér, þanns mestum stýrir
> mætti, hverrar ættar,
> þvít veglyndum vanda
> vin þínum skalk, Rínar,
> brag þeims bjartleyg fögrum
> bauð ótta, goð dróttinn.
>
> 2. Mætr hefr minna látit
> mik stólkonungr sólar
> snjallr, an sómði þolli
> sverðéls, bragar verðan ;
> þó vilk Þróttar skýja
> þeim, es engr vas beima,
> eldveitanda ítrum,
> alfríðri, lof smíða.[90]

Dróttkvætt

Form
Country of Origin: Iceland
Distribution: Norse
Century: 9th – 12th centuries

Dróttkvætt was a Norse metrical form, employing 8-line stanzas with three stresses per line. The full stanzas were

---

[90] https://notendur.hi.is/eybjorn/ugm/skindex/odt.html, March 10, 2016

called *vísuorð*, and were broken down into two half stanzas called *helmingar*. The last two syllables of each line should be stressed-unstressed. The rhyme was variable but always included alliteration and internal rhyme. For odd lines, the internal rhyme can be half-rhyme or full rhyme, whereas even lines must be full rhymes. The first half of the rhyme can be anywhere in the line, but the second half of the rhyme must be the second last syllable of the line.

As for the alliteration, within each pair of lines the same sound was used three times on the first or third syllable of the first line, the fifth syllable of the first line and the first syllable of the second line. (All vowels alliterated with each other.) This can be visualized as follows using lines of six syllables:

(a) - (a) - A - *
A - - - - - - **

* (The two lowercase a's are the two optional places for alliteration.)

** (The capital A's are syllables that must alliterate.)

Dróttkvætt were often written as boasts, either about the poet themselves, or about someone they wanted to glorify. They often made use of *kennings*.

The following is a **dróttkvætt** attributed to Egill Skallagrímsson (c. 904 – c. 995). As in my source for this stanza I have bolded the alliteration and underlined the rhymes.

> Tí<u>tt</u> erum **ver**ð at vá<u>tt</u>a,
> **væ**<u>tt</u>i ber ek at ek h**æ**tta
> **þ**u<u>ng</u> til **þ**essar g<u>o</u> <u>ng</u>u,
> **þ**i<u>nn</u>, kinnalá mi<u>nn</u>i.

Margr velr **gestr** þar er **gist**ir,
gjǫld, finnumsk vér sjaldan,
Ármóði liggr, œðri,
ǫlðra dregg í skeggi.[91]

Dúnadh
Device
Country of Origin: Ireland
Distribution: Irish
Century: 8th – 19th centuries

Dúnadh (conclusion) is when a poem began and ended on the same sound (the same letter, word or syllable). It can also refer to chain rhyme where the last syllable of one line rhymes with the first syllable of the next.

Angus the Culdee (8th century) wrote a *conachlonn* using **dúnadh** called *Féilré*. Translated into English, the opening stanzas read:

> Bless O Christ my speaking
>> King of heavens seven,
> Strength and wealth and power
>> In this hour be **given**;
>
> **Given** O thou brightest
>> Destined not to sever,
> King of angels glorious
>> And victorious *ever*,
>
> *Ever* o'er us shining
>> Light to mortals given,
> Beaming daily, nightly,

---

91 Debbie Potts: 16.

Dyfalu

Genre
Country of Origin: Wales
Distribution: Welsh
Century: 14th century

A **dyfalu** (plural *dyfaliad*) is a poetic technique in which poets dwell on an object and then compare it to other objects in nature. Metaphors, similes and parallels abound. These poems were sometimes riddles (in fact, **dyfalu** means "to guess".

A famous **dyfalu**, written using *cywydd*, is "*Y Gwynt*" (The Wind") by Dafydd ap Gwilym (c. 1315 – c. 1350). The first two stanzas are quoted below:

> Yr wybrwynt, helynt hylaw,
> Agwrdd drwst a gerdda draw,
> Gŵr eres wyd garw ei sain,
> Drud byd heb droed heb adain.
> Uthr yw mor eres y'th roed
> O bantri wybr heb untroed,
> A buaned y rhedy
> Yr awr hon dros y fron fry.
>
> Dywaid ym, diwyd emyn,
> Dy hynt, di ogleddwynt glyn.
> Hydoedd y byd a hedy,
> Hin y fron, bydd heno fry,
> Och ŵr, a dos Uwch Aeron
> Yn glaer deg, yn eglur dôn.
> Nac aro di, nac eiriach,

---

[92] Douglas Hyde: 157.

Nac ofna er Bwa Bach,
Cyhuddgwyn wenwyn weini.
Caeth yw'r wlad a'i maeth i mi.[93]

[Welkin's wind, way unhindered,
Big blusterer passing by,
A harsh-voiced man of marvels,
World-bold, without foot or wing,
How strange that sent from heaven's
Pantry with never a foot,
Now you can race so swiftly
Over the hillside above.
No bridge over stream, no boat;
Forewarned, you remain undrowned,
A free and easy crossing.
Winnowing leaves, you steal nests,
None charge you, you're not halted
By armed band, lieutenant's hand,
Blue blade or flood or downpour.
No sheriff or troop takes you,
Pruner of the treetop plumes.
No mother's son slays, crime's tale,
Fire burns, deceit undoes you.[94]]

93

http://www.dafyddapgwilym.net/AnaServer?dafydd+96320+printPoemEng.anv+poe
m=Edited%20Text:%20%2047%20-%20Y%20Gwynt, March 10, 2016

[94] http://www.poetrynook.com/poem/wind-26, March 10, 2016

E

Echraid
Device
Country of Origin: Ireland
Distribution: Irish
Century: unknown

Meaning "riding", **echraid** is alliteration within stanzas and rhyming the final lines of each one.

Endecasilabos sueltos
Form
Country of Origin: Spanish
Distribution: Spanish
Century: 16th century

Created by Garcilaso de la Vega (c. 1501 – 1536) this form consisted of unrhymed lines of 11-syllables.

x x x x x x x x x x x
x x x x x x x x x x x
…

Endecasillabi sciolti
(Form, Italian)

See *versi sciolti*.

Endecasillabo tronco
(Device, Italian)

See *verso sdrucciolo*.

English madrigal
(Form, English)

See *madrigal*.

Englyn
Form
Country of Origin: Wales, Cornwall
Distribution: Welsh, Cornish
Century: 6th – 15th centuries

Englyn (pronounced eng'-lin; plural *englynion*) is a short poem form in the Welsh and Cornish tradition. It uses quantitative meters, involving the counting of syllables, as well as rigid patterns of rhyme and half rhyme. Each of the lines contains a repeating pattern of consonants and accent (*cynghanedd*).

Types of *englynion* include:

Englyn penfyr (pronounced eng'-lin pen'veer; "short-ended englyn"): This is one of the twenty-four codified Welsh meters of *cerdd dafod*. It consists of three lines, with the first line having 10-syllables, while the other two have seven each. The last three syllables of the first line is a *gair cyrch*. The seventh, eighth or ninth syllable of the first line introduces the rhyme and it is repeated on the last syllable of the other two lines. The fourth syllable of the second line echoes the final syllable of the first through either consonance or rhyme. The *caesura* before the *gair cyrch* could be shown as a dash.

x x x x x x a x x b *
x x b x x x a
x x x x x x a

* (The a could be on the 7th, 8th or 9th syllable.)

Englyn milwr (pronounced eng'-lin mih'-loor; "the soldier's englyn"): This is one of the twenty-four codified Welsh meters of *cerdd dafod*. It consists of three 7-syllable lines, with all three lines rhyming.

x x x x x x a
x x x x x x a
x x x x x x a

Englyn unodl union (pronounced eng'-lin ee-nah'-dl een'-yon; "straight one-rhymed englyn"): This is one of the twenty-four codified Welsh meters of *cerdd dafod*. It consists of four lines of ten, six, seven and seven syllables. The first two lines are called *paladr* (shelf) while the second two lines are galled *esgyll* (wings). Each line makes use of *cynghanedd*. The last three syllables of the first line are a *gair cyrch*. The seventh, eighth or ninth syllable of the first line introduces the rhyme and it is repeated on the last syllable of the other three lines. The part of the first line following the rhyme alliterates with the first part of the second line. The *caesura* before the *gair cyrch* could be shown as a dash.

x x x x x x a x x b *
x x b x x a
x x x x x x a
x x x x x x a

* (The a could be on the 7th, 8th or 9th syllable.)

Englyn unodl crwca (pronounced eng'-lin ee-nah'-dl croo'ca; "crooked one-rhyme englyn"): This is one of the twenty-four codified Welsh meters of *cerdd dafod*. It consists of four lines of seven, seven, ten and six syllables. The last syllables of the first, second and last lines and the seventh, eighth or ninth syllable of the third line all rhyme. The last three syllables of the third line are a *gair cyrch*. The *caesura* before the *gair cyrch* could be shown as a dash. It is basically an *englyn unodl union* with the *paladr* and *esgyll* switched.

x x x x x x a
x x x x x x a
x x x x x x a x x b *
x x b x x a

* (The a could be on the 7th, 8th or 9th syllable.)

Englyn cyrch (pronounced eng'-lin kirch): This is one of the twenty-four codified Welsh meters of *cerdd dafod*. It consists of four lines of seven syllables each. The final syllables of the first, second and fourth line rhyme, while the last syllable of the third line rhymes with the second, third or fourth syllable of the last line.

x x x x x x a
x x x x x x a
x x x x x x b
x x x b x x a *

* (The b could be on the 2nd, 3rd or 4th syllable.)

This selection from the anonymous Anglo-Saxon *Gnomic Verses*, here translated into English, is in *englyn cyrch*:

Frost shall freeze, fire shall eat wood,

Ice will bridge and the earth brood.
Water shall wear winter's shield,
Yet the field will be renewed.

Frost's fetters shall free the grain,
Wonderlock will yield to rain,
And there shall be fair weather
When the winter goes to wane.

Sun-warmed summer! What was dumb
Shall find voice. The body, numb,
When the deep wave was most dark,
Will feel when the lark has come.[95]

Englyn proest dalgron (pronounced eng'-lin pro'-est dal'-gron):
This is one of the twenty-four codified Welsh meters of *cerdd dafod*. It consists of four 7-syllable lines that use slant rhymes using either all short vowels (such as in bet or hit) or all long vowels (such as in hate or height).

x x x x x x a
x x x x x x a
x x x x x x a
x x x x x x a

The Welsh poet Dafydd Benfras (c. 1230 – 1260) wrote "The Grave" using *englyn proest dalgron*. It is presented here in English.

Everyman comes to the dank earth.
Folk, forlorn and small, perish.
What wealth rears is wracked by death.
In an hour dirt devoureth.

---

[95] Lines 71-80. Lewis Turco: 180-181.

Great maw, end of what I clutch,
What I loved you turned to filth.
Mine will be a chill stone hearth—
Life was not meant for a youth.

Each man's cold estate is death;
He walks alone on the heath
That will take him in its clinch,
Come at last to the cromlech.[96]

Englyn lleddfbroest (pronounced eng'-lin clethev'-broist): This is one of the twenty-four codified Welsh meters of *cerdd dafod*. It consists of four 7-syllable lines that half-rhyme with each other, but the half rhymes must use the ae, oe, wy and ei diphthongs (in Welsh) or as in boil, fuel, vial or vowel (if you are trying to write the form in English).

x x x x x x a
x x x x x x a
x x x x x x a
x x x x x x a

Englyn proest cadwynog (pronounced eng'-lin pro'-est god-win'-og; "chain half-rhyme englyn"): This is one of the twenty-four codified Welsh meters of *cerdd dafod*. It consists of four 7-syllable lines with first line slant rhyming with the second and full rhyming with the third. The second line full rhymed with the fourth. (For example: rod/dead/nod/led.)

x x x x x x a
x x x x x x *a*
x x x x x x a

---

[96] Lewis Turco: 181-182.

Englyn proest cyfnewidiog (reciprocal half-rhyme englyn): consists of four 7-syllable lines with all four lines half-rhyming. Also includes other aspects of *cyngnanedd*. It is similar to the *englyn lleddfbroest,* which has the same stanza structure and rhyming scheme but must use diphthongs in tis half rhymes.

Englyn toddaid: The first two lines follow a regular **englyn** pattern, followed by two more lines of 10 syllables each.

Englyn cil-dwrn: The first two lines follow a regular **englyn** pattern, followed by one more line of three syllables or less, which follows the rhyme of the first two lines.

Englyn cil-dwrn
(Form, Welsh, Cornish)

See *englyn.*

Englyn cyrch
(Form, Welsh, Cornish)

See *englyn.*

Englyn lleddfbroest
(Form, Welsh, Cornish)

See *englyn.*

Englyn milwr
(Form, Welsh, Cornish)

See *englyn.*

Englyn penfyr
(Form, Welsh, Cornish)

See *englyn.*

Englyn proest cadwynog
(Form, Welsh, Cornish)

See *englyn.*

Englyn proest cyfnewidiog
(Form, Welsh, Cornish)

See *englyn.*

Englyn proest dalgron
(Form, Welsh, Cornish)

See *englyn.*

Englyn toddaid
(Form, Welsh, Cornish)

See *englyn.*

Englyn unodl crwca
(Form, Welsh, Cornish)

See *englyn.*

Englyn unodl union
(Form, Welsh, Cornish)

See *englyn*.

Ensalada
Form
Country of Origin: Iberian Peninsula (Spain, Portugal)
Distribution: Iberian
Century: 16th century

The **ensalada** (salad, mix-up, medley) appeared in the mid to late 1500s, and was apparently not very popular[97]. It was a poem consisting of lines and strophes of varying lengths and rhyme schemes, generally dependent on the accompanying music. The earliest known **ensalada** was written either by Fray Ambrosio Montesinos (d. c. 1512) or Gil Vincente (c. 1465 – c. 1536). They were often lyrical and a sub-form of the *quodlibet*. It is possible that **ensaladas** were theatrical when performed. **Ensalada** poets made use of satire, quotations from popular songs, dramatic exchanges, quotations from scripture, liturgicals, and classic authors.[98]

Mateo Flecha el viejo (1481 - 1553) wrote a famous **ensalada** called *La Bomba* (el dindirindín). There is a long version and a short (carol) version, which is printed below:

> Ande, pues, nuestro apellido,
> el tañer con el cantar
> concordes en alabar
> a Jesús rezién nascido.
>
> Bendito el que ha venido
> a librarnos de agonía.

---

[97] Stephe Cushman: 436.

[98] Sarah Gilbert: unnumbered page.

Bendito sea este día
que nasció el contentamiento.

Remedió su advenimiento mil enojos,
Benditos sean los ojos
que con piedad nos miraron
y benditos que ansí amansaron tal fortuna.[99]

Enuech
(Genre, French)

See *enuig*.

Enueg
(Genre, French)

See *eunig*.

Enug
(Genre, French)

See *eunig*.

Enuig
Genre
Country of Origin: Occitania (southern France, Monaco, Italy, Spain)
Distribution: Occitan
Century: examples dated from at least the 14th century

Enuig was one of the genres of lyric poetry practiced by the

99   http://www.simbiontes.com/archives/a-pecho-descubierto/la-bomba-ensalada.php, March 11, 2016

troubadours. In general, the **enuig** is a litany of complaints (a song of annoyance), with few of them topically linked to the rest.

"Sonnet LXVI" by William Shakespeare is considered an English **enuig**:

> Tired with all these, for restful death I cry,
> As, to behold desert a beggar born,
> And needy nothing trimm'd in jollity,
> And purest faith unhappily forsworn,
> And guilded honour shamefully misplaced,
> And maiden virtue rudely strumpeted,
> And right perfection wrongfully disgraced,
> And strength by limping sway disabled,
> And art made tongue-tied by authority,
> And folly doctor-like controlling skill,
> And simple truth miscall'd simplicity,
> And captive good attending captain ill:
> Tired with all these, from these would I be gone,
> Save that, to die, I leave my love alone.[100]

See also *complaint*.

Escondich
Genre
Country of Origin: Occitania (southern France, Monaco, Italy, Spain)
Distribution: Occitan
Century: late 12th or early 13th century

The **escondich** was a poem of excuses. Bertran de Born (1140s

---

[100] http://www.poetrymagnumopus.com/index.php?/topic/680-enuig/, March 11, 2016

– c. 1215) wrote the only extant example of this genre[101] known as *Le m'escondisc* ("He Protests His Innocence to a Lady") which begins:

> Ieu m'escondisc, domna, que mal no mier
> de so que.us an de me dich lauzengier;
> per merce.us prec qu'om no puoscha mesclar
> lo vostre cors fi, leial, vertadier,
> umil e franc, cortes e plazentier
> ab me, domna, per menzonjas comtar.[102]

Espinela
Form
Country of Origin: Spain
Distribution: Spanish
Century: 16th century

An **espinela** is a late 16th century octosyllabic 10-line stanza rhyming aabba/accdc. This was sometimes augmented by two more lines rhyming ed. This form evolved from the *décima* and is also known as *décima espanela*.

x x x x x x x a
x x x x x x x a
x x x x x x x b
x x x x x x x b
x x x x x x x a
x x x x x x x a
x x x x x x x c
x x x x x x x c
x x x x x x x d

---

[101] Frank W. Chambers 1: 158.

[102] Ibid.

x x x x x x x c
(x x x x x x x e
x x x x x x x d)

Estampa
(Genre, Occitan, Catalan, Italian)

See *estampie*.

Estampida
Genre
Country of Origin: Provence (France)
Distribution: Provençal
Century: at least 12th century

The **estampida** ("uproar") is related to the Old French *estampie*. **Estampida** employed regular stanza structures and a single-rhyme scheme.[103]

Raimbaut de Vaqueiras or Vaqueyras (fl. 1180 – 1207) wrote an **estampida** known as *"Kalenda maia"* that was an exchange between a knight and his lady. It begins:

> Kalenda maia
> Ni fueills de faia
> Ni chans d'auzell ni flors de glaia
> Non es qe.m plaia,
> Pros dona gaia,
> Tro q'un isnell messagier aia
> Del vostre bell cors, qi.m retraia
> Plazer novell q'amors m'atraia
> E jaia,

---

[103] Frank W. Chambers 1: 215.

E.m traia
Vas vos, donna veraia,
E chaia
De plaia
.l gelos, anz qe.m n'estraia.

Ma bell' amia,
Per Dieu non sia
Qe ja.l gelos de mon dan ria,
Qe car vendria
Sa gelozia,
Si aitals dos amantz partia;
Q'ieu ja joios mais non seria,
Ni jois ses vos pro no.m tenria;
Tal via
Faria
Q'oms ja mais no.m veiria;
Cell dia
Morria,
Donna pros, q'ie.us perdria.[104]

[Neither calends of May,
nor leaves of beech
nor songs of bird, nor gladiolus flowers
are of my liking,
o noble and merry lady,
until I have a fleet messenger
of your beautiful person to tell me
of new pleasures love and joy
are bringing;
and I repair
to you, true lady;

---

[104]

http://www.trobar.org/troubadours/raimbaut_de_vaqueiras/raimbaut_de_vaqueiras_
15.php, March 24, 2016

and let me crush
and strike
the jealous, before I depart from here.

My beautiful friend
by God, this never be:
that out of jealousy one scoffs at my harm,
he'd command a dear price
for his jealousy
if it were such as to part two lovers;
Since never again I'd be happy
nor would I know happiness, without you;
I'd take
such a way
that I'd never be seen by men again;
that day
I'll die,
brave lady, in which I lose you.][105]

Estampie
Genre
Country of Origin: Occitania (southern France, Monaco, Italy, Spain), Catalonia (Spain), Italy
Distribution: Occitan, Catalan, Italian
Century: at least 12th century

Known in Catalan as *estampa* and Italian as *istampitte*, the **estampie** was not just a poetic form but also a dance and musical form. Unlike the *estamida*, the **estampie** does not use rigid stanza structure or mono-rhyme.[106]

---

[105] Ibid.

[106] Frank W. Chambers 1: 215.

Estancia
Form
Country of Origin: Spanish
Distribution: Spanish
Century: 16th century

Created by Garcilaso de la Vega (c. 1501 – 1536) this form consisted of lines of 11- and 7-syllables.

x x x x x x x x x x x

x x x x x x x

Estrambote
(Device, Spanish)

See *estribote*.

Estribillo
Device
Country of Origin: Spain
Distribution: Spanish
Century: examples found by at least the 11th century

An **estibillo** ("little stirrup") was a refrain used in lyrics and ballads that was adapted from the Arabic *zéjel*. (In the 14th century the *zéjel* also developed into the *cantigo*.) Originally, the **estribillo** was the introductory stanza that stated the theme of the poem (and was often called the *cabeza* or *texto*). It was repeated (in whole or in part) at the end of each stanza and at the end of the poem. Later it was sometimes found at the end of each stanza only. The **estribillo** could consist of two to four lines.

An example of an **estribillo** is the following couplet:

Ay mar braba esquiba, de ti doy querella,
fazes(me) que viba con tan grant manzela.[107]

In the following anonymous poem you can see an example of a three line **estribillo** where the second and third lines are repeated at the end of each stanza:

Tres morillas m'enamoran
en Jaén,
Axa ya Fátima y Marién.

Tres morillas tan garridas
Yvan a coger olivas,
Y hallávanlas cogidas
en Jaén,
Axa ya Fátima y Marién.

Y hallávanlas cogidas,
Y tornaban desmaídas
Y las colores perdidas
en Jaén,
Axa ya Fátima y Marién.

Tres moricas tan loçanas,
Tres moricas tan loçanas,
Yvan a coger manzanas
en Jaén,
Axa ya Fátima y Marién.[108]

Estribot
(Device, Spanish)

---

[107] Richard Macpherson: 536.

[108] Karl Reichi: 47.

See *estribote*.

Estribote
Device
Country of Origin: Spain
Distribution: Spanish
Century: unknown

Also known as *estrambote, estribot, estrybote* and *strambotto*, **estribote** were composed with a *zéjel*-like rhyme scheme aabbba and functioned the same as an *estribillo*.

Estrybote
(Device, Spanish)

See *estribote*.

Exemplum
Genre
Country of Origin: unknown
Distribution: Unknown
Century: unknown

An **exemplum** was a short narrative used to illustrate a moral point, used chiefly in sermons. In poetry the genre of **exemplum** is essentially preaching in poetic form. Perhaps the most famous example of an **exemplum** is the anonymous 14th century poem *Patience*, which begins:

> Pacience is a poynt, Þa3 hit displese ofte.
> When heuy herttes ben hurt wyth heÞyng oÞer elles,
> Suffraunce may aswag[en] hem & Þe swleme leÞe,
> For ho quelles vche a qued & quenches malyce;
> For quoso suffer cowÞe syt, sele wolde fol3e,

& quo for Þro may no3t Þole, Þe Þikker he sufferes.
Þen is better to abyde Þe bur vmbestoundes
Þen ay Þrow forth my Þro, Þa3 me Þynk ylle.
I herde on a halyday, at a hy3e masse,
How Mathew melede Þat his Mayster His meyny con teche.[109]

---

[109] http://rpo.library.utoronto.ca/poems/patience, March 11, 2016

F

Fabla
Genre
Country of Origin: unknown
Distribution: unknown
Century: unknown

The **fabla** were fable poems.

Fabliau
Genre
Country of Origin: France
Distribution: French
Century: 12th – 15th century

The **fabliaux** were short comic tales written by jongleurs in northeast France between ca. 1150 and 1400. Thematically, the **fabliaux** featured sexual and scatological obscenity and expressed opinions contrary to the establishment (the church and the nobility).

A **fabliau** was usually written in octosyllabic couplets, numbering between 300 and 400 lines. They employed puns and other verbal wordplay. Paranomasia and catacheresis were commonly used.

There is evidence that **fabliaux** were written for both a bourgeois and noble audience, with the portrayal of peasants (French villains) and nobles differing appropriately. They employed a wide range of stock characters which includes cuckolded husbands, ribald clergy, foolish peasants, beggars, thieves and whores.

Eustache d'Amien's poem *Le boucher d'Abbeville* (The Butcher of Abbeville) is an example of a 13th century French **fabliaux**. It begins:

> Un Boucher d'Abbeville et caustique et malin,
> Pars le nuit surprise en chemin,
> Résolut de coucher dans le prochain village.
> Il arrive; et soudains s'informe, en homme sage,
> De quellqu'auberge où l'étranger
> Commodément puisse loger.[110]

Chaucer wrote English **fabliaux**, as exemplified in the "Miller's Prologue" of the *Canterbury Tales* (this stanza's first line is the second half of a distich started in the previous stanza; the last couplet's concluding line is likewise at the beginning of the next stanza):

> "Now herkneth," quod the Millere, "alle and some!
> But first I make a protestacioun
> That I am dronke; I knowe it by my soun.
> And therfore if that I mysspeke or seye,
> Wyte it the ale of Southwerk, I you preye.
> For I wol telle a legende and a lyf
> Bothe of a carpenter and of his wyf,
> How that a clerk hath set the wrightes cappe."[111]

["Now listen," said the Miller, "everyone!

---

[110] Barthélemy Imbert: 63.

[111] Lines 3136-3143, https://sites.fas.harvard.edu/~chaucer/teachslf/milt-par.htm#PROLOGUE, March 14, 2016

But first I make a protestation
That I am drunk; I know it by my sound.
And therefore if that I misspeak or say (amiss),
Blame it on ale of Southwerk, I you pray.
For I will tell a legend and a life
Both of a carpenter and of his wife,
How a clerk has set the carpenter's cap (fooled
    him)."[112]]

Fatras
Form
Country of Origin: France
Distribution: French
Century: 14th – 17th centuries

The **fatras** first appeared in the 1320s and was an obscure form utilizing 11-lines preceded by a couplet whose lines frame the rest of the poem. Therefore there is a couplet, then the first line of the couplet is repeated, followed by nine more lines, and then the last line of the couplet is repeated. The **fatras** could use rhyme or not and did not need to have a set meter. They tend to be satirical and absurd and full of word play and nonsense. They often mocked courtly love.

The basic form of the **fatras** is also known as the *fatras simple*. A *fatras double* is when two 11-line stanzas are formed, with the lines of the distich reversed in the second stanza. The last line is a restatement of line one of the poem. The *fatras possible* allows for coherent text, whereas the *fatras impossible* is nonsense verse.

The **fatras** is also known as *resverie* and is sometimes used as another name for *fatrasie*.

---

[112] Ibid.

Examples of stanza structure below are using octosyllablic lines.

Fatras simple   OR

x x x x x x x A
x x x x x x x B
x x x x x x x A
x x x x x x x x
x x x x x x x x
x x x x x x x x
x x x x x x x x
x x x x x x x x
x x x x x x x x
x x x x x x x x
x x x x x x x x
x x x x x x x x
x x x x x x x B

fatrras double

x x x x x x x A   x x x x x x x B
x x x x x x x B   x x x x x x x A
x x x x x x x A   x x x x x x x B
x x x x x x x x   x x x x x x x x
x x x x x x x x   x x x x x x x x
x x x x x x x x   x x x x x x x x
x x x x x x x x   x x x x x x x x
x x x x x x x x   x x x x x x x x
x x x x x x x x   x x x x x x x x
x x x x x x x x   x x x x x x x x
x x x x x x x x   x x x x x x x x
x x x x x x x x   x x x x x x x x
x x x x x x x B   x x x x x x x A

See also *fatrasie*.

Below is a **fatras** written by Guillaume Flamant (1455 – 1520):

> O poison pire que mortel,
> Me ferez-vous crever le cœur ?
> O poison pire que mortel,
> Qui me tient en telle tutelle
> Que n'ai ni force ni vigueur;
> Envieuse et fausse querelle,
> Plus pute que n'est maquerelle,
> Trop me plains de votre rigueur.
> Où est Satan, mon gouverneur,
> Qui ne vient pas quand je l'appelle ?
> O folle, infernale fureur;
> Diables pleins de toute cautelle,
> Me ferez-vous crever le cœur ?

Fatras double
(Form, French)

See *fatras*.

Fatras impossible
(Form, French)

See *fatras*.

Fatras possible
(Form, French)

See *fatras*.

Fatras simple
(Form, French)

See *fatras*.

Fatrasie
Form
Country of Origin: France
Distribution: French
Century: 13th century

Similar to the *fatras* (it is sometimes considered to be the same thing), this 13th century form had a different structure. It was comprised of 11-lines, the first six having five feet and the following five having seven feet. It used the rhyme scheme aabaabcabab. **Fatrasie** were sometimes used to criticize those in power and made use of absurdity and impossibility with animals carrying out human activities, animate objects and so on. Scatological references are common, as is other vulgarity.

Also known as *fratrasie*.

x x x x x a
x x x x x a
x x x x x b
x x x x x a
x x x x x a
x x x x x b
x x x x x x c
x x x x x x a
x x x x x x b
x x x x x x a
x x x x x x b

Pascal Kaeser wrote a series of **fatrasies**, including *I*:

Un lérot marin
Jouait du surin
Pour tailler un lemme,
Un rohart d'airain
Signait au burin
L'armet d'une gemme ;
Si ne fût un vieil oedème
Qui dirimait le purin
Et s'entait à un poème,
Le rachis d'un mandarin
Les eût engeignés à Brême.[113]

This anonymous poem from the 13th century is often attributed to Jehan Bodel and is known as *Fatrasies of Arras* (though you will note it breaks the rules for the rhyme scheme and the number of lines):

Le son d'un cornet
Mangeait au vinaigre
Le coeur d'un tonnerre
Quand un béquet mort
Prit au trébuchet
Le cours d'une étoile
En l'air il y eut un grain de seigle
Quand l'aboiement d'un brochet
Et le tronçon d'une toile
Ont trouvé foutu un pet
Ils lui ont coupé l'oreille.

Un ours emplumé
Fit semer un blé
De Douvres à Oissent.

---

[113] http://worldserver2.oleane.com/fatrazie/fatras_et_fatrasie.htm, October 13, 2002

Un oignon pelé
S'était apprêté
A chanter devant.[114]

Finida
Device
Country of Origin: Spain
Distribution: Spanish, Portuguese
Century: 14th – 16th centuries

In the 14th to 16th century, the **finida** served as a conclusion to a poem (like the *remate* of the later *canción petrarquista*). It repeats the rhyme order of the second part of the last stanza in cases where it has the same number of verses. Otherwise it may have one verse more or less than the last half stanza. The Portuguese also used the **finida**, regarding it as an essential part of perfect composition. In Portuguese, it may have one to four verses and must rhyme with the last stanza or, if the poem was a *cantiga de refam*, with the refrain.

Flabel
Genre
Country of Origin: France?
Distribution: unknown
Century: unknown

Also known as *fablel*, **flabel** were "little-fables".

Flokkr
(Form, Norse)

See *drápa*.

---

114 Ibid.

Flyting

Genre
Country of Origin: England, Scotland, Scandinavia
Distribution: Anglo-Saxon, Norse, Scottish
Century: 5th – 16th centuries

Flyting was a boasting match in verse, often between warriors before battles, or between bards. Each participant would insult the other using scatological references and other words of abuse. It was a common element in Anglo-Saxon and Norse verse. In the 15th and 16th centuries it became a popular practice in Scotland.

In *Lokasenna*, a saga likely from the 12th century, Loki insults another god by saying:

> "Give heed now, Njorth, | nor boast too high,
> No longer I hold it hid;
> With thy sister hadst thou | so fair a son,
> Thus hadst thou no worse a hope."[115]

A famous example of Scottish flying is the poem "The Flyting of Dunbar and Kennedy" by William Dunbar (1459 – unkn). Dunbar's initial exchange with his opponent reads in part:

> "…But wonder loth were I to be a bard.
> Flyting to use right greatly I eschame,
> For it is neither winning nor reward,
> But tinsel both of honour and of fame,
> Increase of sorrow, slander, and evil name.
> Yet might they be so bold in their backbiting
> To gar me rhyme and raise the fiend with flyting

---

[115] http://www.sacred-texts.com/neu/poe/poe10.htm, March 14, 2016

And through all countries and kingrics them
proclaim."[116]

Folía
Form
Country of Origin: Spain
Distribution: Spain
Century: 16th century

A **folía** was a 4-line stanza; a variation of the *seguidilla*. It is likely related to a Portuguese dance-song form which normally expressed a nonsensical or ridiculous thought. The lines may be octosyllabic or shorter. If the lines are not of equal length then the even numbered lines are generally shorter and very often oxytonic (stressed on the last syllable).

(x x x x x x x) x
(x x x x x x x) x *
(x x x x x x x) x
(x x x x x x x) x *

* (If lines are uneven, this line is shorter.)

Formes fixes
Form
Country of Origin: France
Distribution: French, Italian
Centuries: 14th – 15th centuries

The "fixed forms" are three 14th and 15th century French poetic forms: the *ballade*, *rondeau* and *virelai*. They each also have a musical form, usually a *chanson*, and they all consisted of

---

[116] http://www.thomondgate.net/docs/dunbar/dunbar3_flytingglossed.pdf, March 14, 2016

complex patterns of verse repetition and a refrain with musical content in two main sections.

Forms from other countries are also sometimes referred to as **formes fixes**, such as the Italian *madrigal*, the Italian *ballata*, the Italian *barzelletta*, the German *bar form*, the Spanish *cantiga*, the Spanish *canción*, and the Italian *villancico*.

Fornyrðislag
Form
Country of Origin: Iceland, Scandinavia
Distribution: Norse
Century: 8th – 13th century

Fornyrðislag (pronounced fort-near-this-lagh; "meter of ancient words") is an Eddic verse form consisting of a 4-line stanza, each line divided by a caesura into two half-lines, which in turn have two accented syllables and two or three unaccented ones. There are six variations of half-lines that could be used. In the following examples the x represents one or more unstressed syllables.

/ x / x
x / x /
x / / x
/ / x x
/ x x /
x x / /

The two half-lines are linked together by alliteration, which in case of the first line could fall on one or the other of the stressed syllables, but in the second half-line had to fall on the first stressed syllables. The alliteration of the first half-line was called *stuðlar* (props), the one in the second half-line *höfuðstafr* (head-stave). The alliteration is actually an initial rhyme consisting of consonants alliterating with the same consonants, except sk, sp and st, which could be alliterated with themselves, and of a vowel alliterating with any other vowel, as well as with j.

```
/ x / x  | / x / x          *
x / x /  | x / x /
x // x  | x // x
// x x  | // x x
/ x x /  | / x x /
x x //  | x x //
```

* (In the first half-line the alliteration can be on either stressed syllable.)

The *Völuspá* (13ᵗʰ century) was written in **fornyrðislag**; the first three stanzas read:

> 1. Hljóðs bið ek allar helgar kindir,
> meiri ok minni mögu Heimdallar;
> viltu, at ek, Valföðr! vel framtelja forn spjöll fíra,
> þau er fremst um man.
>
> 2. Ek man jötna ár um borna,
> þá er forðum mik fœdda höfðu;
> níu man ek heima, níu íviði,
> mjötvið mœran fyr mold neðan.
>
> 3. Ár var alda þar er Ýmir bygði,
> vara sandr né sær né svalar unnir,
> jörð fannsk æva né upphiminn,
> gap var ginnunga, en gras hvergi.[117]

---

[117] http://www.voluspa.org/voluspa1-5.htm, March 14, 2016

[1. Hearing I ask | from the holy races,
From Heimdall's sons, | both high and low;
Thou wilt, Valfather, | that well I relate
Old tales I remember | of men long ago.

2. I remember yet | the giants of yore,
Who gave me bread | in the days gone by;
Nine worlds I knew, | the nine in the tree
With mighty roots | beneath the mold.

3. Of old was the age | when Ymir lived;
Sea nor cool waves | nor sand there were;
Earth had not been, | nor heaven above,
But a yawning gap, | and grass nowhere.[118]]

Fratrasie
(Form, French)

See *fatrasie*.

Frau Minne
Device
Country of Origin: Germany
Distribution: German
Century: 12th to at least 15th century

Frau Minne was a personification of courtly love in Middle High German literature who is often addressed in poetry by the poet.

In the poem *Parzival* by Wolfram von Eschenbach (c. 1160/1180 – c. 1220), **Frau Minne** is often addressed, as shown

---

[118] Ibid.

translated below:

> Frau Minne now bethink thee, for sore this shameth
> thee.
> For an one should wrong a peasant in this wise speech
> will be,
> 'My Lord will sure repay thee.' Vengeance from thee
> he'd seek.
> Methinks, this gallant Waleis, an thou wouldst let him
> speak.[119]

French sonnet
(Form, French)

See *rondel*.

Frottola
Form
Country of Origin: Italy
Distribution: Italian
Century: 14th – 16th centuries

The **frottola** emerged in the 14th century as a satiric, rambling
verse form utilizing irregular meters and stanzas, reflecting
the fact that the subject matter was usually unconnected,
bizarre and sometimes senseless. They could be composed of
couplets of unrhymed pentameter, heptameter or
hendecasyllabic lines with internal rhyme (though some
experts also believe there were blank form **frottola**[120]). In the
15th century the form became known as the *frottola-barzelleta*
where it became a sub-species of *canto carnascialesco* (carnival

---

[119] W. J. Stein: 159.

[120] Lewis Turco.

song), set to music, following the structure of the *balata grande* and being octosyllabic. At the beginning of the 14th century it was used for moral instruction, but by the end of that century it had assumed artistic proportions with moral, political or satirical themes. It also made use of proverbs and witty instructional content (didacticism).

Frottola-barzellta
(Form, Italian)

See *barzeletta*.

G

Gair cyrch
Device
Country of Origin: Wales
Distribution: Welsh
Century: 6th – 15th centuries

A **gair cyrch** was a tail or addendum to a line, following the placement of the main rhyme and after a caesura. The caesura is sometimes represented as a dash.

The following example of a **gair cyrch** occurs in verse written by Tudor Aled (c. 1500):

> Mae'n wir y gwelir argoelyn — **difai**
> Werb dyfiad y brigyn
> A bysbys y dengys dyn
> O ba radd y bo'i wriddyn.[121]

> [It is true that one sees a faultless sign
> In the growth of the shoot;
> And man manifestly shows
> From what grade his root is.[122]]

Gaita gallega

---

[121] John T. Koch: 699.

[122] Ibid.

Form
Country of Origin: Galicia (Spain, Portugal)
Distribution: Galician
Century: unknown

Gaita gallega was a verse form with a variable number of syllables per line (usually averaging ten to twelve). The lines were split into two hemistichs. There were two principal stresses being the second last syllable in each hemistich. The secondary stresses could be displaced to any position. It used an anapestic decasyllable meter. The gaita is a Galician form of the bagpipes and these poems were likely written to be accompanied by them featuring ternary movement.

(x /) x x / x | x / x x / x

Gap
(Genre, Provençal)

See *sirventes*.

Gasconade
Genre
Country of Origin: unknown
Distribution: unknown
Century: unknown

A **Gasconade** was a *rant* and apparently derives its name from a belief that Gascons were naturally boastful.

Gest
Genre
Country of Origin: unknown
Distribution: English, French?
Century: at least 15th – 17th centuries

A **gest** is a tale of war or adventure. One famous example is the Middle English "A Gest of Robyn Hood" (c.1450), which begins:

> LYTHE and listin, gentilmen,
> That be of frebore blode;
> I shall you tel of a gode yeman,
> His name was Robyn Hode.
> Robyn was a prude outlaw,
> [Whyles he walked on grounde;
> So curteyse an outlawe] as he was one
> Was never non founde.[123]

See also *chansons de geste*.

Gilozesca
(Genre, Occitan)

See *mal mariée*.

Glosa
Form
Country of Origin: Spain, Portugal
Distribution: Spanish, Portuguese, English
Century: 14th – 15th centuries

A metric form introduced in the late 14th or early 15th century. It is also known as *mote or retruécano*, and is related to the *cantiga*. It consists of a line or short stanza called a *cabeza* (or sometimes *mote*, *letra*, or *texto*) which states the theme of the poem. Sometimes the *cabeza* consisted of lines quoted from

---

[123] http://www.sacred-texts.com/neu/eng/child/ch117.htm, March 15, 2016

another poet. It is followed by one stanza for each line of the *cabeza*, expanding on that line and incorporating it into this explanatory stanza (sometimes the line from the *cabeza* will be requoted verbatim as the last line of each stanza). Strophes may be of any length (though ten lines were common) and rhyme scheme (including not having any rhyme at all). Spanish **glosa** usually employed octosyllabic lines whereas those written in English were often iambic pentameter. The sixth and ninth lines should rhyme with line ten.

Using octosyllabic lines and a 2-line *cabeza* the form looks like the following:

x x x x x x x A
x x x x x x x B

x x x x x x x x
x x x x x x x x
x x x x x x x x
x x x x x x x x
x x x x x x x x
x x x x x x x a
x x x x x x x x
x x x x x x x x
x x x x x x x a
x x x x x x x A

x x x x x x x x
x x x x x x x x
x x x x x x x x
x x x x x x x x
x x x x x x x x
x x x x x x x b
x x x x x x x x
x x x x x x x x

x x x x x x x b
x x x x x x x B

Goliardic verse
Genre
Country of Origin: France, England, Germany
Distribution: French, English, German
Century: 12th – 13th century

Goliardic verse was a lyric poetical genre popular in the 12th and 13th centuries. It celebrated hedonistic love and drinking, while also satirizing the clergy. It was practiced by wandering students who enjoyed making up ribald and satirical songs composed in Latin. The best known collection of Goliardic verse is the *Carmina Burana* written in the 11th century. One of those poems was called "Let's Away with Study":

> Let's away with study,
>   Folly's sweet.
> Treasure all the pleasure
>   Of our youth:
> Time enough for age
>   To think on truth.
> So short a day,
> And life so quickly hasting,
> And in study wasting
>   Youth that would be gay!
>
> 'Tis our spring that slipping,
>   Winter draweth near,
>   Life itself we're losing,
>   And this sorry cheer
> Dries the blood and cheers the heart,
>   Shrivels all delight.
> Age and all its crowd of ills

terrifies our sight.
So short a day,
And life so quickly hasting,
And in study wasting
　　Youth that would be gay!

Ley us as the gods so,
　'Tis the wiser part:
Leisure and love's pleasure
　Seek the young in heart
Follow the old fashion,
　Down into the street!
Down among the maidens,
　And the dancing feet!
So short a day,
And life so quickly hasting,
And in study wasting
　　Youth that would be gay!

There for the seeing
　Is all loveliness,
White limbs moving
　Light in wantonness.
Gay go the dancers,
　I stand and see,
Gaze, till their glances
　Steal myself from me.
So short a day,
And life so quickly hasting,
And in study wasting
　　Youth that would be gay![124]

Gran chan

[124] http://www.historyguide.org/intellect/goliard.html, March 15, 2016

(Form, French)

See *grand chant*.

Grand chant
Genre
Country of Origin: France
Distribution: French
Century: 12th – 13th centuries

The **gran(d) chan(t)**, also known as the *grand chant courtois*, was an Old French genre of lyric poetry devised by the trouvères in the 12th to 13th centuries. It was adapted from the Occitan *canso* of the troubadours. Like the *canso* it explored courtly love, but it could also be used to expound on many other topics or themes. It tended to be monophonic (meaning it had a single vocal melody).

Gwawdodyn
(Form, Welsh)

See *awdl*.

Gwawdodyn hir
(Form, Welsh)

See *awdl*.

H

Helmingar
Form
Country of Origin: Iceland, Scandinavia
Distribution: Norse
Century: 8th – 13th century

A **helmingar** was a half-stanza or half-verse in Old Norse.

See also *vísuhelmingr*.

Heroldsdichtung
(Genre, German)

See *wappendichtung*.

Hir a toddaid
(Form, Welsh)

See *awdl*.

Hrynhent
Device
Country of Origin: Iceland, Scandinavia
Distribution: Norse
Century: 11th – 13th century

Hrynhent was a skaldic meter, consisting of an 8-line stanza which is otherwise similar to *dróttkvætt* (except for the fact that each line has an added trochee which meant each line had four stresses rather than three). It was used in court poetry in the 11th to 13th centuries; in the 14th century it turned into the *liljulag*.

The following couplet by Arnórr (c. 1012 – 1070s) in his *Hrynhenda* is written in this meter (with the alliteration bolded):

> **M**agnús, hlýð til **m**áttigs óðar;
> **m**anngi veit ek fremra annan;[125]

Huitain
Form
Country of Origin: France
Distribution: French, English
Century: 15th – 18th centuries

The **huitain** (pronounced wit-tain) is a 15th century 8-line strophe with 8-syllable lines (French) or 10-syllable lines (English), using three rhymes with one of these appearing four times and with the same rhyme for the fourth and fifth lines. The rhyme scheme is usually ababbcbc, and sometimes abbaacac. The **huitain** could be a standalone poem, or used as a unit in longer poems. Sometimes multiple poets would each supply hutains to make a longer piece. It was most popular in the 15th – 16th centuries; in the 18th it was used for epigrams. There are those who think this French form is based on an older Spanish one[126].

---

[125] https://www.abdn.ac.uk/skaldic/m.php?p=doconw&i=622, March 16, 2016

[126] Travis Lyons: 219.

Version 1	Version 2
(x x) x x x x x x x a OR	(x x) x x x x x x x a
(x x) x x x x x x x b	(x x) x x x x x x x b
(x x) x x x x x x x a	(x x) x x x x x x x b
(x x) x x x x x x x b	(x x) x x x x x x x a
(x x) x x x x x x x b	(x x) x x x x x x x a
(x x) x x x x x x x c	(x x) x x x x x x x c
(x x) x x x x x x x b	(x x) x x x x x x x a
(x x) x x x x x x x c	(x x) x x x x x x x c

An example of the **hutain** is this octave by Pernette du Guillet (c. 1520 – 1545):

> Plus je desire, et la fortune adverse
> Moins me permect que puisse celuy veoir,
> A qui elle eust par mainte controverse
> Faict mainct ennuy, si ne fust son sçavoir
> Qui des Cieulx a ce tant heureux pouvoir
> De parvenir tousjours à son entente :
> Dont avec luy ce soulas puis avoir
> Que, luy content, je demure contente.[127]

---

[127] Cathy M. Yandell: 104.

I

Istampitte
(Genre, Occitan, Catalan, Italian)

See *estampie*.

Ir
(Device, Welsh)

See *odl*.

J

Jeu parti
(Genre, French)

See *partimen*.

Joc partif
(Genre, Occitan)

See *partimen*.

K

Keen

Genre
Country of Origin: Ireland
Distribution: Irish, Scottish
Century: 7th – 18th centuries

A **keen** (*caoineadh* in Gaelic, meaning "to weep") was a funeral song which could include genealogical details of the deceased, praise for the departed, and a description of the woe felt by those left behind. The first written record of these keenings was in the 16th century but there are references to the practice from at least the 7th century. These songs were sung by one or more women though the chorus may have been sung by all present.

Fearflatha O'Gniamh was an olamb (bard) to the O'Neil of Clanaboy circa 1556. The following are the first two (translated) stanzas of his **keen** that began "*Mo thruaid mar atáid gaoidhil*":

> How dimmed is the glory that circled the Gael,
> And fall'n the high people of Innisfail;
> The sword of the Saxon is red with their gore;
> And the mighty of nations is mighty no more!
>
> Like a bark on the ocean, long shattered and tost
> On the land of your fathers at length you are lost;
> The hand of the spoiler is stretched on your plains,

And you're doomed from your cradles to bondage and chains.[128]

Kenning
Device
Country of Origin: Scandinavia? Iceland?
Distribution: Norse, Anglo-Saxon
Century: 9th – 12th centuries

A figurative phrase used in Old Germanic languages as a synonym for a simple word (such as "swan's road" to refer to the sea). Some kennings were purposely obscure and challenged the listen to figure out what they referred to.

Knittel
(Form, German)

See *knittelvers*.

Knittelvers
Form
Country of Origin: Germany
Distribution: German, Swedish
Century: 15th – 18th centuries

Knittelvers ("knit verse" or "cudgel verse") was a Germanic verse meter which originated in the 15th century, relying on rhyme and assonance. *Strict knittel* has eight or nine syllables on each line, while *free knittel* has no restriction. The lines tended to have four stresses and were paired into rhyming couplets. Before the 16th century the meter used an indeterminate number of unstressed syllables per line, but

---

[128] Thomas Crofton Croker: 2.

later was restricted to eight or nine syllables per line. Some poets looked down on **knittelvers** for being too simple or clumsy a form. It was also often seen as satirical or vulgar. By the 17th century the form dipped in popularity but experienced a rebirth in the 18th.

In Sweden both the *Eufemiavisorna* and the *Erikskrönikan* were written using **knittelvers**. The prologue to *Erikskrönikan* begins:

Gud hawe heder äro ok looff
han er til alskons dygd vphooff
all jorderikis frygd ok hymmerikis nade
thz han er welduger ouer them bade
at giffwa ok läna hwem han thz an
wel er then thz forskylla kan
werldena hauer han skipat swa weel
hwar her swa liffuer tha er han sääl
Thz han gömer hans helgha budh
tha faar han hymmerikis friid mz gud
Verldena hauer han skipat swa widha
skogh ok marka bergh ok lidha
lööff ok gräss vatn ok sand
mykin frögd ok margh land
Ok eth ther med som swerighe heter
hwar som nor i werldena lether
Tha faar han fynna huar thz er
godha tiägna finder man ther
ridderskap ok häladha godha
the Didrik fan berner vel bestodo
huro herra ok första hawa ther liffuat
thz finder man her i bokenne scriffuit
huro the hawa liffuat giort ok farit
her star thz scriwat huru thz hauer warit
hwo thz hauer ey förra hört sakt

nw ma han thz höra hauer han tess akt
fore lust at höra fagher ordh
ok skämptan oss til wy gaa til bordh[129]

[God let us praise and celebrate!
For he did all good things create,
all earthly joy and heaven's repose,
Over them both he does dispose
to give and grant to who he please.
Who them deserves will be at ease!
The world by him was made so well
that all are blessed who therein dwell
if His commands they but uphold;
they shall God's peace in heaven behold!
The world He made so much contains:
woodland, pastures, hills and plains,
leaves and grass, water and sand,
so much joy and many a land,
and there among them Sweden lies.
He who northward turns his eyes
will that country see outlined.
There good warriors you will find,
many a hero and noble knight,
who bravely Theodric of Bern did fight.
How lords and princes once lived there
is all in writing recorded here:
their lives, their deeds and how they fared,
are here set down as they appeared.
Those who wish to hear the tale,
if they pay heed, I shall regale
with words as well as I am able,
before we all sit down at table.][130]

---

[129] http://runeberg.org/erikkron/01.html, March 16, 2016

[130] Erik Carlquist and Peter C. Hogg: 31-32.

Kviðuháttr
Form
Country of Origin: Scandinavia? Iceland?
Distribution: Norse
Century: 9th – 12th centuries

Kviðuhátr was an 8-line alliterative verse form, resembling *fornyrðislag* except that its lines alternate between three and four syllables[131]. Alternatively, other sources say it is line 3, 5 and 7 that are 3 syllables with the rest being four[132]. The alliteration can also carry over from one line to the next (so a word in line one alliterates with a word in line two, a word in line three with line four, and so on).

Version 1		*Version 2*
x x x	OR	x x x x
x x x x		x x x x
x x x		x x x
x x x x		x x x x
x x x		x x x
x x x x		x x x x
x x x		x x x
x x x x		x x x x

Egill Skallagrímsson (c. 905 – c. 995) used **kviðuhátr** when writing his *Sonatorrek*, which opens as follows (the alliteration is bolded):

> Mjök erum **t**regt
> **t**ungu at hrœra

---

[131] https://www.abdn.ac.uk/skaldic/m.php?p=doconw&i=624, March 15, 2016

[132] http://www.trobar.org/prosody/pnort.php, March 16, 2016

með loptvætt
ljóðpundara;
esa nú vænligt
of Viðurs þýfi,
né hógdrœgt
ór hugar fylgsni.[133]

Kyrielle

Form
Country of Origin: France
Distribution: French
Century: unknown

The **kyrielle** is named after the Kyrie (part of Christian liturgy). It is a French verse form using short, octosyllabic, rhyming couplets. When written in English the lines are generally iambic tetrameters. These couplets were often paired into quatrains and employed a refrain that was sometimes a single word, and sometimes the full second line of the couplet, or the full fourth line of the quatrain. There is no limit to the number of stanzas in a **kyrielle**, though three is considered the accepted minimum. The form takes its name from the Old French *kiriele*, which is a derivative of the word *kyrie* (a form of Christian liturgical prayer).

If the poem is written in couplets, the rhyme scheme will be aA, aA. If written in quatrains there is greater freedom in the rhyme scheme, such as aabB, ccbB or abaB, cbcB.

Version 1		*Version 2*	
x x x x x x x a	OR	x x x x x x x a	OR
x x x x x x x A		x x x x x x x a	
x x x x x x x a		x x x x x x x b	

---

[133] https://notendur.hi.is/eybjorn/ugm/skindex/egst.html, March 16, 2016

x x x x x x x A   x x x x x x x B

                                   x x x x x x x c
                                   x x x x x x x c
                                   x x x x x x x b
                                   x x x x x x x B

Version 3

x x x x x x x a
x x x x x x x b
x x x x x x x a
x x x x x x x B

x x x x x x x c
x x x x x x x b
x x x x x x x c
x x x x x x x B

L

Lai
Genre
Country of Origin: France
Distribution: French
Century: 12th – 14th centuries

A **lai** (also known as a *lay lyrique* or "lyric lay" to distinguish it from a *Breton lay*) is a lyrical, narrative poem written in octosyllabic couplets. They often dealt with tales of adventure and romance. The terms *note*, *nota* and *notula* also appeared to be synonyms for **lai**.

A **lai** usually had several stanzas, none of which had the same form. As a result, the accompanying music did not repeat itself. Towards the end of the 14th century some **lais** began repeating stanzas, but usually only in longer examples.

The earliest **lais** known were by Marie de France and were written in the 1170s. The **lai** *Bisclavret* by Marie concerned the case of an unhappy werewolf. The first stanza reads as follows:

> quant de lais faire m'entremet,
> ne voil ublïer Bisclavret:
> Bisclavret ad nun en bretan,
> garwaf l'apelent li Norman.
> jadis le poeit hume oïr
> e sovent suleit avenir,

humes plusurs garual devindrent
e es boscages meisun tindrent.
Garualf, c[eo] est beste salvage:
tant cum il est en cele rage,
hummes devure, grant mal fait,
es granz forez converse e vait.
cest afere les ore ester;
del Bisclavret [vus] voil cunter.[134]

[Since I'm making lais, Bisclavret
Is one I don't want to forget.
In Breton, "Bisclavret"'s the name;
"Garwolf" in Norman means the same.
Long ago you heard the tale told —
And it used to happen, in days of old —
Quite a few men became garwolves,
And set up housekeeping in the woods.
A garwolf is a savage beast,
While the fury's on it, at least:
Eats men, wreaks evil, does no good,
Living and roaming in the deep wood.
Now I'll leave this topic set.
I want to tell you about Bisclavret.][135]

Lai Breton
(Genre, French)

See *Breton lay*.

Laisse

---

[134] https://fr.wikisource.org/wiki/Lais_de_Marie_de_France/Bisclavret, February 28, 2016

[135] http://users.clas.ufl.edu/jshoaf/marie/bisclavret.pdf, February 28, 2016

Form
Country of Origin: France
Distribution: French
Century: 11th – 15th century

A **laisse** was a stanza, of variable length used in French poetry (especially epic poetry like the *chanson de geste*). In earlier works the **laisse** was made up of mono- assonanced verses (though this became much rarer in later years). Within a poem, each **laisse** could be of different length while the metric length of the verse was invariable (each verse had the same syllable length, usually decasyllabic or, occasionally, *alexandrines*). Masculine and feminine rhymes could not be mixed in the same laisse.

The **laisse** employs stereotyped phrases and formulas, frequently repeating themes and motifs, including repetitions of lines or words from one **laisse** to another. These types of devices are commonly used in oration. When a poet repeated content (with different wording or assonance/rhyme) from one **laisse** to another, they were called *laisses similaires*.

La Chanson de Roland (The Song of Roland) written in the 11th or 12th century used **laisses**; the first reads:

> The king our Emperor Carlemaine,
> Hath been for seven full years in Spain.
> From highland to sea hath he won the land;
> City was none might his arm withstand;
> Keep and castle alike went down
> Save Saragossa, the mountain town.
> The King Marsilius holds the place,
> Who loveth not God, nor seeks His grace:
> He prays to Apollin, and serves Mahound;

But he saved him not from the fate he found.[136]

Laisse similaires
(Form, French)

See *laisse*.

Lament
Genre
Country of Origin: unknown
Distribution: across Europe
Century: unknown to present

A **lament** was a poem expressing grief and it existed in nearly (if not all) societies. In the 10th century an Anglo-Saxon scop named Deor wrote a **lament** to relate his feelings of distress and sorrow over being replaced at court with another minstrel. The poem is called *Deor* or *Deor's Lament*.

> Wēlund him be wurman   wræces cunnade,
> ānhȳdig corl   earfþa drēag,
> hæfde him to gesīþþe   sorge ond ongþ,
> wintercealde wræce;   wean oft onfond,
> siþþan hine Nīðhād on   nēde legde,
> swoncre seonobende   on syllan monn.
> Þæs oferēode,   þisses swā mæg!
> Beadohilde ne wæs   hyre brōþre dēaþ
> on sefan swā sār   swā hyre sylfre þing,
> þæt hēo gearolīce   ongieten hæfde
> þæt hēo ēacen wæs;   æfre ne meahte
> þrīste geþencan   hū ymb þæt sceolde.
> Þæs oferēode,   þisses swā mæg!

---

[136] https://legacy.fordham.edu/halsall/basis/roland-ohag.asp, March 16, 2016

Wē þæt Mǣðhilde   monge gefrugnon
Wurdon grundlēase   Gēates frige,
Þæt hī sēo sorglufu   slǣp ealle binom.
Þæs oferēode,   þisses swā mæg!
Đēodrīc āhte   þrītig wintra
Mǣringa burg;   þæt wæs monegum cūþ.
Þæs oferēode,   þisses swā mæg!
Wē geāscodan   Eormanrīces
Wylfenne geþōht;   āhte wide folc
Gotena rīces.   Þæt wæs grim cyning.
Sæt secg monig   sorgum gebunden
wean on wēnan,   wyscte geneahhe
þæt þæs cynerīces   ofercumen wǣre.
Þæs oferēode,   þisses swā mæg!
Siteð sorgcearig   sǣlum bidǣled
on sefan sweorceð,   sylfum þinceð
þæt sȳ endelēas   earfoða dǣl.
Mæg þonne geþencan,   þæt geond þās woruld
wītig dryhten   wendeþ geneahhe,
eorle monegum   āre gescēawað,
wislīcne blǣd,   sumun wēana dǣl.
Þæt ic bi me sylfum   secgan wille
þæt ic hwīle wæs   Heodeninga scop,
dryhtne dȳre.   Mē wæs Dēor noma.
Āhte ic fela wintra   folgað tilne,
holdne hlāford,   oþþæt Heorrenda nū,
lēoðcræfting monn   londryht geþah,
þæt mē eorla hlēo   ǣr gesealde.
Þæs oferēode,   þisses swā mæg!¹³⁷

[Weland endured the agony of exile.
That indomitable smith was wracked by grief.
He suffered countless sorrows;

---

¹³⁷ Jackson J. Campbell and James L. Rosier: 32-34.

indeed, sorrows were his only companions
in that frozen island dungeon
where Nithad fettered him,
so many strong-but-supple sinew-bands
binding the better man.
  That passed away; this also may.

Beadohild mourned her brothers' deaths
but bemoaned even more her own sad state
once she discovered herself with child.
She knew nothing good could ever come of it.
  That passed away; this also may.

We have heard that the Geat's moans for Matilda,
his lady, were limitless,
that his sorrowful love for her
robbed him of regretless sleep.
  That passed away; this also may.

For thirty winters Theodric ruled
the Mæring stronghold with an iron hand;
many acknowledged this and moaned.
  That passed away; this also may.

We have heard too of Ermanaric's wolfish ways,
of how he cruelly ruled the realm of the Goths.
That was a grim king! Many a warrior sat,
full of cares and maladies of the mind,
wishing constantly that his kingdom might be
overthrown.
  That passed away; this also may.

If a man sits long enough, sorrowful and anxious,
bereft of joy, his mind constantly darkening,
soon it seems to him that his troubles are endless.
Then he must consider that the wise Lord

often moves through the earth
granting some men honor, glory and fame,
but others only shame and hardship.
This I must say for myself:
that for awhile I was the Heodeninga's scop,
dear to my lord. My name was Deor.
For many winters I held a fine office,
faithfully serving a just lord. But now Heorrenda
a man skillful in songs, has received the estate
the protector of warriors promised me.
That passed away; this also may.][138]

See also *complaint*.

Lauda
Genre
Country of Origin: Italy
Distribution: Italian
Century: 13th – 19th centuries

The **lauda** originated in the 13th century and was also known as *laude, laudi* and *laudi spirituali*. These *laude* (which is the plural) was a verse form with religious content, usually adapting church liturgy. It generally followed the *ballata* in form, or the octosyllabic *sestina*, with alternating rhyme in quatrain, followed by a rhymed stich. *Laude*, with their ties to the liturgy, were initially written in Latin but eventually were composed in vernacular language.[139] Those who composed *laude* were known as Laudisti.

Iacopone da Todi (c. 1230/1236 – 1306) wrote many *laude*

---

[138] http://www.thehypertexts.com/Deor's%20Lament%20Translation.htm, March 16, 2016

[139] Gaetana Marrone: 955.

including *De la beata Vergine Maria e del Peccatore*:

—O Regina cortese, —io so a voi venuto
ch'al mio cor feruto —deiate medecare.

Io so a voi venuto —com'omo desperato
da omn'altro aiuto; —lo vostro m'è lassato;
se ne fusse privato, —faríeme consumare.

Lo mio cor è feruto, —Madonna, nol so dire;
ed a tal è venuto, —che comenza putire;
non deiate soffrire —de volerm'aiutare.

Donna, la sofferenza —sí m'è pericolosa;
lo mal pres'ha potenza, —la natura è dogliosa;
siate cordogliosa —de volerme sanare.

Non aio pagamento, —tanto so anichilato;
faite de me stromento, —servo recomperato;
donna, el prez'è dato: —quel ch'avest'a lattare.

Donna, per quel amore —che m'ha avut'el tuo figlio
dever'aver en core —de darm'el tuo consiglio;
succurrime, aulente giglio, —veni e non tardare.

—Figlio, poi ch'èi venuto, —molto sí m'è 'n piacere;
adomandimi aiuto, —dollote voluntere;
ètte oporto soffrire —co per arte voglio fare.

Medecaro per arte —emprima fa la diita;
guarda li sensi da parte —che non dien piú ferita
a la natura perita —che se possa aggravare.

E piglia l'oximello, —lo temor del morire;
ancora si fancello, —cetto ce de' venire;

vanetá lassa gire, — non pò teco regnare.

E piglia decozione — lo temor de lo 'nferno;
pens'en quella prescione — non escon en sempiterno;
la piaga girá rompenno — farallate revontare.

Denante al preite mio — questo venen revonta,
ché l'officio è sio; — Dio lo peccato sconta;
ca se 'l Nemico s'aponta, — non aia que mostrare.[140]

Laude
(Form, Italian)

See *lauda*.

Laudi
(Form, Italian)

See *lauda*.

Laudi spirituali
(Form, Italian)

See *lauda*.

Lay
(Genre, French)

See *lai*.

Lay lyrique
(Genre, French)

---

[140] http://www.gutenberg.org/files/29977/29977-h/29977-h.htm, March 16, 2016

See *lai*.

Leathrann
Device
Country of Origin: Ireland
Distribution: Irish
Century: unknown

The **leathraan** is a half-*rann*; a couplet.

Lehrgedicht
Genre
Country: Germany
Distribution: German
Centuries: unknown

Lehrgedicht were didactic or "wisdom" poems.

Leich
Form
Country of Origin: Germany
Distribution: German
Century: 13th – 14th centuries

Leich was a lyric form, similar to the French *descort*, which was widely used between circa 1200 and 1350. Poems written as a **leich** were designed to be sung. It could use irregular stanza forms and could be non-repetitive (or it could use a standard stanza form and repeat verses). Regardless of its regularity or irregularity of stanzic form, it was isostrophic (which meant all stanzas conform to the first stanza). They generally had a lot of short rhyming units and could use different types of rhyme. **Leich** were frequently split into two parts (while the *tanzleich* was split in three parts). There were three kinds of **leich**: the *Tanzleich* (which was a dance lyric), the *religiöse leich* (a religious lyric), and the *Minneleich* (the love lyric). After the 14th century only the religious version was still used.

A famous **leich** was *Marienleich* (Mary's Song) by Frauenlob (1250/1260 – 1318). Below you can see the first four stanzas, and see how the second conforms to the first in form, as the fourth also conforms to the third.

> 1. Ei ich sach in dem trone
> ein vrouwen, die was swanger.
> die trug ein wunderkrone
> vor miner ougen anger.
>
> sie wolte wesen enbunden,
> sust gie die allerbeste,
> zwelf steine ich zu den stunden
> kos in der krone vest.
>
> 2. Nu market,
> wie sie trüge,
> die gefüge,
> der naturen zu genüge
> mit dem sie was gebürdet,
> den sach sie vor ir sitzen mit witzen
> in siben liuchteren
> und sach in
> doch besundert
> in eines lammes wise
> uf Sion, dem berge gehiuren
>
> Sie tet rechte
> als sie solde,
> ja, die holde

trug den blumen same in tolde.
vrouwe, ob ir muter würdet
des lammes und der tuben, iur truben
ir liezet iuch sweren?
da von mich
nicht enwundert,
ob iuch die selbe spise
kan wol zu der früchte gestiuren.[141]

[1. Listen! I saw a vision:
a Lady on a throne
Great with child, that woman
wore a wondrous crown.

How she ached for the hour
of birth, the best of women!
In her crown of power
I saw twelve gemstones glisten.

2. Now see
how she
so meekly
bowed to Nature's ways.
With visionary gaze
she saw the child in her womb
enthroned amid lampstands seven,
and yet again she saw him
in the form of a Lamb
high on Mount Zion,
the mount of Heaven.

She did
as she should,

---

[141] Barbara Newman: 2-7.

noble and good,
bore a flower like a scepter.
Lady, if you would be
mother of both Lamb and Dove,
could you bear the weight
of the vineyard's grape?
I'll not be amazed
if the fruit of that vine
makes you fruitful from above.[142]

Letra
(Form, Spanish)

See *cabeza*.

Lethrannaegecht morb
Form
Country of Origin: Ireland
Distribution: Irish
Century: unknown

Lethrannaegecht morb were an *oglachas* version of *dán direach* that were quatrains consisting of 5-syllable lines. The lines rhymed xaxa xbxb (and so forth, where the x lines were unrhymed). Lines one and two were linked by assonance; the end of line three rhymed internally with line four or line one and line three consonate with line two and four. The poem concludes with *dunadh*.

x x x x x
x x x x a
x x x x b

---

[142] Ibid.

Letrilla
Genre
Country of Origin: Spain
Distribution: Spanish
Century: 14th – 16th centuries

The **letrilla** was a poem generally written in small lines (often 6 or 8 syllables, but could be even shorter), often using a refrain (*estribillo*). The topics were usually light hearted or satiric but sometimes religious. They were written as early as the 14th century.

Poderosos caballero es don Dinero by Francesco de Quevedo (1580-1645) is an example of a **letrilla**:

> Madre, yo al oro me humillo
> el es mi amante y mi amado,
> pues de puro enamorado,
> anda contino amarillo;
>
> que pues doblon o sencillo,
> hace todo cuanto quiero
> poderoso caballero
> es don Dinero.[143]

Lied
Genre
Country of Origin: Germany
Distribution: German
Century: 12th – 19th centuries

---

[143] http://www.poetrymagnumopus.com/index.php?/topic/1866-letrilla/, March 16, 2016

The **lieder** (the plural of **lied**) were several types of German songs as they were referred to in English and French writings. The earliest examples are from the 12th and 13th centuries and were the works of the Minnesingers.

The **lied** proper usually had two sections. The first phrase of music (a) repeated with different words, and the second phrase (B), again with different words (aaB). This is the *bar form* which was favoured by many German composers.

The courtly *minnelieder* were monophonic (a single melodic line). As musical notation of this period was not precise, the rhythmic interpretation is open to debate.

In the 14th century the monophonic **lied** went into decline, while the polyphonic **lied** was introduced (for two or more voices or voice and instruments).

In the 15th century the polyphonic **lieder** expanded to having up to four voices, and were addressed to scholars and clergy.

A manuscript compiling **lieder** was known as a *liederhandschrift*.

One popular **lied** was *"Wach auff myn Hort"* ("Awake, my darling") by Oswald of Wolkenstein (1377–1455). The opening stanzas read:

> Wach auf, mein Schatz! Es leuchtet dort
> der helle Tag vom Orient entgegen.
> Schau durch die Lider, sieh den Glanz,
> wie gar zart blau die Himmelskrone
> sich auf rechte Weise durch das Grau mengt.
> Ich befürchte einen baldigen Tagesanbruch.

Ich beklage das Unheil, das ich nicht möchte,
man hört die Vögel im Gebüsch
schon mit hellem Klang erklingen.
O Nachtigall, dein verkündender Ton
bringt mir Qual, die ich nicht belohne.
Einer Frau unwürdig muss ich klagen.

Mit deinem Segen gehen! Der Speer deines Herzens
verwundet mich, weil ich nicht bleiben darf.
Der Schmerz des Scheidens bringt mir Traurigkeit,
dein rotes Mündlein beklemmt mich sehnsuchtsvoll,
der bittere Tod bedrückt mich weniger.
Das Scheiden lässt mich verzagen.[144]

Liljulag
Form
Country of Origin: Iceland
Distribution: Norse
Century: 14th – 18th centuries

The 14th century Icelandic poem *Lilja* ("Lily") by Eysteinn was written using the *hrynhent* meter. Due to *Lilja's* popularity, Icelanders began to refer to *hrynhent* as **liljulag** ("Lilja's tune" or "Lilja's meter") instead.[145] This ode to the Virgin Mary begins:

Almáttugr guð allra stètta,
yfirbjóðandi eingla ok þjóða,
ei þurfandi staði nè stundir,

---

[144] https://www.uni-due.de/~hg0222/images/stories/pdfs/tagelied/Folie_Text_Oswald_mhd_und_nhd.pdf, March 16, 2016

[145] J. M. Fladmark: 102. Daisy Neijmann: 51

staÍ haldandi I kyrrleiksvaldi;
senn verandi úti ok inni,
uppi ok niðri ok þar i miðju,
lof sè þèr um aldr ok aefi,
eining sönn i þrennum greinum![146]

[Almighty God of all beings!
who reignest over angels and men,
independent of space and time,
abiding in the realm of tranquility;
at once existing both without and within,
above and below, and in the midst,
praise be to thee through time and eternity,
true unity in three branches!]

Lira
Form
Country of Origin: Spain
Distribution: Spanish
Century: 16th century

The **lira** is a shortened variation of the *canción* and was invented by Garcilaso de la Vega (c. 1501 – 1536). The most popular form of the **lira** is a quintain stanza where the second line repeats in line five and has a rhyme scheme of aBabB. The lines had either seven or eleven syllables.

x x x x x x x a
x x x x x x x x x x B
x x x x x x a
x x x x x x b
x x x x x x x x x x B

---

[146] George B. Marsh: 147-148.

Liturgical Poetry
Genre
Country of Origin: unknown
Distribution: across Europe
Century: unknown

Liturgical poetry is any poem concerning religion (including rites and ceremonies).

An example of liturgical poetry is "Psaume XXIII" by Clément Marot (1496-1544):

Dominus regit me

Mon Dieu me paît sous sa puissance haute,
C'est mon berger, de rien je n'aurai faute.
En toi bien sûr, joignant les beaux herbages,
Coucher me fait, me mène aux clairs rivages,
Traite ma vie en douceur très humaine,
Et pour son nom par droits sentiers me mène
Si sûrement, que quand au val viendroye
D'ombre de mort, rien de mal ne craindroye,
Car avec moi tu es à chacune heure,
Puis ta houlette et conduit m'asseure.
Tu enrichis de vivres necéssaires.
Ma table, aux yeux de tous mes adversaires.
Tu oins mon chef d'huiles et senteurs bonnes
Et jusqu'aux bords pleine tasse me donnes,
Voire, et feras que cette faveur tienne,
Tant que vivrai compagnië me tienne,
Si que toujours de faire ai espérance
En la maison du Seigneur demeurance.[147]

---

[147] Alan Boase: 53.]

Ljóðaháttr
Form
Country of Origin: Iceland
Distribution: Norse
Century: unknown

Ljóðaháttr was an Eddic meter of six lines (two units of three lines). The first and second lines are *fornyrðislag* and are linked by alliteration, while the third lines alliterate with themselves. The first two lines have at least two syllables whereas the third lines have at least three.

The following quotation from the *Hávamál* is written in ljóðaháttr:

Sá einn veit
er víða ratar
ok hefir fjöld um farið
hverju geði
stýrir gumna hver
sá er vitandi er vits.
Deyr fé
Deyja frændr
Deyr sjálfr ið sama
En orðstír
Deyr aldregi
Hveim er sér góðan getr[148]

[He is truly wise
who's travelled far
and knows the ways of the World.
He who has travelled
can tell what spirit

---

[148] http://www.trobar.org/prosody/pnort.php, March 16, 2016

governs the men he meets.
Cattle die
kinsmen die
all men are mortal
words of praise
will never perish
nor a noble name.[149]]

M

Madrigal
Form
Country of Origin: Italy
Distribution: Italian, English, French, Spanish
Century: 14th -18th centuries

The **madrigal** (known in its native Italian as the *madrigale*) is a form of poetry whose exact nature has never been agreed upon in English. Though sometimes said to be short lyrical poems about love, some **madrigals** are long and about other subjects.

Madrigal is sometimes used in a derogatory sense, referring to works that are sentimental and of trifling expression.

Italian **madrigals** averaged nine to eleven lines, with a 6-syllable opening line and the other lines never being longer than 10-syllables.

French **madrigals** were short pieces of verse and seen as trifling pieces of erotica.

In England, *English madrigals* were introduced in the 16th century and were seen as the chief form of secular vocal music. They often dwelt on the topic of love. Both William Drummond (1585 – 1649) and Chaucer have been credited with creating the *English madrigal*. Drummond's version is a poem of between six and fourteen lines, with the lines alternating between six and ten syllables. The rhyme schemes were variable.

x x x x x
x x x x x x x x x
x x x x x
x x x x x x x x x
x x x x x
x x x x x x x x x
(x x x x x
x x x x x x x x x
x x x x x
x x x x x x x x x
x x x x x
x x x x x x x x x
x x x x x
x x x x x x x x x x)

An example of Drummond's English madrigal is "Her Passing":

> THE beauty and the life
> --- Of life's and beauty's fairest paragon
> —O tears! O grief! —hung at a feeble thread
> To which pale Atropos had set her knife;
> --- The soul with many a groan
> --- Had left each outward part,
> And now did take his last leave of the heart:
> Naught else did want, save death, ev'n to be dead;
> When the afflicted band about her bed,
> Seeing so fair him come in lips, cheeks, eyes,
> Cried, 'Ah! and can Death enter Paradise?'[150]

---

[150]   http://www.poetrymagnumopus.com/index.php?/topic/671-english-madrigal/, March 16, 2016

The version of the *English madrigal* credited to Chaucer is made up of a tercet, a quatrain and a sixain. They were written in iambic pentameter and rhymed AB^1B^2 $abAB^1$ $abbAB^1B^2$ making use of repeated lines.

x x x x x x x x x A
x x x x x x x x x B^1
x x x x x x x x x B^2

x x x x x x x x x a
x x x x x x x x x b
x x x x x x x x x A
x x x x x x x x x B^1

x x x x x x x x x a
x x x x x x x x x b
x x x x x x x x x b
x x x x x x x x x A
x x x x x x x x x B^1
x x x x x x x x x B^2

Madrigale
(Form, Italian)

See *madrigal*.

Mal mariée
Genre
Country of Origin: France
Distribution: French, Italian
Century: 13th – 16th centuries

Also called a *chanson de mal mariée*, a **mal mariée** ("badly married") was an Old French song in which a married woman is overheard lamenting her marriage and calling upon her lover. Sometimes the lover will appear to save her. A common variant involves a nun who wants her lover to take her away from the convent. **Mal mariée** often used the *ballade* meter and employed a 2-line refrain.

In Occitan the **Mal mariée** was known as the *gilozesca*[151].

The anonymous poem *Chanson de mal-mariée* (written in the late 12th or early 13th century) is, unsurprisingly, a **mal mariée**:

> Pancis amerouzement
> De Tornai parti l'autrier;
> En un pre lons un destour
> Vi trois dames ombroier,
> Mariees de novel.
> Chascune ot un vert chapel.
> La moinee a dit ansi:
> "Je servirai mon mari
> Lealment en leu d'ami."
>
> La moinee par baudour
> Fu vestue au tens d'esté
> D'un riche drap de colour,
> D'un vert qui fait a louer.
> En avoit robe et mantel
> Et chantoit cest chant novel,
> Si ke je l'ai bien oï:
> "S'on trovast leal ami,
> Ja n'eüsse pris mari."[152]

[151] Stephen Cushman: 842.

[152] F. Brittain: 157-158.

Málaháttr
Form
Country of Origin: Iceland
Distribution: Norse
Century: unknown

Málaháttr ("speech meter") is an Eddic measure closely related to *fornyrðislag*. Each line of the 4-line stanza was divided into two half-lines by a caesura. The half-lines had two accented and three or four unaccented syllables. The alliteration used is similar to *fornyrðislag*.

The 12th century poem *Atlamál in grænlenzku* (The Greenlandic Lay of Atli) is the only extant Eddic poem completely composed in **málaháttr**.[153] It begins:

> 1. Frett hefir ₳ld ófo þa,
> er endr vm gorðo
> seggir samkvndo,
> sv var nytt festom,
> ǫ xto einmęli;
> yggr var þeim siþan
> oc iþ sama sonom Givca,
> ęr váro sannraðnir.
>
> 2. Sc₳p ǫ xto scioldvnga
> — scyldoat feigir —,
> illa ręz Atla,
> atti hann þo hyggio;
> feldi stoþ stora,
> striddi ser harþla,
> af bragdi boþ sendi,

---

[153] Seiichi Suzuki: 425.

at qvẹmi brat mágar.[154]

[1. There are many who know | how of old did men
In counsel gather; | little good did they get;
In secret they plotted, | it was sore for them later,
And for Gjuki's sons, | whose trust they deceived.

2. Fate grew for the princes, | to death they were given;
Ill counsel was Atli's, | though keenness he had;
He felled his staunch bulwark, | his own sorrow
fashioned,
Soon a message he sent | that his kinsmen should seek
him.][155]

Measurau
Device
Country of Origin: Wales
Distribution: Welsh
Century: 6th – 15th centuries

The lines of Welsh poetry were written in quantitative verse
(meaning the line is measured by counting the number of long
and short vowel sounds). This is referred to as **measurau**.

Measurau rhyddion
Device
Country of Origin: Wales
Distribution: Welsh
Century: 16th century

This term is used to identify any poem not written in one of

---

[154] http://etext.old.no/Bugge/atlamal.html, March 17, 2016

[155] http://www.sacred-texts.com/neu/poe/poe35.htm, March 17, 2016

the twenty-four official codified meters (*cerdd dafod*).

Mester de clerica
(Form, Catalan)

See *cuaderna via*.

Mesur tri-thrawiad
Form
Country of Origin: Wales
Distribution: Welsh
Century: 17th century

Mesur tri-thrawiad was a meter consisting of dactylic half-lines of a set number of syllables (6, 6, 6, 5; 6, 6, 6, 3). There were three stresses on the last line. This form was not very common until the 17th century.

x x x | x x x
x x x | x x x
x x x x x

x x x | x x x
x x x | x x x
x x x

Minnelied
Form
Country of Origin: Germany
Distribution: German
Century: 12th – 15th centuries

A **minnelied** was a song or poem written by a minnesinger (though some scholars say that if it was not sung it was a *spruch* and not a **minnelied**[156]). **Minnelieder** (which is the plural) were written in many forms. One example of a **minnelied** was six lines long with a rhyme scheme of aabbaa. The first two lines had 6-syllables, the following two had 5-syllables, and the last two lines had 7-syllables.

x x x x x a
x x x x x a
x x x x b
x x x x b
x x x x x x a
x x x x x x a

A famous **minnelied** is *Unter der Linden* ("Under the linden trees") by Walther von der Vogelweide (c. 1170 – c. 1230):

> Under der linden
> an der heide,
> dâ unser zweier bette was,
> dâ muget ir vinden
> schône beide
> gebrochen bluomen unde gras.
> Vor dem walde in einem tal,
> tandaradei,
> schône sanc diu nahtegal.[157]
>
> [Under the linden tree,
> on the open field,
> where we two had our bed,
> you can still see
> lovely both

[156] A. E. Kroeger: 10.

[157] http://www.germany.info/Vertretung/usa/en/__pr/GIC/TWIG__WoW/2013/25-Minnelied.html, March 17, 2016

broken flowers and grass.
On the edge of the woods in a vale,
tandaradei,
sweetly sang the nightingale.][158]

Minnerede

Genre
Country of Origin: Germany
Distribution: German
Century: 14th – 15th centuries

A type of poem made up of rhymed couplets which explored love and numbered between 100 and 2000 verses. A commonly seen motif was the act of eavesdropping.

One example of the **minnerede** was the poem *Stiefmutter und Tochter* ("Stepmother and Daughter"), ca. 1395, which begins:

Ich gieng ains nachts von huse spat
und kam fur liebs kemnat
Do hort ich reden zway daarynn.
Das merck ich wol in meinem synn,
Ain muoter und ir dochterlein. [159]

[I left the house late one night and passed by the chamber of love. There I overheard two people speaking. I noted it well in my mind: it was a mother and her young daughter.][160]

---

[158] Ibid.

[159] Ann Marie Rassmussen: 1.

[160] Ibid.

Monk's Tale Stanza
Form
Country of Origin: France
Distribution: French
Century: 15th century

This stanza form was developed in France (as a *ballade* stanza), but took its name from the work of Chaucer (specifically "The Monk's Tale"). It was popular in the 15th century and was composed of eight lines of iambic pentameter, rhyming ababbcbc.

x x x x x x x x x a
x x x x x x x x x b
x x x x x x x x x a
x x x x x x x x x b
x x x x x x x x x b
x x x x x x x x x c
x x x x x x x x x b
x x x x x x x x x c

The Monk's Tale begins:

> I wol biwaille in manere of tragedie
> The harm of hem that stoode in heigh degree,
> And fillen so, that ther nas no remedie
> To brynge hem out of hir adversitee.
> For certein, whan that Fortune list to flee,
> Ther may no man the cours of hire withholde;
> Lat no man truste on blynd prosperitee;
> Be war of thise ensamples, trewe and olde.[161]

> [I will bewail in manner of tragedy

---

[161] http://www.librarius.com/canttran/monktrfs.htm, March 18, 2016

The ills of those that stood in high degree
And fell so far there was no remedy
To bring them out of their adversity;
For certain 'tis, when Fortune decides to flee,
There may no man the course of her withhold;
Let no man trust in blind prosperity;
Be warned by these examples true and old][162]

Mineleich
(Form, German)

See *leich*.

Mote
Form
Country of Origin: Spain
Distribution: Spanish
Century: 15th century

A popular form in the 15th century, the **mote** (pronounced moat) was usually one or two lines (though sometimes more) and contained a complete thought. It can be used as part of a longer poem.

Also, see *glosa*.

Mudanza
Device, form
Country of Origin: Spain
Distribution: Spanish
Century: unknown

---

[162] Ibid.

A **mudanza** is a mono-rhymed tercet, used as an opening to a poem.

N

Narrative lay
(Genre, French)

See *Breton lay*.

Neapolitan octave
(Form, Italian)

See *Octave, Sicilian*.

Neufain
Form
Country of Origin: France
Distribution: French
Century: unknown

The **neufain** ("heroical verse") appears to be an expanded *huitain* with 9-lines. The rhyme scheme could be aabaabbab, aababbcbc, aabaabbcc or ababbcbbc.

In tetrameter **neufain** could look like the following:

Version 1		*Version 2*	
x x x x x a	OR	x x x x x a	OR
x x x x x a		x x x x x a	
x x x x x b		x x x x x b	
x x x x x a		x x x x x a	
x x x x x a		x x x x x b	

x x x x x b	x x x x x b
x x x x x b	x x x x x c
x x x x x a	x x x x x b
x x x x x b	x x x x x c

Version 3		Version 4
x x x x x a	OR	x x x x x a
x x x x x a		x x x x x b
x x x x x b		x x x x x a
x x x x x a		x x x x x b
x x x x x a		x x x x x b
x x x x x b		x x x x x c
x x x x x b		x x x x x b
x x x x x c		x x x x x b
x x x x x c		x x x x x c

Nekuia
Genre
Country of Origin: unknown
Distribution: across Europe
Century: unknown

Nekuia (pronounced ne-kwee-a) was a genre encompassing visits to the land of the dead, especially by a living person (such as in Dante's *Divine Comedy*). This genre dates back to the ancient world, and **nekuia** is a term applied to Book IX of Homer's *Odyssey*. [163]

In "Canto 3" of *The Inferno*, Dante approaches the vestibule of Hell on his way to entering the underworld:

> Per me si va ne la città dolente,
> per me si va ne l'etterno dolore,

---

[163] Jay Parini: 408.

per me si va tra la perduta gente.

Giustizia mosse il mio alto fattore:
fecemi la divina podestate,
la somma sapienza e 'l primo amore.[164]

Dinanzi a me non fuor cose create
se non etterne, e io etterno duro.
Lasciate ogne speranza, voi ch'intrate.

[Through me the way is to the city dolent;
Through me the way is to eternal dole;
Through me the way among the people lost.

Justice incited my sublime Creator;
Created me divine Omnipotence,
The highest Wisdom and the primal Love.

Before me there were no created things,
Only eterne, and I eternal last.
All hope abandon, ye who enter in!][165]

Neufs preuses, Les
(Device, French)

See the *Nine Worthy Women*.

Neufs preux, Les
(Device, French)

See the *Nine Worthies*.

---

[164] http://www.divinecomedy.org/divine_comedy.html, March 18, 2016

[165] Henry Wadsworth Longfellow, trans. Canto 3: lines 1-9.
http://www.divinecomedy.org/divine_comedy.html, March 18, 2016

Nine Valiants, The
(Device, French)

See the *Nine Worthies*.

Nine Worthies, The
Device
Country of Origin: France
Distribution: French, English
Century: 14th century

The idea of the *Neufs preux* (Nine Valiants) was introduced by Jacques de Longuyon in 1312. These Nine Worthies were nine individuals that were thought to represent the ideals of chivalry (as it was then understood). These worthies would be depicted in art and invoked in literature. Three of the worthies were pagans (Hector, Alexander the Great, Julius Caesar), three were Jews (Joshua, David and Judas Maccabeus), and three were Christians (King Arthur, Charlemagne, Godfrey of Bouilon). They were referred to as Princes, no matter what titles they may actually have held.

See also *Nine Worthy Women*.

Nine Worthy Women
Device
Country of Origin: France
Distribution: French, English
Century: 14th century

In the late 14th century a female pantheon of Worthies began to appear, though its membership varied from region to region, and artist to artist.

See also the *Nine Worthies*.

No-sai-que-s'es
Genre
Country of Origin: France
Distribution: French
Century: unknown

The no-sai-que-s'es (I-don't-know-what-it-is) is a genre of poetry listed in some works on the troubadours, though without any further elaboration as to what it concerned.[166] William D. Paden and Francis Freeman Paden list it as a "pseudo-genre" in their collection of troubadour poetry.[167]

Escotatz, mas no say que s'es by Raimbaut d'Aurenga, also known as Raimbaut of Orange, (c. 1147 – 1173) is called a **no-sai-que-s'es** in at least one collection[168]. The poem begins:

> Escotatz, mas no say que s'es
> Senhor, so que vuelh comensar.
> Vers, estribot, ni sirventes
> Non es, ni nom no·l sai trobar;
> Ni ges no say co·l mi fezes
> S'aytal no·l podi'acabar,
>
> Que ia hom mays non vis fag aytal ad home ni a femna
>   en
>   est segle ni en l'autre qu'es passatz.
>
> Sitot m'o tenetz a foles

---

[166] Frank M. Chambers 1: 86.

[167] William D.s Paden and Francis Freeman Paden: 278.

[168] Samuel N. Rosenberg, et al: v.

Per tan no m poiria layssar
Que ieu mon talan non disses:
No m'en cujes hom castiar;
Tot cant es non pres un pojes
Vas so c'ades vey et esgar,

E dir vos ay per que. Car si ieu vos o avia mogut, e
no us
    o trazia a cap, yenriatz m'en per fol. Car mais
    amaria seis deniers en mon punh que mil sols
    el cel.[169]

[Listen, but I don't know what it is,
gentlemen, that I want to start:
it is not verse nor estribot
nor a sirventes: I can't give it a name;
and I don't know how I might write it
if I weren't able to finish it

in such a manner that one never saw a similar one,
made by a man or by a woman, either in this age or in
the other one that has passed.

Although you think it foolish of me,
I still can't resist
expressing what I think;
one ought not to blame me for it;
I don't give a damn about all that exists
as opposed to what I see and watch,

and I shall tell you why. It is because, if I had begun,
and never reached a conclusion, you would consider
me a fool. It is because I would better like to have six

---

[169] Lines 1-14. Robert Kehew: 120.

sous in my hand than a thousand suns in the sky.][170]

Nota
(Genre, French)

See *lai*.

Note
(Genre, French)

See *lai*.

Notula
(Genre, French)

See *lai*.

Novas rimadas
Form
Country of Origin: France
Distribution: Provençal
Century: 13th century

A non-lyric poem, usually written in octocyllabic rhymed couplets. They could be narrative or didactic. A famous example of the **novas rimados** form is the poem *Flamenca* (13th century).

x x x x x x x a
x x x x x x x a
x x x x x x x b
x x x x x x x b

Nueva maestria
(Form, Catalan)

See *cuaderna via*.

O

Octava de arte mayor
(Form, Castilian)

See *arte mayor*.

Octava real
(Form, Spanish)

See *octave, Sicilian*.

Octave
Form
Country of Origin: Italy
Distribution: Italian, English
Century: unknown

In English, an **octave** consists of 8-lines of iambic pentameter, while in Italian it is hendecasyllabic. The most common rhyme scheme for an *octave* was abba abba. An octave can be its own poem, strophe or part of the structure of another poetry form (such as a *Petrarchan sonnet*).

English   *Italian*

x x x x x x x x x a   OR   x x x x x x x x x x x a
x x x x x x x x x b   x x x x x x x x x x x b
x x x x x x x x x b   x x x x x x x x x x x b
x x x x x x x x x a   x x x x x x x x x x x a

x x x x x x x x x a
x x x x x x x x x b
x x x x x x x x x b
x x x x x x x x x a

x x x x x x x x x x x a
x x x x x x x x x x x b
x x x x x x x x x x x b
x x x x x x x x x x x a

Also, see *Octave, Sicilian*.

Octave, Sicilian
Form
Country of Origin: Sicily (Italy)
Distribution: Sicilian, English
Century: 14th – 16th century

Also known as the *ottava siciliana*, *ottava napoletana*, and the "Neapolitan octave", the **Sicilian octave** was a verse form that consisted of eight lines of eleven syllables each (hendecasyllabic). The form is common in late period Italian poetry. In English, iambic pentameter was often used. The rhyme scheme was abababab.

This form is a variant of the *strambotto* and is also called the *octava real*.

Sicilian   OR   *English*

x x x x x x x x x x x a   x x x x x x x x x a
x x x x x x x x x x x b   x x x x x x x x x b
x x x x x x x x x x x a   x x x x x x x x x a
x x x x x x x x x x x b   x x x x x x x x x b
x x x x x x x x x x x a   x x x x x x x x x a
x x x x x x x x x x x b   x x x x x x x x x b
x x x x x x x x x x x a   x x x x x x x x x a
x x x x x x x x x x x b   x x x x x x x x x b

Odl

Device
Country of Origin: Wales
Distribution: Welsh
Century: 6th – 15th centuries

Literally "rhyme". The Welsh used both end rhyme and internal rhyme, and would commonly rhyme stressed and unstressed syllables. *Ir* is a rhyme where only the vowels correspond while the consonants following them needed to belong to the same phonetic group. *Proest* was when the consonants following the vowel corresponded exactly and the vowels are of the same length.

Also see *awdl*.

Óglachas
(Form, Irish)

See *dán díreach*.

Old English Versification
Form
Country of Origin: England
Distribution: Anglo-Saxon
Century: 5th – 12th centuries

The oral **Old English versification** tradition was brought to England from Germany by the Anglo-Saxons in the 5th century. It therefore shares many (if not all) characteristics with *Old German versification*.

The lines of verse (which were not recorded in written form until the 8th century[171]) were alliterative, of variable length,

---

[171] Richard Dance: 35.

and divided by a caesura. The third stressed syllable in each line had to alliterate with either or both of the first two, while the fourth did not alliterate. All vowels and diphthongs alliterated with each other. Sc, sp and st usually only alliterated with themselves. The disposition of stressed syllables is the same as the Sievers' types described in *Old German versification*.

Synonyms and compound words were widely used (likely to assist with alliteration). Kennings, though not common, were sometimes used. Sometimes the words used could have multiple meanings (though whether this was done on purpose is open to debate).[172] Variation (using multiple names for the same subject within the same lines) was also used and poets would often reuse lines or word patterns from earlier poems by other poets.

Beowulf (between 8th and 11th century) is the most famous example of Old English alliterative verse. It begins:

> Hwæt! We Gardena   in geardagum,
> þeodcyninga,   þrym gefrunon,
> hu ða æþelingas   ellen fremedon.
> Oft Scyld Scefing   sceaþena þreatum,
>
> monegum mægþum,   meodosetla ofteah,
> egsode eorlas.   Syððan ærest wearð
> feasceaft funden,   he þæs frofre gebad,
> weox under wolcnum,   weorðmyndum þah,
> oðþæt him æghwylc   þara ymbsittendra
>
> ofer hronrade   hyran scolde,
> gomban gyldan.   þæt wæs god cyning!

---

[172] Ibid: 47.

ðæm eafera wæs   æfter cenned,
geong in geardum,   þone god sende
folce to frofre;   fyrenðearfe ongeat

þe hie ær drugon   aldorlease
lange hwile.   Him þæs liffrea,
wuldres wealdend,   woroldare forgeaf;
Beowulf wæs breme   (blæd wide sprang),
Scyldes eafera   Scedelandum in. [173]

[LO, praise of the prowess of people-kings
of spear-armed Danes, in days long sped,
we have heard, and what honor the athelings won!
Oft Scyld the Scefing from squadroned foes,
from many a tribe, the mead-bench tore,
awing the earls. Since erst he lay
friendless, a foundling, fate repaid him:
for he waxed under welkin, in wealth he throve,
till before him the folk, both far and near,
who house by the whale-path, heard his mandate,
gave him gifts: a good king he!
To him an heir was afterward born,
a son in his halls, whom heaven sent
to favor the folk, feeling their woe
that erst they had lacked an earl for leader
so long a while; the Lord endowed him,
the Wielder of Wonder, with world's renown.
Famed was this Beowulf: far flew the boast of him,
son of Scyld, in the Scandian lands.][174]

Old German Versification

---

[173] Lines 1-19. http://www.sacred-texts.com/neu/ascp/a04_01.htm, March 21, 2016

[174] http://www.poetryfoundation.org/poem/180445, March 21, 2016

Form
Country of Origin: Germany
Distribution: German
Century: examples from at least the 4th century

This form is made up of lines divided into hemistichs by a caesura. Each hemistich had at least two stressed syllables and at least two unstressed syllables. The syllables in each hemistich almost always followed one of the following metrical patterns (called Sievers' types[175]). Note that a forward slash represents a primary stressed syllable, a back slash represents a secondary stressed syllable and an x represents an unstressed syllable. The most common lines are:

The A-line: / x / x (**Hostig Har**drad)
The B-line: x / x / (On **call** or **free**)
The C-line: (x) x / / x (The **red blood** fell)
The D1-line: / / \ x (**bright arch**angels)
The D4-line: / / x \ (**bold braz**enfaced)
The E-line: / \ x / (**High**-seated **thegn**)[176]

Within the main lines there are further variations.

The A2-line: (x) x / x / x (as the A-line, but begins with one or two extra unstressed syllables: neither **age** nor **wis**dom)
The A3-line: / x x (x x) / x (Modern scholars believe this tupe of line only had one lift (stressed syllable) preceeded by a long string of unstressed syllable, while Sievers felt the first syllable was stressed: **so** that he will **see** us)
The C2-line: (x) x / / x (Structurally this looks the same as the regular C-line, however it features suspension of resolution,

---

[175] Named after Edward Sievers, a 19th century scholar.

[176] Paul Deane, 2000. http://alliteration.net/field12.htm, March 21, 2016

wherein the second syllable of the end word would normally be resolved as part of the lift, but is here allowed to be the final dip (unstressed syllable: a **dark pre**sence)

The D2-line: / / x x (Like in the C2-line there is a suspension of resolution, here on the secondary stress in the dip with a single short accented syllable: **bold bread**-winners)

The D3-line: / / x x (Like in the C2-line there is a suspension of resolution, here on the second lift which is a short accented syllable: **half-wi**llingly)

The D*-line: / x / \ x or / x / x \ (The same as the D1 or D4-lines, but with an extra syllable between the lifts: **ev**il **el**ements)

The E2-line: / \ x / (The secondary stress is a single short accented syllable with suspension of resolution: **learn** ever **less**)[177]

Alliteration had to occur between at least one stressed syllable in each half-line. It should be noted that all vowels alliterated, and so did any words starting with the letter G (whether the syllables had assonance or not).

Ottava napoletana
(Form, Italian)

See *Octave, Sicilian.*

Ottava rima
Form
Country of Origin: Tuscany (Italy)
Distribution: Tuscan, Spanish, Portuguese, English
Century: 13th – 18th centuries

---

[177] Ibid.

This was a stanza consisting of eight hendecasyllabic lines, which rhymed abababcc. It was used in religious verse by the late 13th century, and became very popular. It spread to Spain and Portugal in the 16th century. In England in the 18th century it was used for heroic poetry, though it was sometimes changed to having 10-syllable lines.

Tuscan	OR	*English*
x x x x x x x x x x a		x x x x x x x x x x a
x x x x x x x x x x b		x x x x x x x x x x b
x x x x x x x x x x b		x x x x x x x x x x b
x x x x x x x x x x b		x x x x x x x x x x b
x x x x x x x x x x b		x x x x x x x x x x b
x x x x x x x x x x b		x x x x x x x x x x b
x x x x x x x x x x c		x x x x x x x x x x c
x x x x x x x x x x c		x x x x x x x x x x c

La Teseide ("The Book of Thesus") by Giovanni Boccaccio (1313-1375) was written in 1340 mainly using ottava rima. Following the opening argument, Stanza I reads:

> O Sorelle Castalie, che mel monte
> Elicona contente dimorate
> D'intorno al sacro, gorgonce fonte,
> Sottesso l'ombra delle frondi amate
> Da Febo, delle quali aucor la fronte
> Spero d'ornaraui sol che 'l concediate,
> Le sante oreachie a'miei preghi porgete,
> E quegli udoite come roi dovete.[178]

Ottava siciliana
(Form, Italian)

---

[178] Giovanni Boccaccio: 1837.

See *Octave, Sicilian.*

Ottava Toscana
(Form, Tuscan)

See *strombotto Tuscano.*

P

Padairin
(Device, Irish)

See *conachloon*.

Partia
(Genre, Occitan)

See *partimen*.

Partimen
Genre
Country of Origin: Occitania (southern France, Monaco, Italy, Spain)
Distribution: Occitania, Catalonia, France
Century: 12th – 13th centuries

A genre of Occitan and Old French lyric poetry composed between two troubadours. It is a subgenre of the *tenso* or *cobla* (a poetic debate).

Unlike a *tenso*, the first speaker in the **partimen** presents a problem with two solutions and leaves his opponent to choose which solution to defend and then taking up the second option themselves. Therefore the debate is not based on conviction but simply for the sake of discussion. However, this distinction does not appear to have been seen in period, with troubadours and trouvères using both interchangeably.

One of the most common themes in **partimen** was courtly love. Each speaker (sometimes the same poet, sometimes two different poets) contribute three stanzas and an *envoi* in which he appeals to someone to be his judge. In some poems the two participants appeal to the same person, but more often each participant chose their own judge.

The Catalan name for this genre is *pariment*, whereas the French called it *jeux parti* (plural jeux parties). In Occitan it was also known as *partia*.

The **partimen** between Folquet de Marseille and Tostemps (written in the early 13th century) is an excellent example of the genre. The final stanza of the poem reads:

> Tostemps, de tort say dreg fayre,
> per c'a mi platz esta razos;
> e s'ie.us en vens, joi n'ayatz gran,
> car vos sofretz los companhos,
> mas eu n'am tal que.m fay semblan
> d'amor e no.y ay cofrarie.
> Folquetz, tostemps gabayre!
> jutjada si' esta razos:
> a Na Gaucelma vuelh que.s n'an,
> e si ieu am ab companhos,
> ja per so no.y ira duptan
> que be crey n'er fis jutjaire.[179]

[Tostemps, I know how to turn wrong into right, therefore this subject gives me pleasure; and if I defeat you in this way, be very glad, as you put up with companions whereas I love a lady who shows me her love and I do not have any fellow-lovers.

---

[179] Lines 61-72. Glynnis M. Cropp: 99.

Folquet, you always liked to joke! let this subject be judged: I wish it to be sent to Lady Gaucelma, and if I have rival companions in loving, she will not be fearful because of this, as I believe she will be an excellent judge.][180]

Pariment
(Genre, Catalan)

See *partimen*.

Passus
Device
Country of Origin: unknown
Distribution: unknown
Century: unknown

From the Medieval Latin *pace* (meaning "step") **passus** was a term used for a main division of a poem or story.[181] The poem *Piers Plowman* (c. 1370-90) is divided into sections called **passus**.

Pastorela
Genre
Country of Origin: Occitania (southern France, Monaco, Italy, Spain)
Distribution: Occitan
Century: 12th century

Meaning the "little or young shepherdess", the **pastorela** was

---

[180] Ibid.

[181] John Strachan and Richard Terry: 185

an Occitan lyric genre employed by the troubadours and which inspired the Old French *pastourelle*. The topic of these poems was an encounter between a knight and a shepherdess which could end any number of ways and were often humourous. Some of these poems tended to have long stanzas with short verses.[182]

L'autrier jost'una sebissa ("The other day, by a hedgerow"), by Marcabru (fl. 1130 – 1150), is an excellent example of the **pastorela**. It begins:

> L'autrier jost'una sebissa
> trobei tozeta mestissa,
> de joi e de sen masissa,
> si con fillia de vilaina
> chap' e gonel' e pellissa
> viest, e camiza traslissa,
> sotlars e caussas de laina.
>
> A leis vinc per la chalmissa,
> "Bela," fiz m'ieu, "res faitissa,
> dol ai car lo fregz vos fissa."
> "Segner," so.m ditz la vilaina,
> "merce Dieu e ma noirissa,
> pauc o prez si.l venz m'erissa
> c'alegreta.n soi e sana."
>
> [The other day, by a hedgerow,
> I met a common little girl,
> full of high spirits and good sense.
> Like the daughter of a peasant woman
> she wore a cape, a tunic lined with fur,
> a rough chemise,

---

[182] Darcy Butterworth Kitchin: 18.

shoes, and woolen stockings.[183]

I approached her across the heath,
"Pretty girl," I said, "you beautiful thing,
it pains me that you are pierced by the cold."
"Milord," said the peasant girl,
"I thank God and my nurse,
I don't care if the wind ruffles me,
for I'm happy and healthy."][184]

Pastorella
(Genre, French)

See *pastourelle*.

Pastorelle
(Genre, French)

See *pastourelle*.

Pastorita
(Genre, French)

See *pastourelle*.

Pastourelle
Genre
Country of Origin: Provence (France)
Distribution: Provençal, German, English, Welsh
Century: at least 12th – 18th century

---

[183] Lines 1-14. Anne L. Klink: 65.

[184] Ibid.

A **pastourelle** was an Old French lyrical genre concerning a meeting between a knight and a shepherdess. In early **pastourelles** the shepherdess bests the knight in a battle of wits and displays a sense of coyness. The knight (who is the narrator of the poem) usually has sex with the shepherdess (sometimes willingly and sometimes not), and then either departs or escapes. In later **pastourelles** sometimes a shepherd would be added to the cast, and sometimes a quarrel would occur.

The **pastourelle** was based on the Occitan *pastorela*, and went on to influence the Spanish *serranilla*. In the 15th century there are examples of **pastourelles** in French, German, English and Welsh.

The following translation of a poem by Theobald I of Navarre (also known as Thibault of Champagne, 1201 – 1253) is an example of a **pastourelle**:

> The other day I went wandering
> Without any companion
> On my palfrey, thinking
> To make a song,
> When I heard—I don't know how—
> Near a bush
> The voice of the most beautiful child
> That any man has ever seen;
> And she was not a child,
> For she was fifteen and a half years old.
> I have never seen anyone
> With such a noble face.
> Laughing, I rode towards her
> And made this speech:
> 'Beautiful one, tell me,
> By God, what your name is.'

But she jumped up
With her crook:
'If you come any nearer,
You'll get a blow from this.
Sir, get away from here!
I don't care for a friend such as you,
And I'd rather choose
A more handsome one called Robin!'

When I saw that she was scared
So thoroughly
That she wouldn't look at me
Or give any other positive sign,
Then I began to think
How to make her
Fall in love with me
And change her mind.
I sat down on the ground beside her,
And the more I looked upon her bright face,
The more it fired my heart,
Which doubled my desire.

Then I took upon myself to ask her,
In the most beautiful terms,
To look at me
And give me a different expression.
She started to cry
And said thus:
'I cannot look at you;
I don't even know what you're after.'
I leant towards her, and told her:
'My beautiful one, by God, your mercy.'
She laughed and responded:
'You make folk scared.'

Then I took her up before me
And made straightaway
In the direction of a small, green wood.
Across the fields I saw
And heard calling out
Two shepherds amongst the wheat;
They came shouting
And raising a great cry.
And I accomplished nothing more than I have said.
I let her down and fled from there;
I didn't care for such folk.[185]

Pie quebrado
Device
Country of Origin: Spain
Distribution: Spanish
Century: 14th century

Meaning "broken foot" or "limping verse", the **pie quebrado** is a short line (often 4-syllables) that followed other longer lines (a tail). It was often used in the *copla*. It usually followed an octocyllabic couplet. Indeed the medieval stanza in which the **pie quebrado** was introduced was made up of 6-lines, with line one, two, four and five of 8-syllables, and lines three and six made of 4-syllables[186]. (So two couplets, each followed by a **pie quebrado**.)

Planh
Genre
Country of Origin: Provence (France)

---

[185] http://www.poemhunter.com/poem/pastourelle/, March 21, 2016

[186] Howard Mancing: 566.

Distribution: Provençal
Century: at least the 12th century

The **planh** is a funeral lament and could be seen as a specialized variety of *sirventes*. They were usually written for famous people. They praised the departed, prayed for their soul and stated the author's sense of loss (though sometimes the sincerity was left in question).

Bertran de Born wrote a **planh** for Geoffrey of Brittany, who died in 1186. The first stanza reads:

> A totz dic qe ja mais non voil
> viure ni ja joi non aurai
> tan gran con lo jorn q'ieu morrai;
> pos sai hai mon Rassa perdut,
> lai lo volri'aver cobrat.
> Ai! Segner, car ses vos remain
> totz temps n'aurai lo cor irat
> duscha qe vos aia segut.[187]

Plazer
Genre
Country of Origin: Occitania (southern France, Monaco, Italy, Spain)
Distribution: Occitan
Century: unknown

The **plazer** was a song of pleasure.

Poulter's Measure
Form

---

[187] William D. Paden, et al: 349.

Country of Origin: England
Distribution: English
Century: 16th century

A meter composed of rhyming couplets made up of a line of iambic hexameter followed by a line of iambic heptameter. A Poulter's measure was similar to a baker's dozen, in that it could number more than twelve (hence the lines of 12 and 14-syllables.

x x x x x x x x x x x x

x x x x x x x x x x x x x x

Below is an example of a couplet written in **Poulter's Measure** from *the Literary Encyclopedia*:

The **doubt** | of **fu** | ture **foes** | exiles | my **pre** | sent **joy** |
And **wit** | me **warns** | to **shun** | such **snares** | as **threa** | ten **min**
e | annoy | [188]

Pregunta
Genre
Country of Origin: Spain
Distribution: Spanish
Century: 14th – 15th centuries

The **pregunta** (or *requesta*), with corresponding *respuesta* (answer), was a form of poetic debate in the Spanish courts in the late 14th and 15th century. One poet would present his question in a poem, while a second answered in another poem using identical form and rhymes.

---

[188] Peter Lewis Groves.

See also *débat* and *partimen*.

Priamel
Genre
Country of Origin: Germany
Distribution: German
Century: 12th – 16th centuries

The **priamel** (plural **priameln**) was a series of seemingly unrelated and unconnected ideas taken from everyday life which are brought together with a surprising effect in the last line. They made much use of wit, and often of vulgarity. There are antecedents of this form all over the world dating back at least to ancient Greece.[189]

An example of a **priamel** was printed in Reverend Metcalfe's 19th century work on German literature:

> He who will wash a raven white,
> And does the same with all his might,
> Or by the sun-light dry the snow,
> And box up all the winds that blow;
> Who'll cry 'Bad luck, who'll buy, who'll buy?'
> To shave bald pates industrious try,
> To make fools wise will undertake,--
> Why, he's an ass, and no mistake."[190]

Proest
(Device, Welsh)

See *odl*.

---

[189] Wiliam H. Race: 64.

[190] Rev. Frederick Metcalfe: 250.

Quintilla

Form
Country of Origin: Spain
Distribution: Spanish
Century: 16th century

The **quintilla** (pronounced kwin-tee-uh) was a Spanish form that used iambic tetrameter. The rhyme scheme could vary, but only two consecutive lines could have the same rhyme pattern. Therefore there were the following choices of rhyme scheme: ababa, abbab, abaab, aabab, or aabba. **Quintilla** were used to express deep emotions.

Version 1		*Version 2*	
x x x x x x x a	OR	x x x x x x x a	OR
x x x x x x x b		x x x x x x x b	
x x x x x x x a		x x x x x x x b	
x x x x x x x b		x x x x x x x a	
x x x x x x x a		x x x x x x x b	

Version 3		*Version 4*	
x x x x x x x a	OR	x x x x x x x a	OR
x x x x x x x a		x x x x x x x a	
x x x x x x x b		x x x x x x x b	
x x x x x x x a		x x x x x x x b	
x x x x x x x b		x x x x x x x a	

Version 5

x x x x x x x a
x x x x x x x b
x x x x x x x a
x x x x x x x a
x x x x x x x b

R

Rann
Form
Country of Origin: Ireland
Distribution: Irish
Century: unknown

A *rann* is a piece of verse, usually a stanza (and most often a quatrain).

Rannaicheacht randaigecht chethar-chubaid garit rocamarach
(Form, Irish)

See *rannaighheacht*.

Rannaighheacht
Form
Country of Origin: Ireland
Distribution: Irish
Century: 12th – 19th centuries

Rannaighheacht (pronounced ron-a'yach; "versification") were a *bruilingeacht* version of *dán díreach*. All versions of **rannaigheacht** made use of *dunadh*.

Basic **rannaighheacht** were quatrains consisting of 7-syllable lines. Two words in each line alliterate and rhymed xaxa xbxb (and so forth, where the x lines are unrhymed). Lines one, two and four consonate; line one and line two are true rhymes. The last word in line three should be two syllables.

x x x x x x *a* (line one does not rhyme with lines two and four, but it consonates)
x x x x x x a
x x x x x **x x**
x x x x x x a

Rannaighheacht bheag (pronounced ron-a'yach voig; "little verse") consisted of quatrains with line numbering 8-, 6-, 8- and 6-syllables. Each line had two words that alliterated and all end words were two syllables and consonated. The last word of line four alliterated with the previous stressed word. They also made use of internal rhyme, where the internal rhyme of the first line could consonate rather than be true thyme. In the second couplet however the rhyme had to be true.

x x x x b x **x a**
x x a x **x b**
x b x x x x **x a**
x a x x **x b**

Rannaighheacht ghairid (pronounced ron-a'yach cha'r-id; short-line versification) consisted of quatrains made up of one 3-syllable lines and followed by three 7-syllable lines. Two words in each line must alliterate. The lines rhymed aaba with the end word of line three rhyming internally with line four.

x x a
x x x x x x a
x x x x x x b
x x b x x x a *

* (The internal rhyme could take place on the first to fifth syllable.)

Rannaighheacht mhor (pronounced ron-a'yach voor; great versification) consisted of quatrains made of 7-syllable lines. Two words in each line must alliterate; lines rhymed abab and so forth. The end words rhymed internally in opposite lines of each couplet. The end word of line three rhymes internally with line four. The last word of line four alliterates with the previous word.

x x x x b x a
x x x a x x b
x b x x x x a
x x a x x x b

Rannaighheacht mhor gairit (shortened line great versification) consisted of quatrains made of one 3-syllable line followed by three 7-syllable lines. Two words in each line must alliterate; lines rhymed aaba, ccdc and so forth. If line three ends in a 2-syllable word aicill is used and the end word of line three rhymes internally in line four.

Version 1		*Version 2*
x x a	OR	x x a
x x x x x x a		x x x x x x a
x x x x x x b		x x x x x **x b**
x x x x x x a		x x **b** x x x a

Rannaichheacht randaigecht chethar-chubaid garit rocamarach (clipped versification with two syllable end words) were quatrains consisting of a 3-syllable line followed by three 7-syllable lines. Two words alliterated in each line. Made use of *aicill*, so line three rhymed internally with line four. Each line ended in a 2-syllable word.

x **x** **a**
x x x x x **x** **a**
x x x x x **x** **b**
x x b x x **x** **a**

Rannaighheacht bheag
(Form, Irish)

See *rannaighheacht.*

Rannaighheacht ghairid
(Form, Irish)

See *rannaighheacht.*

Rannaighheacht mhor
(Form, Irish)

See *rannaighheacht.*

Rannaighheacht mhor gairit
(Form, Irish)

See *rannaighheacht.*

Rant
Genre
Country of Origin: unknown
Distribution: unknown
Century: unknown

A **rant** was blustering and boastful, full of vainglorious speech.

See also *Gasconade*.

Redondilla
Form
Country of Origin: Castile (Spain)
Distribution: Castilian
Century: 16th century

A **redondilla** was a stanza form consisting of four trochaic lines, usually octocsyllabic, and using a rhyme scheme of abba. Quatrains in this form, but using a rhyme scheme of abab, are sometimes called *serventesios*. **Redondilla** is derived from the Spanish word for "round" and has been common in Castilian poetry since the 16th century.

Redondilla	OR	*Serventesios*
x x x x x x x a		x x x x x x x a
x x x x x x x b		x x x x x x x b
x x x x x x x b		x x x x x x x a
x x x x x x x a		x x x x x x x b

Refrein
Form
Country of Origin: The Netherlands
Distribution: Dutch
Century: 15th – 16th centuries

The refrain was a 15th and 16th century form with four or more stanzas of identical length and rhyme scheme, each of which ended with an identical line. The number of syllables is variable. The last stanza (which may be shorter than the others) is usually directed towards the "prince" of rhetoric or some other person. The initial letters of the lines are sometimes used acrostically to form the name of the poet.

Reicne dechubaid
Device
Country of Origin: Ireland
Distribution: Irish
Century: unknown

Reicne dechubaid was a sequence of two or three alliterating words separated by one word which did not alliterate. For example: go get three geese.

Reimrede
(Form, German)

See *spruch*.

Reimspruch
(Form, German)

See *spruch*.

Religiöse leich
(Form, German)

See *leich*.

Remate
Device
Country of Origin: Spain
Distribution: Spanish
Century: unknown

A **remate** is a refrain used in *canción petrarquista*; similar to the *finida.*

Retroencha
Form
Country of Origin: Occitania (southern France, Monaco, Italy, Spain)
Distribution: Occitan
Century: at least by the 13th century

Retroencha (Occitan) also known as *rotrouenge* (Provençal) was a lyric form almost identical to the *vers* or *chanso*, except it has a refrain at the end of each stanza.

Retroensa
(Form, Provençal)

See *retroencha*.

Retruécano
(Form, Spanish)

See *glosa*.

Reverdie
Genre
Country of Origin: France
Distribution: French
Century: unknown

An old French genre that celebrates the arrival of Spring. In fact, the poet will often encounter a beautiful woman personifying the season. The **reverdie** originated in the troubadour ballads of the early Middle Ages and were very popular during the time of Chaucer. Occasionally a reverdie would serve as an introduction to a longer poem.[191]

"Sumer is y-cumen in" (Cummer Canon, or, The Cuckoo Song), written in the mid-13th century, possibly by W. de Wycombe (late 13th century), is an example of a reverdie:

> Sumer is y-cumen in,
> Ludė sing, cuccu!
> Groweth sed and bloweth med,
>   And springth the wudė nu.
>   Sing, cuccu!
> Awė bleteth after lamb,
>   Lowth after calvė cu;
> Bulluc sterteth, buckė ferteth.
>   Merië sing, cuccu!
>   Cuccu, cuccu,
> Wel singės thu, cuccu;
> Ne swik thu never nu!
>
> Sing, cuccu, nu! Sing, cuccu!
> Sing, cuccu! Sing, cuccu, nu![192]

Reversie
(Format, French)

See *fatras*.

Rhupunt
(Form, Welsh)

See *awdl*.

---

[191] Laura Cooner Lambdin and Robert Thomas Lambdin: 308.

[192] Celia Sisam: 15-16.

Rhupynt
(Form, Welsh)

See *awdl*.

Rhyme Royal
Form
Country of Origin: England
Distribution: English
Century: 14th - 16th centuries

A **rhyme royal** was a stanza consisting of seven lines, usually in iambic pentameter, and using a rhyme scheme of ababbcc. It could be constructed either as a tercet and two couplets (aba, bb, cc) or a quatrain and a tercet (abab, bcc). This meter was introduced by Chaucer and became one of the standard narrative meters in the late Middle Ages.

x x x x x x x x x a
x x x x x x x x x b
x x x x x x x x x a
x x x x x x x x x b
x x x x x x x x x b
x x x x x x x x x c
x x x x x x x x x c

The Man of Law's Tale from the "Canterbury Tales", written by Chaucer around 1387, made use of the **rhyme royal**. Here is a section from the poem's prologue:

> O hateful harm, condicion of poverte!
> With thurst, with coold, with hunger so confoundid!
> To asken help thee shameth in thyn herte;
> If thou noon aske, with nede artow so woundid

That verray nede unwrappeth al thy wounde hid!
Maugree thyn heed, thou most for indigence
Or stele, or begge, or borwe thy despence![193]

[O hateful harm, condition of poverty!
By thirst, by cold, by hunger so distressed!
To ask help thou art ashamed in thy heart;
If thou ask for none, thou art so wounded by need
That true need reveals all thy hidden wound!
Despite all you can do, thou must for indigence
Either steal, or beg, or borrow thy living expenses!][194]

Riddle

Genre
Country of Origin: unknown
Distribution: Anglo-Saxon and others
Century: unknown

Riddles were short didactic poems containing hints as to their subject matter with roots dating back to ancient and biblical times.

See also *dyfalu*.

Exeter Riddle 35 is an Anglo-Saxon **riddle** from the 10th century:

> Mec se wæta wong, wundrum freorig,
> of hi innaþe ærist cende.
> Ne wat ic merc beworhtne wulle flysum,
> hærum þurh heahcræft,   hygeþoncum min.

---

[193] Lines 99-105. http://sites.fas.harvard.edu/~chaucer/teachslf/mlt-par.htm, March 21, 2016

[194] Ibid.

Wundene me ne beoð wefle.   Ne ic wearp hafu,
ne þurh þreata geþræcu   þræd me ne hlimmeð,
ne mec ohwonan   sceal amas cnyssan.
Wyrmas mec ne awæfan   wyrda cræftum,
þa þe geolo godwebb   geatwum frætwað.
Wile mec mon hwæþre seþeah   wide ofer eorþan
hatan for hæleþum hyhtlic gewæde.
Saga soðwidum,   searoþoncum gleaw,
wordum wisfæst,   hwæt þis gewædu sy.[195]

[The wet ground, incredibly cold, first produced me from its innards. I do not know myself in my mind's considerations to be made with wool fleeces, from hair through great skill. There are no woofs woven in me, nor do I have warps, nor does thread resound in me through the thrustings of pressers, nor does whizzing shuttle glide in me, nor must the sley knock me anywhere. Worms did not weave me with the skills of the fates, those which adorn the costly yellow cloth with decorations. But nevertheless, widely across the earth, I am wont to be called desirable clothing amongst heroes. Nor do I dread terror from the peril of a flight of arrows, though it might be taken eagerly from the quivers. Person clever in your ideas, wise in your words, say in truthful utterance what this clothing might be.][196]

The answer is mail coat.

Ríma
Genre form

---

[195] Richard Dance: 40.

[196] Ibid: 40-41.

Country of Origin: Ireland
Distribution: Irish
Century: 14th – 19th centuries

A **ríma** (plural **rímur**) was a genre form used between the 14th and 19th centuries. They were based on heroic tales and chivalric romances. They used alliterative 4-line stanzas and made use of *kennings*. There are over two thousand recorded rhyme schemes used in **rímur**.

Rimas dissolutas
Form
Country of Origin: France
Distribution: French
Century: 12th – 13th centuries

This form of the troubadours consisted stanzas with no set syllable count (though all lines must have the same number of syllables). There is no end rhyme within a stanza, but each line of a stanza must correspond with the same line in the next stanza. So a **rimas dissolutas** written as two quatrains would rhyme abcd abcd.

Rime Couée
Form
Country of Origin: Provence (France)
Distribution: Provençal
Century: 12th century

A 12th century tail-rhymed verse form used by the troubadours. It was written in any number of sixains (each made up of two tercets). The lines were accentual and followed the meter of normal speech. Lines one, two, four and five were longer lines (of similar length) while lines three and six are shorter lines (by one foot[197]) of the same length. A typical rhyme scheme was aabccb, ddeffe. Below is how a **rime couée** might look with lines of 8- and 6-syllables.

x x x x x x x a
x x x x x x x a
x x x x x b
x x x x x x x c
x x x x x x x c
x x x x x b

x x x x x x x d
x x x x x x x d
x x x x x e
x x x x x x x f
x x x x x x x f
x x x x x e

This form can be found in the following strophe of the poem "Of Sir Thomas Norray" by William Dunbar (1459 – unkn):

> "Now lythis of ane gentill Knycht,
> Schir Thomas Norray, wyse and wicht,
>   And full of chivalrie;
> Quhais father was ane Grand Keyne,
> His mother was ane Farie Queybe,
>   Gotten by sossery."[198]

Rime royal
(Form, English)

---

[197] John Small: 190.

[198] Ibid.

See *rhyme royal.*

Rionnaird
Form
Country of Origin: Ireland
Distribution: Irish
Century: 12th – 19th centuries

Rionnaird (pronounced ru'n-ard) were quatrains consisting of 6-syllable lines. All end words had 2-syllables, lines one and three consonate. The lines rhymed axax where the x lines were unrhymed. The poem concludes with *dunadh.*

x x x x **x a**
x x x x **x x**
x x x x **x a**
x x x x **x x**

Rionnaird Tri-Nard (pronounced ru'n-ard tree-nard) were quatrains consisting of 6-syllable lines. All end words had 2-syllables; the lines rhymed abxb and each line alliterated. Line two and four rhymed while line three consonated with it. The last syllable of line one alliterates with the first stressed word in line two. *Aicill* (cross-rhyme) occurs twice in the second couplet. The poem concludes with *dunadh.*

x x x x **x a**
x a x x **x b**
x *b* x x **x** *b* (consonates with line two and four)
x x *b* x **x b**

Rionnaird Tri-Nard
(Form, Irish)

See *rionnaird.*

Rispetto

Form
Country of Origin: Tuscany (Italy)
Distribution: Tuscan, English
Century: at least 13th – 15th centuries

Meaning "respect," the **rispetto** (plural **rispetti**), was a Tuscan folk verse and a version of the *strambotto*. A **rispetto** was generally composed of eight hendecasyllabic lines. The earlier **rispetti** used a rhyme scheme of abababcc. Later **rispetti** used ababccdd (as well as other variations). The form reached its peak during the 14th and 15th centuries making its way into English in the 16th century. In English the **rispetto** may be part of a longer poem.

Version 1		Version 2
x x x x x x x x x x a	OR	x x x x x x x x x x x a
x x x x x x x x x x b		x x x x x x x x x x x b
x x x x x x x x x x a		x x x x x x x x x x x a
x x x x x x x x x x b		x x x x x x x x x x x b
x x x x x x x x x x a		x x x x x x x x x x x c
x x x x x x x x x x b		x x x x x x x x x x x c
x x x x x x x x x x c		x x x x x x x x x x x d
x x x x x x x x x x c		x x x x x x x x x x x d

"Gascoigne's Lullaby" by George Gascoigne (c. 1534-1577) opens with a **rispetto**:

> Sing lullaby, as women do,
> Wherewith they bring their babes to rest;
> And lullaby can I sing to,
> As womanly as can the best.
> With lullaby they still the child,
> And if I be not much beguil'd,

Full many wanton babes have I,
Which must be still'd with lullaby.[199]

Ritornello

Form
Country of Origin: Italy
Distribution: Italian
Century: 14th century

A group of one to five lines (though often two or three) repeated like a refrain at the end of each stanza of a poem. The last two lines form a couplet (though the first line can combine with them to form a couplet or can rhyme with a line of the preceding stanza). It was an emotional response to the idea presented in the stanza and may have originated as a sermonic device.

See *madrigal* and *ballata*.

Roman

Genre
Country of Origin: France
Distribution: French, English
Century: 12th – 15th centuries

A broad term used to refer to long narrative poems concerned with chivalry and love and usually written in octosyllabic rhymed couplets. There are two named categories of **roman**: the "Matter of Britain" (concerned with Arthurian romance and Celtic legends) and the "Matter of Rome" (concerned with Roman-era heroes and exploits). A third unnamed category

---

199
https://www.wwnorton.com/college/english/nael/noa/pdf/27636_16u18Gascoigne.1_7.tp.pdf, March 22, 2016

exists of **roman** set in Byzantium.

Famous examples of the roman include *King Horn, Havelok, Sir Gawain and the Green Knight,* and *Sir Orfeo.*

Sometimes called a *romance* in English (not to be confused with the Spanish form of the same name).

See also *roman de geste* and *Breton lai.*

The following is the beginning of the anonymous *Sir Orfeo* (14th century or early):

> We reden ofte and finde y-write,
> As clerkès don us to wite,
> The layès that been of harping
> Been y-founde of frely thing:
> Sum been of wele, and sum of wo,
> And sum of joy and merthe also;
> Sum of bourdes, and sum of ribaudry,
> And sum ther been of the faièry;
> Sum of treachery, and sum of gile,
> And sum of happes that fallen by while;
> Of allè thing that men may see
> Most to lowe forsooth they be.
> In Britain these layes aren y-write,
> First y-founde and forth y-gete,
> Of àventures that fillen by dayes,
> Wherof they ight owher heren
> Of àventures that ther weren.
> They her harpès tooke with game,
> Maden layes and yaf it name.[200]

---

[200] Lines 1-20. Sisam: 76.

Romance
(Form, English)

See *roman*.

Romance
Form
Country of Origin: Spain
Distribution: Spanish
Century: 16th century

A romance was an indefinite series of octosyllabic verses using assonance in the even lines. This form was full of exposition and used for narration and description.

x x x x x x x x
x x x x x x x x (this line features assonance)
x x x x x x x x
x x x x x x x x (this line features assonance)
…

See also *romancillo*.

Romancillo
Form
Country of Origin: Spain
Distribution: Spanish
Century: 15th century

The **romancillo** was a version of the *romance* with 6- or 7-syllable lines with assonance on every second line.

Version 1		*Version 2*
x x x x x x x	OR	x x x x x x
x x x x x x x *		x x x x x x *

```
x x x x x x x            x x x x x x
x x x x x x x *          x x x x x x *
...
```

* (These lines feature assonance.)

Roman de Geste
(Genre, French)

See *chanson de geste*.

Rondeau
Form
Country of Origin: France
Distribution: French, English
Century: 12th – 16th centuries

The **rondeau** (plural **rondeaux**) was one of the *formes fixes* in French lyric poetry and song. Older **rondeau** forms are the *triolet* and *rondel*, while in the 15th century the **rondeau** was made up of 15-lines divided into a quintet, a quatrain and a sestet with a rhyme scheme of aabba aabR aabbaR (where the R is a refrain using a shorter line and based on the first line of the poem). French rondeaux had open meter and were not bound by this rhyme pattern. English rondeaux were often in tetrameter or pentameter and were much more dour in tone.

"Listen, Everyone!" is a 14th century rondeau written by Jehan Valliant (fl. 1360 – 1390) and was written in the English style:

> Listen, everyone! I have lost my girl
> For he who finds her, on my soul
> Even though she is fair and kindly
> I give her up heartily
> Without raising a stink at all.

This girl knows her graces well
God knows, she loves and is loyal
For heaven's sake, let him keep her secretly
Listen, everyone! I have lost my girl

Look after her well, this pearl
Let no one hurt or wound her
For by heaven, this pretty
Is sweetness itself to everybody
Woe is me! I cry to the world
Listen, everyone! I have lost my girl[201]

Rondeau redouble

Form
Country of Origin: France
Distribution: French
Century: 16th – 17th centuries

The **rondeau redouble** (pronounced ron-dough ray-dub-lay) was one of the *forme fixes*. Written using two rhymes in five stanzas of four lines each and one stanza of five lines. Each of the lines in the first stanza are repeated individually in turn as the fourth lines in the following stanzas. The first part of the first line is also repeated as a short fifth line (tail) to conclude the sixth stanza. The rhyme scheme is therefore A1,B1,A2,B2 b,a,b,A1 a,b,a,B1 b,a,b,A2 a,b,a,B2 b,a,b,a,*A1*.

The following is a **rondeau redouble** written by Vincent Voiture (1597 – 1648):

Si l'on en trouve, on n'en trouvera guère

---

[201]   http://www.webexhibits.org/poetry/explore_classic_rondeau_examples.html,
March 22, 2016

De ces rondeaux qu'on nomme redoublés,
Beaux et tournés d'une fine manière
Si qu'à bon droit la plupart sont sifflés.

A six quatrains les vers en sont réglés
Sur double rime et d'espèce contraire.
Rimes où soient douze mots accouplés,
Si l'on en trouve, on n'en trouvera guère.

Doit au surplus fermer son quaternaire
Chacun de vous au premier assemblés,
Pour varier toujours l'intercalaire
De ces rondeaux qu'on nomme redoublés.

Puis par un tour, tour des plus endiablés,
Vont à pieds joints, sautant la pièce entière
Les premiers mots qu'au bout vous enfilez,
Beaux et tournés d'une fine manière.

Dame Paresse, à parler sans mystère,
Tient nos rimeurs de sa cape affublés:
Tout ce qui gêne est sûr de leur déplaire,
Si qu'à bon droit la plupart sont sifflés.

Ceux qui de gloire étaient jadis comblés,
Par beau labeur en gagnaient le salaire:
Ces forts esprits, aujourd'hui cherchez-les;
Signe de croix on aura lieu de faire
Si l'on en trouve.[202]

Rondel
Form
Country of Origin: France

---

[202] http://www.trobar.org/prosody/pfor1.php, March 22, 2016

Distribution: French, English
Century: 13th – 16th centuries

The **rondel** is a 13th century fixed poetic form, a variant of the *rondeau*, that runs on two rhymes. It usually consisted of thirteen lines with a free meter (though often eight or ten syllables) divided into three stanzas (two quatrains and a quintet), with the first two lines of the first stanza serving as a refrain of the second and third stanzas. The rhyme scheme is therefore ABba abAB abbaB with no rhyme words being repeated. Sometimes the term **rondel** and *rondeau* were used interchangeably.

(x x) x x x x x x x A
(x x) x x x x x x x B
(x x) x x x x x x x b
(x x) x x x x x x x a

(x x) x x x x x x x a
(x x) x x x x x x x b
(x x) x x x x x x x A
(x x) x x x x x x x B

(x x) x x x x x x x a
(x x) x x x x x x x b
(x x) x x x x x x x b
(x x) x x x x x x x a
(x x) x x x x x x x A

In the 16th century the *rondel supreme* was introduced (also known as *French sonnet)* which added a fourteenth line, making the concluding quintain a sestet. The rhyme scheme was ABba abAB abbaAB. In French it is often written in *alexandrines*, though the lines could be any length as long as it remained constant (8-syllables were also common). In English

they were usually written in iambic pentameter or
alexandrines.

(x x x x) x x x x x x x A
(x x x x) x x x x x x x B
(x x x x) x x x x x x x b
(x x x x) x x x x x x x a

(x x x x) x x x x x x x a
(x x x x) x x x x x x x b
(x x x x) x x x x x x x A
(x x x x) x x x x x x x B

(x x x x) x x x x x x x a
(x x x x) x x x x x x x b
(x x x x) x x x x x x x b
(x x x x) x x x x x x x a
(x x x x) x x x x x x x A
(x x x x) x x x x x x x B

The following poem by Charles d'Orléans (1394-1465) is a
rondel:

En mes pays, quand me trouve à repos,
Je m'ébahis, et n,y sais contenance,
Car j'ai appris travail dès mon enfance,
Don't Fortune m'a bien chargé le dos.

Que voulez que vous die à briefs mots?
Ainsi m'est-il, ce vient d'accoutu mance,
En mes pays, quand me trouve à repos,
Je m'ébahis, et n,y sais contenance.

Tout à port moi, en penser m'enclos,
Et fais châteaux en Espagne et eb France;

Outre les monts forge mainte ordonnance,
Chacun jour j'ai plus de mille propos,
    En mes pays, quand me trouve à repos.[203]

Rondel supreme
(Form, French)

See *rondel*.

Rondelet
Form
Country of Origin: France
Distribution: French
Century: 12ᵗʰ – 20ᵗʰ century

The **rondelet** is a brief poem containing a refrain, a strict rhyme scheme and a distinct meter. The **rondelet** is essentially a short version of the *rondel*. It had seven lines with the following syllabic count: 4, 8, 4 (being line one repeated), 8, 8, 8, 4 (being line one repeated). The rhyme scheme is AbAabbA. While the refrained lines contained the same words, the punctuation could be changed.

x x x A
x x x x x x x b
x x x A
x x x x x x x a
x x x x x x x b
x x x x x x x b
x x x A

Rondelle

---

[203] Alan Boase: 16.

(Form, French)

See *Rondel*.

Rotrouenge
(Form, Provençal)

See *retroencha*.

Roundelay
Form
Country of Origin: France
Distribution: French
Century: likely the 16th century

A **roundelay** was a 24-line poem (four sestets) written in trochaic tetrameter which used a refrain and was set to music and meant to be danced to. The **roundelay** has a complex rhyme scheme where the middle couplet of each stanza repeats as the first couplet of the next stanza. The final couplet of the first stanza serves as a refrain as the last two lines of each stanza. When the *roundeau* and *rondel* are also set to music they can also be called a **roundelay**.

x x x x x x x a1
x x x x x x x b1
x x x x x x x A1
x x x x x x x B1
x x x x x x x A2
x x x x x x x B2

x x x x x x x A1
x x x x x x x B1
x x x x x x x A3
x x x x x x x B3

x x x x x x x A2
x x x x x x x B2

x x x x x x x A3
x x x x x x x B3
x x x x x x x A4
x x x x x x x B4
x x x x x x x A2
x x x x x x x B2

x x x x x x x A4
x x x x x x x B4
x x x x x x x a2
x x x x x x x b2
x x x x x x x A2
x x x x x x x B2

The following roundelay is by John Dryden (1631 – 1700):

Chloe found Amyntas lying,
　　All in tears, upon the plain,
Sighing to himself, and crying,
　　"Wretched, I, to love in vain!
Kiss me, dear, before my dying;
　　Kiss me once and ease my pain!"

Sighing to himself, and crying,
　　"Wretched, I, to love in vain!
Ever scorning, and denying
　　To reward your faithful swain:
Kiss me, dear, before my dying;
　　Kiss me once and ease my pain!"

"Ever scorning, and denying
　　To reward your faithful swain."

Chloe, laughing at his crying,
　　Told him that he loved in vain.
"Kiss me, dear, before my dying;
　　Kiss me once and ease my pain!"

Chloe, laughing at his crying,
　　Told him that he loved in vain.
But repenting, and complying,
　　When he kissed, she kissed again—
Kissed him up before his dying;
　　Kissed him up and eased his pain.[204]

---

[204] Lewis Turco: 244-245.

S

Salut
(Form, Occitan)

See *salut d'amor*.

Salut d'amor
Form
Country of Origin: Occitania (southern France, Monaco, Italy, Spain)
Distribution: Occitan
Century: 12th – 13th century

Derived from the *canso*, **salut d'amor** were epistolary love poems, written in octosyllabic rhymed couplets and broken into introduction, main body and conclusion.

x x x x x x x a
x x x x x x x a
…

The first known **salut d'amor** was written by Raimbaut d'Aurenga (c. 1147 – 1173) and begins:

> Donna, cel qe us es bos amics,
> A cui vos etz mals et enics,
> Vos clama merce d'una re:
> C'aujaz so qe us vol dir per be
> Aici en esta carta escrit,

Ez escoutaz com o a dit;
E prega ·us qe non respondaz
Tro qe tot auzit o aiaz;
Qe tal ren i aura ben leu
Al fenir qe ja no ·us er greu.[205]

[Lady, he who is a good friend of yours,
and to whom you are harsh and hostile,
begs you to have mercy in one thing:
that you hear properly what he means to tell you
here, ([it is] written in this letter)
and that you listen to the way he tells it;
and he begs you not to answer it
until you have listened to it all,
for there could easily be something
at the end that won't displease you.][206]

Séadna
Form
Country of Origin: Ireland
Distribution: Irish
Century: unknown

Séadna (pronounced shay'-na) were *dán direach* verse forms and concluded with *dunadh*.

The regular **séadna** were quatrains made up of lines of 8-, 7-, 8- and 7-syllables. Lines one and three end on two syllable words, while lines two and four end with one syllable lines. Line two and four shared end rhyme while line three rhymed with the word preceding the final word of line four. There are

---

[205] Lines 1-10. http://www.trobar.org/troubadours/aurenga/aa23.php, March 22, 2016

[206] Ibid.

two *aicill* rhymes in the second couplet. Each line featured alliteration; the final word of line four also alliterated with the preceding stressed word. The final syllable of line one alliterates with the stressed word of line two.

x x x x x x **x a**
x x x x x x b
x x x b x **x c**
x x x c x x b

Séadna mheadhanach were the same as the regular **séadna** except the first and third lines ended in 3-sylable words, while the second and fourth ended on 2-syllable words.

x x x x x x **x a**
x x x x x **x b**
x x x b x **x c**
x x x c x **x b**

Séadna mòr (pronounced shay'-na mor) were the same as regular **séadna** except lines two and four ended on three syllable words instead of single syllable words.

x x x x x x **x a**
x x x x **x x b**
x x x b x **x c**
x x x c **x x b**

Séadna mheadhanach
(Form, Irish)

See *séadna*.

Séadna mòr
(Form, Irish)

See *séadna*.

Séimhiú
Device
Country of Origin: Irish
Distribution: Irish
Century: unknown

Also known as *lenition*, **séimhiú** is a feature of the Irish language which generally makes it easier and more natural to speak it, while losing some grammatical complexity. It alters consonants and makes them more vowel-like. It is represented by a letter h after the first consonant of certain words (and only at certain times).

Senhal
Device
Country of Origin: Provence (France)
Distribution: Provençal
Century: unknown

Senhal (or secret name[207]) is a fanciful name used to address ladies, patrons or friends in Old Provençal poetry, especially for a beloved person. The **senhal** will encapsulate some aspect of the person's character. The most famous examples are Dante's Beatrice ("bringer of blessings") and Petrarch's Laura ("Laurel").[208]

Septain
Form

---

[207] William D. Paden et al: 38.

[208] Virginia Cox: unnumbered page in the Glossary.

Country of Origin: France
Distribution: French
Century: unknown

Also known as a *settain*, the **septain** ("Trolius' verse") is a contracted version of the *huitan* with 7-lines which rhymed ababbcc.

An example in tetrameter would look like the following:

x x x x x a
x x x x x b
x x x x x b
x x x x x b
x x x x x c
x x x x x c

Serena
Genre
Country of Origin: unknown
Distribution: unknown
Century: unknown

The **serena** were evening songs often concerning a lover waiting for the sun to set so he can meet with his beloved.

Serrana
(Genre, Spanish)

See *serranilla*.

Serranilla
Genre
Country of Origin: Spain
Distribution: Spanish

Century: 13th – 15th centuries

This later medieval genre concerned the meeting of a gentleman and a pretty country girl. They were light hearted in tone and often seen as a parody of the *pastourelle*. They were composed in any short meter (but especially *arte mayor* half-line). **Serranillas** ("mountain songs") were also sometimes called *serrana* (especially if they were octosyllabic).

Íñigo López de Mendoza y de la Vega, Marquis of Santillana (1398 – 1458) wrote several serranillas, including *"La vaquero de Morana"*:

> En toda la Sumontaña,
> de Trasmoz a Veratón,
> non vi tan gentil serrana.
>
> Partiendo de Conejares,
> allá suso en la montaña,
> cerca de la Travesaña,
> camino de Trasovares,
> encontré moça loçana
> poco más acá de Añón,
> riberas de una fontana.
>
> Traya saya apertada,
> muy bien fecha en la cintura;
> a guisa de Estremadura,
> cinta e collera labrada.
>
> Dixe: 'Dios te salve, hermana;
> aunque vengas de Áragón'
> d'esta serás castellana'.
>
> Respondióme: 'Cavallero,

non penséis que me tenedes,
ca primero provaredes
éste, mi dardo pedrero;
ca después d'esta semana
fago bodas con Antón,
vaquerizo de Morana'.[209]

See also *pastourelle* and *pastorela*.

Serventesios
(Form, Spanish)

See *redondilla*.

Serventois
(Form, French)

See *chant royal*.

Sestina
Form
Country of Origin: Occitania (southern France, Monaco, Italy, Spain)
Distribution: Occitan, English
Country: 12th – 16th century

A 12th century fixed verse form consisting of six stanzas, each of six lines, and normally followed by an *envoi* (three lines). The last word of each line of the first stanza were used as line endings in each of the following stanzas, rotated in a set pattern. There is no rhyme scheme. In the original form of the sestina the first line of each stanza had 7-syllables, whereas the

---

[209] 299-300.

other lines had 10-syllables. It was later changed to being completely hendecasyllabic, and over time many other variants appeared.

The pattern of line-ending words is most easily explained if the numbers 1 through 6 are allowed to stand for the end-words of the first stanza. Each following stanza takes its pattern using a bottom-up pairing of the lines of the preceding stanza (that is last and first, then second-last and second, then third-last and third). The pattern for the first stanza is therefore 123456, while the second is 615243, the third is 364125, the fourth is 532614, the fifth is 451362, and the sixth is 246531. There is then an *envoi* (or *tornado*). It consists of three lines that include all six of the line-ending words. This should take the pattern 2-5, 4-3, 6-1. The first word of each pair can appear anywhere in the line, while the second must end the line.

The **sestina** did not enter the English language until the 16th century.

Version 1		*Version 2*
x x x x x x 1	OR	x x x x x x x x x x 1
x x x x x x x x 2		x x x x x x x x x 2
x x x x x x x x 3		x x x x x x x x x 3
x x x x x x x x 4		x x x x x x x x x 4
x x x x x x x x 5		x x x x x x x x x 5
x x x x x x x x 6		x x x x x x x x x 6
x x x x x 6		x x x x x x x x x 6
x x x x x x x x 1		x x x x x x x x x 1
x x x x x x x x 5		x x x x x x x x x 5
x x x x x x x x 2		x x x x x x x x x 2
x x x x x x x x 4		x x x x x x x x x 4
x x x x x x x x 3		x x x x x x x x x 3

x x x x x x 3   x x x x x x x x x x 3
x x x x x x x x x 6   x x x x x x x x x x 6
x x x x x x x x x 4   x x x x x x x x x x 4
x x x x x x x x x 1   x x x x x x x x x x 1
x x x x x x x x x 2   x x x x x x x x x x 2
x x x x x x x x x 5   x x x x x x x x x x 5

x x x x x x 5   x x x x x x x x x x 5
x x x x x x x x x 3   x x x x x x x x x x 3
x x x x x x x x x 2   x x x x x x x x x x 2
x x x x x x x x x 6   x x x x x x x x x x 6
x x x x x x x x x 1   x x x x x x x x x x 1
x x x x x x x x x 4   x x x x x x x x x x 4

x x x x x x 4   x x x x x x x x x x 4
x x x x x x x x x 5   x x x x x x x x x x 5
x x x x x x x x x 1   x x x x x x x x x x 1
x x x x x x x x x 3   x x x x x x x x x x 3
x x x x x x x x x 6   x x x x x x x x x x 6
x x x x x x x x x 2   x x x x x x x x x x 2

x x x x x x 2   x x x x x x x x x x 2
x x x x x x x x x 4   x x x x x x x x x x 4
x x x x x x x x x 6   x x x x x x x x x x 6
x x x x x x x x x 5   x x x x x x x x x x 5
x x x x x x x x x 3   x x x x x x x x x x 3
x x x x x x x x x 1   x x x x x x x x x x 1

x x x x 2 x x x x 5 *   x x x x 2 x x x x 5 *
x x x x 4 x x x x 3   x x x x 4 x x x x 3
x x x x 6 x x x x 1   x x x x 6 x x x x 1

* (The first word can appear anywhere in the line but the
second must end the line.)

Francesco Petrarca, better known as Petrarch, (1304 – 1374) wrote several **sestinas**, including *Sestina V*:

Alia dolce ombra de le belle frondi.

HE TELLS THE STORY OF HIS LOVE, RESOLVING HENCEFORTH TO DEVOTE HIMSELF TO GOD.

Beneath the pleasant shade of beauteous leaves
I ran for shelter from a cruel light,
E'en here below that burnt me from high heaven,
When the last snow had ceased upon the hills,
And amorous airs renew'd the sweet spring time,
And on the upland flourish'd herbs and boughs.

Ne'er did the world behold such graceful boughs,
Nor ever wind rustled so verdant leaves,
As were by me beheld in that young time:
So that, though fearful of the ardent light,
I sought not refuge from the shadowing hills,
But of the plant accepted most in heaven.

A laurel then protected from that heaven:
Whence, oft enamour'd with its lovely boughs,
A roamer I have been through woods, o'er hills,
But never found I other trunk, nor leaves
Like these, so honour'd with supernal light,
Which changed not qualities with changing time.

Wherefore each hour more firm, from time to time
Following where I heard my call from heaven,
And guided ever by a soft clear light,
I turn'd, devoted still, to those first boughs,
Or when on earth are scatter'd the sere leaves,

Or when the sun restored makes green the hills.

The woods, the rocks, the fields, the floods, and hills,
All that is made, are conquer'd, changed by time:
And therefore ask I pardon of those leaves,
If after many years, revolving heaven
Sway'd me to flee from those entangling boughs,
When I begun to see its better light.

So dear to me at first was the sweet light,
That willingly I pass'd o'er difficult hills,
But to be nearer those beloved boughs;
Now shortening life, the apt place and full time
Show me another path to mount to heaven,
And to make fruit not merely flowers and leaves.

Other love, other leaves, and other light,
Other ascent to heaven by other hills
I seek — in sooth 'tis time — and other boughs.[210]

Sestine
(Form, Occitan)

See *sestina*.

Settain
(Form, French)

See *septain*.

Sextain
(Form, Occitan)

---

[210] Petrarch: 140-141.

See *sestina*.

Sextilla
Form
Country of Origin: Spain
Distribution: Spanish
Century: unknown

A **sextilla** was a *stanza* with six octosyllabic or shorter lines, usually rhymed abbaab, ababba, ababab, abbaba, aabbab or abaabb.

Version 1

(x x x x x x) x a   OR
(x x x x x x) x b
(x x x x x x) x b
(x x x x x x) x a
(x x x x x x) x a
(x x x x x x) x b

Version 2

(x x x x x x) x a   OR
(x x x x x x) x b
(x x x x x x) x a
(x x x x x x) x b
(x x x x x x) x b
(x x x x x x) x a

Version 3

(x x x x x x) x a   OR
(x x x x x x) x b
(x x x x x x) x b
(x x x x x x) x a
(x x x x x x) x b
(x x x x x x) x a

Version 4

(x x x x x x) x a   OR
(x x x x x x) x a
(x x x x x x) x b
(x x x x x x) x b
(x x x x x x) x a
(x x x x x x) x b

Version 5

(x x x x x x) x a   OR
(x x x x x x) x b
(x x x x x x) x a
(x x x x x x) x b

Version 6

(x x x x x x) x a
(x x x x x x) x b
(x x x x x x) x a
(x x x x x x) x a

$(x \, x \, x \, x \, x \, x) \, x \, a$
$(x \, x \, x \, x \, x \, x) \, x \, b$

$(x \, x \, x \, x \, x \, x) \, x \, b$
$(x \, x \, x \, x \, x \, x) \, x \, b$

Sextine
(Form, Occitan)

See *sestina*.

Sicilian Strambottos
(Form, Sicilian)

See *strambotto*.

Silva
Form
Country of Origin: Spain
Distribution: Spanish
Century: 16th century

A 16th century poem in Italianate hendecasyllables and heptasyllables in which the poet makes strophic divisions at will, usually in unequal length. Most of the lines are rhymed without a set pattern, and some of the lines are left unrhymed. Other meters may be used. Sometimes considered a form of Italianate *canción* and called a *canción libre*.

Las Soledades ("Solitudes") is a poem by Luis de Góngora, composed in 1613 in **silva**. It begins:

> Pasos de un peregrino son, errante,
> Cuantos me dictó versos dulce Musa
> En soledad confusa,
> Perdidos unos, otros inspirados.
>
> ¡O tú que de venablos impedido

-Muros de abeto, almenas de diamante-,
Bates los montes que de nieve armados
Gigantes de cristal los teme el cielo,
Donde el cuerno, del eco repetido,
Fieras te expone, que - al teñido suelo,
Muertas, pidiendo términos disformes-
Espumoso coral le dan al Tormes!:

Arrima a un frexno el frexno, cuyo acero,
Sangre sudando, en tiempo hará breve
Purpurëar la nieve;
Y, en cuanto da el solícito montero,
Al duro robre, al pino levantado
-Émulos vividores de las peñas-
Las formidables señas
Del oso que aun besaba, atravesado,
La asta de tu luciente jabalina,
-O lo sagrado supla de la encina
Lo Augusto del dosel, o de la fuente
La alta cenefa, lo majestuoso
Del sitïal a tu Deidad debido-,
¡O Duque esclarecido!
Templa en sus ondas tu fatiga ardiente,
Y, entregados tus miembros al reposo
Sobre el de grama césped, no desnudo,
Déjate un rato hallar del pie acertado
Que sus errantes pasos ha votado
A la real cadena de tu escudo.[211]

Sirventes
Genre

---

[211]

http://web.archive.org/web/20080209211215/http://www.geocities.com/revistaverso
ados/webpoemas/webpoemarios/gon-soledades.htm, March 22, 2016

Country of Origin: France
Distribution: Provençal
Century: 12th – 14th centuries

Unlike many other medieval genres, the **sirventes** were not about love. The main themes tend to be about abuse or, occasionally, praise. They were literary satire of a superficial nature, moralizing on the evil state of the world, politics, and current events (including the crusades). They were mostly satiric, with vituperation being common. The **sirventes** were considered subservient to the *chanso* (and often written to adopt the *chanso's* rhyme sounds). **Sirventes** were strophic in form and often told from the point of view of a servant or the troubadour himself who uses the opportunity to malign his fellow composers.

A sub-genre of the **sirventes** is the *gap*, in which the poet informs his audience of his prowess as a writer, a fighter and in the bedroom.[212]

The *canso de crozada* ("crusade song") is another sub-genre of the **sirventes** and were jingoistic propaganda.[213]

Sirventes joglaresc are generally thought to be the sub-genre of **sirventes** that deals with the poet insulting another person[214] (often a joglar[215]).[216] However, some scholars state that other than its name, nothing is known about this genre (three

---

[212] Robert Kehew: 7.

[213] Ibid.

[214] John Scattergood: 501 and Simon Gaunt and Sarah Kay: 57.

[215] A joglar (another word for a jongleur) was an itinerant entertainer.

[216] William W. Kibler: 1667.

troubadours being said to have created this genre but whose works in it have not survived).[217]

Sirventes-ensenhamen is another sub-genre in which a troubadour lists the repertory that a joglar should know.[218]

Yet another sub-genre is the *canso-sirventes* in which the themes of satire and love are mingled.[219]

In *"Cardaillac, per un sirventes"*, the troubadour Girault de Borneil (c. 1138 – 1215) slings some mud at a fellow minstrel. Using the above definitions of the sirventes sub-genres, this poem would be a *sirventes joglaresc*.

> Cardaillac, per un sirventes
> M'es dig q'en ventretz soudadiers;
> Mas enanz que.us obra.l portiers,
> Voill qe m'ofratz de loing merces,
> C'un petit vos flaira l'ales
> E car vos fatz trop presentiers.
> Per qu'es meillz c'un pauc de deniers
> Hom vos envi, c'om plus pres vos atenda;
> C'afanz es granz, qui no.s vir'o no.s benda![220]

> [Cardaillac, they tell me that you are coming in search
> of a sirventes with which to earn yourself some money;
> but before the doorkeeper lets you in I want you to
> thank me from a distance, for your breath is rather bad

---

[217] Frank M. Chambers 1: 180.

[218] William W. Kibler: 1667.

[219] Ibid.

[220] Ruth Verity Sharman: 399.

and you are apt to come too close. This is why a man is better off sending you a few pence rather than waiting for you to approach; for he suffers great torment if he does not turn away his face or cover his nose!][221]

Sirventes-ensenhamen
(Genre, French)

See *sirventes*.

Sirventes joglaresc
(Genre, French)

See *sirventes*.

Sixain
Form
Country of Origin: France
Distribution: French, English
Century: unknown

The **sixain** (also spelled *sixaine*; "common verse") was a stanza or poem of 6-lines that rhymed ababcc (tough in the late 16th century England saw an explosion of **sixain** variations with at least fifty-seven versions appearing[222]). In tetrameter this would look like:

x x x x x a
x x x x x b
x x x x x a
x x x x x b

---

[221] Ibid. 401.

[222] Kent Cartwright: 249.

x x x x x c
x x x x x c

Skeltonic verse
Form
Country of Origin: England
Distribution: English
Century: 15th century

Invented by John Skelton (1460 – 1529) in the late 15th century, this verse form consisted of short lines rhymed in groups of varying length with no stanza break. The lines were dipodic, meaning they had two stressed syllables and any number of unstressed syllables. The lines all rhymed until the poet felt the urge to switch to a new line. **Skeltonic verse** was used to convey unconventionality and a lack of dignity. It was a form of doggerel.

John Skelton's *The Tunnyng of Elynour Rummyng* (c. 1545) begins with the following *passus*:

> TELL you I chyll,
> If that ye wyll
> A whyle be styll,
> Of a comely gyll
> That dwelt on a hyll :
> But she is not gryll,
> For she is somwhat sage
> And well worne in age ;
> For her vysage
> It would aswage
> A mannes courage.
>   Her lothely lere
> Is nothynge clere,
> But vgly of chere,

Droupy and drowsy,
Scuruy and lowsy ;
Her face all bowsy,
Comely crynklyd,
Woundersly wrynkled,
Lyke a rost pygges eare,
Brystled wyth here.
    Her lewde lyppes twayne,
They slauer, men sayne,
Lyke a ropy rayne,
A gummy glayre :
She is vgly fayre ;
Her nose somdele hoked,
And camously croked,
Neuer stoppynge,
But euer droppynge ;
Her skynne lose and slacke,
Grained lyke a sacke ;
With a croked backe.
    Her eyen gowndy
Are full unsowndy,
For they are blered ;
And she gray hered ;
Jawed lyke a jetty ;
A man would have pytty
To se how she is gumbed,
Fyngered and thumbed,
Gently ioynted,
Gresed and annoynted
Vp to the knockles ;
The bones [of] her huckels
Lyke as they were with buckles
Togyther made fast :
Her youth is farre past :
Foted lyke a plane,

Legged lyke a crane ;
And yet she wyll iet,
Lyke a iolly fet,
In her furred flocket,
And gray russet rocket,
With symper the cocket.
Her huke of Lyncole grene,
It had ben hers, I wene,
More then fourty yere ;
And so doth it apere,
For the grene bare thredes
Loke like sere wedes,
Wyddered lyke hay,
The woll worne away ;
And yet I dare saye
She thynketh herselfe gaye
Vpon the holy daye,
Whan she doth her aray,
And gyrdeth in her gytes
Stytched and pranked with pletes ;
Her kyrtel Brystow red,
With clothes vpon her hed
That wey a sowe of led,
Wrythen in wonder wyse,
After the Sarasyns gyse,
With a whym wham,
Knyt with a trym tram,
Vpon her brayne pan,
Like an Egyptian,
Capped about :
When she goeth out
Herselfe for to shewe,
She dryueth downe the dewe
Wyth a payre of heles
As brode as two wheles ;

She hobles as a gose
With her blanket hose
Ouer the falowe ;
Her shone smered wyth talowe,
Gresed vpon dyrt
That baudeth her skyrt.[223]

Slabhradh
(Device, Irish)

See *conachloon*.

Snam Suad
Form
Country of Origin: Ireland
Distribution: Irish
Century: unknown

Snam suad (pronounced snao sooud; "swimming of the sages" or "floating phrases") were a form of *dán direach*. They were octastitch (8-lined) poems with 3-syllable lines. The lines rhymed aaxbcccb where the x lines were unrhymed. Lines four and eight had to be three syllable words, and the poem concluded with *dunadh*.

x x a
x x a
x x x
x x b
x x c
x x c
x x c
x x b

---

[223] John Skelton: 109-131.

Sneadhbairdne

Form
Country of Origin: Ireland
Distribution: Irish
Century: unknown

Sneadhbairdne (pronounced snay-vuy-erd-ne) were quatrains with line numbering 8-, 4-, 8- and 4-syllables. Each line featured alliteration and ended in two-syllable words. Lines two and four featured end rhyme while line three consonated with that rhyme. Every stressed syllable in line four had to rhyme and the poem concluded with *dunadh*.

x x x x x x **x x**
x x **x** a
x x x x x x **x** a
x a **x** a

Soneto

Form
Country of Origin: Spain
Distribution: Spanish
Century: 15th century

The **soneto** (which had Italian roots) was made up of two quatrains of 11-syllable lines, followed by two 11-syllable tercets. The rhyme scheme was abba abba cdc dcd (though the tercets could mix up the scheme as in cdc cdc or dcc cde).

Version 1	OR	*Version 2*
x x x x x x x x x x a		x x x x x x x x x x a
x x x x x x x x x x b		x x x x x x x x x x b
x x x x x x x x x x b		x x x x x x x x x x b
x x x x x x x x x x a		x x x x x x x x x x a

```
x x x x x x x x x x a        x x x x x x x x x x a
x x x x x x x x x x b        x x x x x x x x x x b
x x x x x x x x x x b        x x x x x x x x x x b
x x x x x x x x x x a        x x x x x x x x x x a
x x x x x x x x x x c        x x x x x x x x x x c
x x x x x x x x x x d        x x x x x x x x x x d
x x x x x x x x x x c        x x x x x x x x x x c
x x x x x x x x x x d        x x x x x x x x x x c
x x x x x x x x x x c        x x x x x x x x x x d
x x x x x x x x x x d        x x x x x x x x x x c
```

Version 3

```
x x x x x x x x x x a
x x x x x x x x x x b
x x x x x x x x x x b
x x x x x x x x x x a
x x x x x x x x x x a
x x x x x x x x x x b
x x x x x x x x x x b
x x x x x x x x x x a
x x x x x x x x x x d
x x x x x x x x x x c
x x x x x x x x x x c
x x x x x x x x x x c
x x x x x x x x x x d
x x x x x x x x x x e
```

Sonnet

Form
Country of Origin: Italy
Distribution: across Europe
Century: at least 13th – 21th century

The **sonnet** ("little poem") originated in Italy and soon spread to other countries. By the 13th century a **sonnet** was considered to be any poem that consisted of 14-lines and followed a set rhyme scheme and structure. Regional variations were eventually created including the *Caudate sonnet, French sonnet, Elizabethan/Shakespearean sonnet, Petrarchan sonnet* and *Spencerian sonnet*.

Sonnet, Caudate
Form
Country of Origin: Italy
Distribution: Italian
Century: 16th century

Created in the 16th century, the **caudate sonnet** is an extended version of the *Petrarchan sonnet* consisting of fourteen lines in a standard *sonnet* form followed by a *coda*. The first fourteen lines are in iambic pentameter with a rhyme scheme of abbaabbacdecde. The *coda's* rhyme scheme is cfffgg, in trimeter. This form was often used for satire.

x x x x x x x x x a
x x x x x x x x x b
x x x x x x x x x b
x x x x x x x x x a
x x x x x x x x x a
x x x x x x x x x b
x x x x x x x x x b
x x x x x x x x x a
x x x x x x x x x c
x x x x x x x x x d
x x x x x x x x x e
x x x x x x x x x c
x x x x x x x x x d
x x x x x x x x x e

x x x x x c

```
x x x x x f
x x x x x f
x x x x x f
x x x x x g
x x x x x g
```

Sonnet, French
(Form, French)

See *rondel*.

Sonnet, Elizabethan
(Form, English)

See *sonnet, Shakespearian*.

Sonnet, Petrarchan
Form
Country of Origin: Italy
Distribution: Italian
Century: 14th – 16th century

The original form of the **Petrarchan sonnet** was divided into an octave and a sestet. The octave's rhyme scheme is usually abbaabba, while the sestet's was more flexible (Petrarch tended to use cdecde or cdcdcd). Other possible rhyme schemes for the sestet included cddcdd, cddece or cddccd. In a strict **Petrarchan sonnet**, the sestet does not end with a couplet, but in English poetry this rule is not always observed (with the rhyme schemes cddcee and cdcdee also being used). This form was introduced to England in the 16th century.

The *octave* is used to pose a problem or question, express a desire or otherwise present a situation that causes the poem's speaker doubt or conflict. The problem is introduced in the first quatrain and developed in the second. The beginning of the sestet is called the *volta* and it introduces a change in tone of the *sonnet* (reflected in the rhyme scheme). The sestet comments on the problem or offers a solution to it.

The conventions of this *sonnet* would sometimes be subverted by court writers during the Renaissance.

The following sonnet was written by Dante Alighieri (1265-1321):

> Ye ladies, walking past me piteous-eyed,
> Who is the lady that lies prostrate here?
> Can this be even she my heart holds dear?
> Nay, if it be so, speak, and nothing hide.
> Her very aspect seems itself beside,
> And all her features of such altered cheer
> That to my thinking they do not appear
> Hers who makes others seem beatified.
>
> 'If thou forget to know our lady thus,
> Whom grief o'ercomes, we wonder in no wise,
> For also the same thing befalleth us,
> Yet if thou watch the movement of her eyes,
> Of her thou shalt be straightaway conscious.
> O weep no more; thou art all wan with sighs.
> (Trans. D.G. Rossetti)[224]

Sonnet, Shakespearian
Form
Country of Origin: England
Distribution: English

[224]   http://www.webexhibits.org/poetry/explore_famous_sonnet_examples.html, March 22, 2016

Century: 16th century

An early 16th century form, introduced and developed by other poets, but made most famous by Shakespeare. It consists of fourteen lines structured as three quatrains and a couplet. The third quatrain usually introduces an unexpected thematic twist (*volta*). In the *sonnets* written by Shakespeare the *volta* usually comes in the couplet and usually summarizes the theme of the poem or introduces a new look at the theme. The meter is almost always iambic pentameter. The usual rhyme scheme is abab, cdcd, efef, gg.

x x x x x x x x x a
x x x x x x x x x b
x x x x x x x x x a
x x x x x x x x x b

x x x x x x x x x c
x x x x x x x x x d
x x x x x x x x x c
x x x x x x x x x d

x x x x x x x x x e
x x x x x x x x x f
x x x x x x x x x e
x x x x x x x x x f

x x x x x x x x x g
x x x x x x x x x g

Below is Shakespeare's "Sonnet XVII":

> Who will believe my verse in time to come,
> If it were filled with your most high deserts?
> Though yet heaven knows it is but as a tomb

Which hides your life, and shows not half your parts.
If I could write the beauty of your eyes,
And in fresh numbers number all your graces,
The age to come would say 'This poet lies;
Such heavenly touches ne'er touched earthly faces.'
So should my papers, yellowed with their age,
Be scorned, like old men of less truth than tongue,
And your true rights be termed a poet's rage
And stretched metre of an antique song:
    But were some child of yours alive that time,
    You should live twice, in it, and in my rhyme.[225]

Sonnet, Spencerian
Form
Country of Origin: England
Distribution: English
Century: 16th century

A variant of the *Elizabethan sonnet* and introduced in the late 16th century by Edmund Spencer (1552/1553 – 1599), a **Spencerian sonnet** does not use its initial octave to pose a problem answered in the closing sestet. Instead the form is treated as three quatrains connected by the interlocking rhyme scheme and closed with a couplet. The rhyme scheme is abab, bcbc, cdcd, ee.

x x x x x x x a
x x x x x x x b
x x x x x x x a
x x x x x x x b
x x x x x x x b
x x x x x x x c
x x x x x x x b

---

[225] http://www.shakespeares-sonnets.com/sonnet/17, March 22, 2016

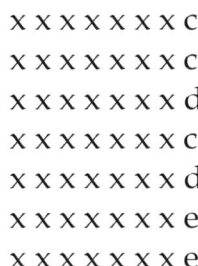

x x x x x x x c
x x x x x x x c
x x x x x x x d
x x x x x x x c
x x x x x x x d
x x x x x x x e
x x x x x x x e

Spencer's "Sonnet 75" from *Amoretti* reads:

> One day I wrote her name upon the strand,
> ··But came the waves and washed it away:
> ··Again I wrote it with a second hand,
> But came the tide, and made my pains his prey.
> Vain man, said she, that doest in vain assay
> ··A mortal thing so to immortalize,
> ··For I myself shall like to this decay,
> And eek my name be wiped out likewise.
> Not so (quoth I), let baser things devise
> ··To die in dust, but you shall live by fame:
> ··My verse your virtues rare shall eternize,
> And in the heavens write your glorious name.
> ··Where whenas Death shall all the world subdue,
> ·Our love shall live, and later life renew.[226]

Sotte amoureuse
(Form, French)

See *chant royal*.

Sotte chanson
(Form, French)

[226] https://poemshape.wordpress.com/2009/01/11/what-is-shakespearean-spenserian-amp-petrarchan-sonnets/, March 22, 2016

See *chant royal*.

Sprechspruch
Form
Country of Origin: Germany
Distribution: German
Century: 12th – 16th centuries

Sprechspruch ("spoken saying") were lyrical poems of the minnesingers which were meant to be spoken and read (as opposed to sung,[227] though a prolific definition on the internet claims otherwise[228]). They were gnomic and contained practical wisdom, religious admonitions and fables with morals (a *bispel*). They had 4-beat lines, arranged in pairs. They were non-strophic but could be subdivided into line groups of varying length.

x x x x
x x x x
…

Spruch
Form
Country of Origin: Germany
Distribution: German
Century: 12th – 16th centuries

Spruch ("saying") were lyrical poems of the minnesingers that often expressed maxims. They were set to music (though some scholars say that if the poem was set to music and sung it was

---

[227] Alex Preminger: 808 and Matthias Konzett: unnumbered page.

[228] http://www.proz.com/?sp=gloss/term&id=7868930, March 22, 2016

more properly called a *minnelied*). They contained subjective emotional elements. They had 4-beat lines, arranged in pairs. They were non-strophic but could be subdivided into line groups of varying length.

x x x x
x x x x
...

The following is the beginning of a **spruch** called *Der Marner*, written sometime between 1230 and 1280:

> Sing ich dien liuten miniu liet,
> sô wil der êrste daz
> wie Dietrîch von Berne schiet.
> der ander, wâ künc Ruother saz,
> der dritte wil der Riuzen sturm, sô wil der vierde
> Ekhartes nôt,
> der fúnfte wen Kriemhilt verriet...[229]

> [When I sing my songs to the people,
> Then the first wants to hear
> How Dietrich parted from Berne.
> The second wants to hear where King Rother lived and
> reigned,
> The third wants to hear the battle of the Riuzen, the
> fourth Ekhart's distress,
> The fifth who was betrayed by Kriemhild...]

Starina
(Form, Slavic)

See *bylina*.

---

[229] Karl Reichl 2: 101.

Strambotto

Form
Country of Origin: Tuscany (Italy)
Distribution: Tuscan, Sicilian, Italian
Century: at least 12th – 19th centuries

The **strambotto** is one of the oldest verse forms in the Italian language. The version used in Sicily and Tuscany employed either six or eight hendecasyllables. The rhyme scheme varied, even within the same area (there are at least five Tuscan versions). The most commonly used rhyme scheme was for the 8-line *strambotto romagnuolo* (ababccdd). The 6-line **strambotto** rhymed ababab or ababcc or aabbcc. There was only one stanza.

Strambotto were sometimes employed as *estribote*.

Strambotto Romagnuolo

x x x x x x x x x x a   OR
x x x x x x x x x x b
x x x x x x x x x x a
x x x x x x x x x x b
x x x x x x x x x x c
x x x x x x x x x x c
x x x x x x x x x x d
x x x x x x x x x x d

Strambotto Tuscano/ Ottava Tuscana V.1

x x x x x x x x x x a   OR
x x x x x x x x x x b
x x x x x x x x x x a
x x x x x x x x x x b
x x x x x x x x x x a
x x x x x x x x x x b
x x x x x x x x x x c
x x x x x x x x x x c

Sicilian Strambottos

x x x x x x x x x x a   OR
x x x x x x x x x x b
x x x x x x x x x x a
x x x x x x x x x x b

Strambotto Tuscano/ Ottava Tuscana V.2

x x x x x x x x x x a   OR
x x x x x x x x x x a
x x x x x x x x x x b
x x x x x x x x x x b

x x x x x x x x x x x a   x x x x x x x x x x x c
x x x x x x x x x x x b   x x x x x x x x x x x c
x x x x x x x x x x x a   x x x x x x x x x x x d
x x x x x x x x x x x b   x x x x x x x x x x x d

Strambotto Tuscano/   *Strambotto Tuscano/*
Ottava Tuscana V.3   *Ottava Tuscana V.4*
x x x x x x x x x x x a   OR   x x x x x x x x x x x a   OR
x x x x x x x x x x x b   x x x x x x x x x x x a
x x x x x x x x x x x a   x x x x x x x x x x x b
x x x x x x x x x x x b   x x x x x x x x x x x b
x x x x x x x x x x x c   x x x x x x x x x x x c
x x x x x x x x x x x c   x x x x x x x x x x x c

Strambotto Tuscano/
Ottava Tuscana V.5
x x x x x x x x x x x a
x x x x x x x x x x x b
x x x x x x x x x x x a
x x x x x x x x x x x b
x x x x x x x x x x x a
x x x x x x x x x x x b

Strambotto Romagnuolo
(Form, Italian)

See *strambotto.*

Strambotto Tuscano
(Form, Italian)

See *strambotto.*

T

Tagelied

Genre
Country of Origin: Germany
Distribution: German
Century: 13th – 16th centuries

Adopted from the Provençal troubadour's *alba*, the **tagelied** (dawn song) was a lyric genre, often told in three verses, concerning the separation of two lovers at dawn.

A popular version of the **tagelied** was the *wächterlied* (watchman's song) in which a trusted watchman warns the male lover (a knight) that he must depart.

The form of a **tagelied** (plural **tagelieder**) was alternating verse, spoken by the knight and the lady (though not directed to each other). The form and prosody used varied over time and by poet.

Important motifs of the **tagelied** were the depiction of daybreak, the warning to depart, the lament at parting, and the lady's permission for the knight to go (the *urloup*).

Below is a section of the **tagelied** of Wolfram von Eschenbach (c. 1160/80 – c. 1220):

> Sîne klâwen durh die wolken sint geslagen,
> er stîget ûf mit grôzer kraft,

ich sih in grâwen tägelîch als er wil tagen,
den tac, der im geselleschaft
erwenden wil, dem werden man,
den ich mit sorgen în verliez.
ich bringe in hinnen, ob ich kan.
sîn vil manegiu tugent michz leisten hiez.[230]

Tanzleich
(Form, German)

See *leich*.

Tawddgyrch cadwynog
(Form, Welsh)

See *awdl*.

Tenso
Genre
Country of Origin: Occitania (southern France, Monaco, Italy, Spain)
Distribution: Occitan
Century: likely around the 12th century

Another of the genres of poetic debate, the **tenso** was a troubadour song. **Tenso** are usually written by two poets and is a debate (quite often about love or ethics). Occasionally the contributing poets may be male and female (especially when the topic is love) or one of them may be a patron dabbling in poetics.[231] Sometimes the poem is only written by a single poet, while the second voice is attributed to an imaginary party (such as God, the poet's horse, or even the poet's cloak).

---

[230] http://www.columbia.edu/~fdc/utf8.html, March 22, 2016

[231] Peire Vidal: 245.

A *cobla exchange* was a **tenso** of only two stanzas.

A *contenson* was a **tenso** where the debate is judged by a third party whose judgement was delivered in a final *tornada*.

The Tenso of Blacatz and Peire Vidal (12th century) is written in four coblas (two per poet):
Blacatz

I. Peire Vidal, pos far m'ave tenso,
No.us sia greu, si.us deman per cabal
Per cal razo avetz sen tan venal
En mains afars que no.us tornon a pro,
Et en trobar avetz saber e sen;
E qui ja veils en aital loc aten
Et en joven n'es atressi passatz,
Meins a de be que sia ja no fos natz.

Peire Vidal

II. Blacatz, no tenh ges vostre chan per bo,
Quar anc partis plait tan descominal;
Qu'ieu ai bon sen e fin e natural
En totz afars, per que.m par be qui so.
E s'ai m'amor meza e mon joven
En la meillor et en la plus valen,
No.n vueill perdre los guizardos ni.ls gratz,
Quar qui.s recre es vilans e malvatz.

Blacatz

III. Peire Vidal, ja la vostra razo
Non vueill aver a mi dons que tan val,
Que.ill vueill server a totz jorns per engal,

E d'ela.m platz, que.m fassa guizardo;
Et a vos lais lo lonc atendemen
Sense jauzir, qu'lieu vueill lo jauzimen,
Es jois perdut, qu'anc uns no.n fo cobratz.

Peire Vidal

IV. Blacatz, no soi eu ges d'aital faiso,
Com vos autre, a cui d'amor non cal;
Gran jornada volh far per bon ostal
E lonc server per recebre getn do.
Non es fis drutz sel que.s camja soven,
Ni bona domna sela qui.l consen;
Non es amors, ans es engans proatz,
S'oi enqueretz e deman o laissatz. (XLV)[232]

[Blacatz

I. Peire Vidal, since I have decided to compose a tenso,
do not be angry if I ask you, first of all,
why you have such a venal sense
in many matters which did not profit you,
but in poetry you have such knowledge and talent;
he who, in old age continues to wait
after spending his youth in such a way,
he has acquired less wealth than if he had never been
        born.

Peire Vidal

II. Blacatz, I do not appreciate your song,
for never have you debated so unconvincingly;
that I possess a good, refined and natural intelligence

---

[232] Peire Vidal: 246-248.

in all matters, for this I am justly recognized.
And since I have placed my love and my youth
in the best and most worthy lady,
I do not wish to lose the rewards or favours,
for he who gives up is base and unworthy.

Blacatz

III. Peire Vidal, I do not wish to pursue your argument
with my lady, who is so worthy,
for I wish to serve her equally every day,
and I like her to give me a reward;
I leave the long wait without joy to you,
what I want is enjoyment,
for you should well know that a song wait without joy
is joy lost, never to be recovered.

Peire Vidal

IV. Blacatz, I am not made like this,
like you others who care little for love.
I want to do a good days work to be well lodged,
and to do a long service to receive a noble gift.
The pure lover does not change so often
nor does a good lady consent to it.
It is not love but obvious deception
if today you request love and tomorrow you abandon
        it.]233

See also *cobla, débat, tenzone* and *partimen.*

Tenson
(Genre, Occitan)

---

233 Ibid.

See *tenso.*

Tenzone
Genre
Country of Origin: France
Distribution: Provençal
Century: 12ᵗʰ – 13ᵗʰ centuries

The **Tenzone** (like the Occitan *tenso*) was a verbal exchange or debate. In the **tenzone** it is done in the form of invective (a verbal duel) expressed through *sirventes* or *coblas*.

Dante Alighieri (c. 1265 – 1321) wrote a famous **tenzone** with Forese Donati (d. 1296).

Tercetos
(Form, Spanish)

See *terza rima.*

Terza rima
Form
Country of Origin: Italy
Distribution: Italian, English
Century: 13ᵗʰ century

A **terza rima** ("third rhyme") is a rhyming verse stanza consisting of an interlocking three-line rhyme scheme first used by Dante Alighieri (c. 1265 – 1321). The stanza uses chain rhyme in a pattern of aba, bcb, cdc, ded. There is no limit to the number of lines but poems (or sections of poems) written in **terza rima** end in either a single line or a couplet that repeats the rhyme of the middle line of the final tercet. Using the above pattern, the two possible endings are therefore ded, e or ded, ee. Though there is no set meter, in English iambic pentameter is preferred.

Using the above example of lines, a terza rima would look like:

Version 1		Version 2
x x x x x x x x x a	OR	x x x x x x x x x a
x x x x x x x x x b		x x x x x x x x x b
x x x x x x x x x a		x x x x x x x x x a
x x x x x x x x x b		x x x x x x x x x b
x x x x x x x x x c		x x x x x x x x x c
x x x x x x x x x b		x x x x x x x x x b
x x x x x x x x x c		x x x x x x x x x c
x x x x x x x x x d		x x x x x x x x x d
x x x x x x x x x c		x x x x x x x x x c
x x x x x x x x x d		x x x x x x x x x d
x x x x x x x x x e		x x x x x x x x x e
x x x x x x x x x d		x x x x x x x x x d
x x x x x x x x x e		x x x x x x x x x e
		x x x x x x x x x e

Dante wrote the *Divina Commedia* ("Divine Comedy") in **terza rima**:

> Nel mezzo del cammin di nostra vita
> mi ritrovai per una selva oscura,
> ché la diritta via era smarrita.
> Ahi quanto a dir qual era è cosa dura
> esta selva selvaggia e aspra e forte
> che nel pensier rinova la paura!

Tant' è amara che poco è più morte;
ma per trattar del ben ch'i' vi trovai,
dirò de l'altre cose ch'i' v'ho scorte.

Io non so ben ridir com' i' v'intrai,
tant' era pien di sonno a quel punto
che la verace via abbandonai.[234]

[Midway in the journey of our life
I came to myself in a dark wood,
for the straight way was lost.
Ah, how hard it is to tell
the nature of that wood, savage, dense and harsh –
the very thought of it renews my fear!
It is so bitter death is hardly more so.
But to set forth the good I found
I will recount the other things I saw.
How I came there I cannot really tell,
I was so full of sleep
when I forsook the one true way.][235]

Tétramère
Form
Country of Origin: France
Distribution: French
Century: unknown

The **tétramère** consists of lines of 12-syllables, with each line having four divisions. There is a caesura after the sixth syllable.

x x x x x x | x x x x x x

---

[234] Lines 1-12. http://etcweb.princeton.edu/dante/pdp/, March 22, 2016

[235] Ibid.

...

Texto
(Form, Spanish)

See *estribillo*.

Toddaid
(Form, Welsh)

See *awdl* and *toddaid byr*.

Toddaid byr
Form
Country of Origin: Wales
Distribution: Welsh
Century: 6th – 15th centuries

A shortened version of a *toddaid*, where the first line has 10-syllables and the second has 6-syllables.

Therefore a **toddaid byr** looks like:

x x x x x x x A x b
x x x b x A

Tornada
Form
Country of Origin: Occitania (southern France, Monaco, Italy, Spain)
Distribution: Occitan, Sicilian
Century: 11th to at least the 14th centuries

Meaning "turned" or "twisted", the **toranda** is a final, shorter *cobla* (stanza) and is the precursor of the French *envoi*. They are composed of a variable number of lines and could therefore be known by other names based on that length (for instance, the 3-line **tornado** in a *sestina* is called a *tercet*).

Tornadas can be used to identify the location and date of the poem's composition and the identities of members of the troubadour's circle, or as a dedication to a friend or patron. They can also serve to focus and reflect on the theme of the poem, commenting on the surrounding material within the poem, or to act as a conclusion.

In the original Occitan model, the **tornada** replicated the meter of the second half (*sirima*) of the preceding strophe. The Sicilian **tornada** is longer and serves as the last strophe of the song or *ballad* being performed and worked as a summation or personification of the poem.

The **tornada** from "*Tant ai mo cor ple de joya*" by Bernart de Ventadorn (fl. 1130 – 1200) reads:

> Messatgers, vai e cor
> e di.m a la gensor
> la pena e la dolor
> que.n trac, e.l martire[236]

> [But the false intriguers have distanced me from her country; and that one has become a spy whom / thought would have helped us, if he knew our souls had one will.][237]

---

[236] Lines 73-75. http://trobadors.iec.cat/veure_d.asp?id_obra=475, March 23, 2016

[237] http://www.poemhunter.com/poem/tant-ai-mo-cor/, Mach 23, 2016

Traethodl

Form
Country of Origin: Wales
Distribution: Welsh
Century: unknown

Traethodl was a Welsh verse form consisting of couplets in which 7-syllabled lines rhyme with alternate accented and unaccented rhyming syllables. It was elaborated upon in the 14th century and evolved into the *cywydd (deuair birion)*. *Cynghanedd* is not required.

x x x x x x a (accented end)
x x x x x x a (unaccented end)
x x x x x x b (accented end)
x x x x x x b (unaccented end)
…

The famous Welsh poet Dafydd ap Gwilm wrote the following in **traethodl**:

> Merch sydd decaf blodeu^n
> Yn y nef ond Duw ei hun.
> O wraig y ganed pob áyn
> O'r hoU bobloedd ond trid^n.
> Ac am hynny nid rhyiedd
> Caru merched a ^TdLgedd.
> O'r nef y cad áìgr'úwch
> Ac o uffern bob irisiwch.[238]

Treochair

Form

---

[238] Lines 43-50. Dafydd ap Gwilm: 19. This is from a scanned copy and may contain scanning errors.

Country of Origin: Ireland
Distribution: Irish
Century: unknown

Treochair were a form of *dán díreach* that were written in tercets featuring line of 3-, 7- and 7-syllables. Line one had two stresses, line two had three stresses and line three had two stresses. The rhyme scheme was axa bxb and so forth, with the x lines being unrhymed, and concluded with axa again. **Treochair** made generous use of alliteration.

x x a

x x x x x x x

x x x x x x a

…

Tri-thrawiad
(Form, Welsh)

See *mesur tri-thrawiad*.

Triad
Form
Country of Origin: Ireland
Distribution: Irish, English
Century: unknown

A **triad** was a poem written in three monorhymed lines (tercets) of variable length and meter where the poet lists three related things and considers their relationship.

The following anonymous poem "The Rule of Three", translated into English from Middle English:

> When I consider these things three,

I say never then blithe be:
The first is that I shall sway;
The second, I know not which day;
The third fills me with my most care—
I know not wither I shall fare![239]

Trian rannaigechta moire
Form
Country of Origin: Ireland
Distribution: Irish
Century: unknown

Trian rannaigechta moire were a form of dán direach written in quatrains of 4-syllable lines with consonant rhyme. The line rhyme xaba xcdc and so on with the x line being unrhymed. If line three ends on a 2-syllable word, aicill is employed and there is a cross-rhyme with the following line. They concluded with *dunadh*.

Version 1		*Version 2*
x x x x	OR	x x x x
x x x a		x x x a
x x x b		x x **x b**
x x x a		x b x a

Trimètre
Form
Country of Origin: France
Distribution: French
Century: unknown – 18th centuries

Trimètre was a 12-syllable *vers romantique* with three divisions

---

[239] Lewis Turci: 277.

per line.

Possibly the same as the *tétramère*.

Triolet
Form
Country of Origin: France
Distribution: French
Century: 13th – 14th centuries

A **triolet** was a stanza poem of 8-lines, written in iambic tetrameter and rhyming ABaAabAB. The first, fourth and seventh lines are identical, as are the second and final lines (thus making the initial and final couplets identical as well). The **triolet** is related to the *rondeau*.

x x x x x x x A
x x x x x x x B
x x x x x x x a
x x x x x x x A
x x x x x x x a
x x x x x x x b
x x x x x x x A
x x x x x x x B

Jean Froissart (1337-1404) wrote a poem called *Rondel* (even though it is a **triolet**):

> Love, love, what wilt thou with this heart of mine?
> Naught see I fixed or sure in thee!
> I do not know thee,–nor what deeds are thine:
> Love, love, what will though with this heart of mine?
>
> Shall I be mute, or vows with prayers combine?
> Ye who are blessed in loving, tell it me:

Love, love, what wilt thou with this heart of mine?
Naught see I permanent or sure in thee![240]

Trobar clus
Genre
Country of Origin: Occitania (southern France, Monaco, Italy, Spain)
Distribution: Occitan
Century: unknown – 12th century

This "closed form" was a complex style of poetry by the troubadours for more discerning audiences. It was willingly written to be ambiguous, using obscure allegories, metaphors, languages and symbols. Due to its inaccessibility it disappeared by 1200.

Trobar leu
Genre
Country of Origin: Occitania (southern France, Monaco, Italy, Spain)
Distribution: Occitan
Century: unknown

A light style of poetry, easily accessible (in contrast to the *trobar clus*) and the most popular style used by the troubadours.

Trobar ric
Genre
Country of Origin: Occitania (southern France, Monaco, Italy, Spain)
Distribution: Occitan

---

[240] http://www.webexhibits.org/poetry/explore_obscure_triolet_examples.html, March 23, 2016

Century: unknown

Trobar ric was a troubadour style distinguished by its verbal complexity. Though more popular than *trobar clus*, it was not as popular as *trobar leu*.

U

Uaim

Device
Country of Origin: Ireland
Distribution: Irish
Century: unknown

Uaim is the use of alliteration in early Irish poetry. Only unaccented syllables should come between alliterated words. 'Fh' is silent, so **uaim** counts for the sound following it. "Ph" alliterates with itself and "f". "Sh" alliterates only with itself. *Urú* does not affect **uaim**, and *séimhiú* only affects "f", "p" and "s".

Uaithne

Device
Country of Origin: Ireland
Distribution: Irish
Century: unknown

Uatihne is the Irish term for consonance. The final consonants of a specific syllable must rhyme, but the preceding vowels cannot.

Urloup

Device
Country of Origin: Germany
Distribution: German
Century: 13th – 16th centuries

In a *tagelied*, the **urloup** is the giving of permission to the knight from her lady love to depart at dawn.

Urú
Device
Country of Origin: Ireland
Distribution: Irish
Century: unknown

Urú is eclipsis; that is the omission of words required to fully express the sense of a phrase. It does not affect *uaim* (alliteration).

V

Vanto
Genre
Country of Origin: France?
Distribution: unknown
Century: unknown

The **vanto** was a boastful poem in the troubadour tradition[241].

Venus and Adonis Stanza
Form
Country of Origin: England
Distribution: English
Century: 16th century

This stanza form, invented by Shakespeare, used six lines written in iambic pentameter and rhyming ababcc. The form takes its name from the poem where Shakespeare introduced it, *Venus and Adonis* (1593).

x x x x x x x x x a
x x x x x x x x x b
x x x x x x x x x a
x x x x x x x x x b
x x x x x x x x x c
x x x x x x x x x c

---

[241] Bernard Dov Cooperman: 155.

Venus and Adonis reads in part:

> Shakespeare. Even as the sun with purple-colour'd face
> Had ta'en his last leave of the weeping morn,
> Rose-cheek'd Adonis hied him to the chase;
> Hunting he loved, but love he laugh'd to scorn;
> Sick-thoughted Venus makes amain unto him,
> And like a bold-faced suitor 'gins to woo him.[242]

Vers

Form
Country of Origin: Provence (France)
Distribution: Provençal
Century: unknown

A **vers** was a song; very similar to the *chanso*. The subject matter of the **vers** could vary widely. They tended to have shorter and less complicated stanzas than the *chanso*, but have more of them.

Vers de société

Genre
Country of Origin: Provence (France)
Distribution: Provençal, English
Century: at least by the 14th – 19th century

Vers de société were light verse, witty and ironic, and intended for a sophisticated audience. This form has antecedents from the time of the Greeks. In the 18th century the form found its way to England.

---

[242] Lines 21-26.
http://www.opensourceshakespeare.org/views/poems/poem_view.php?WorkID=ve nusadonis, March 23, 2016

"To the Virgins to Make Much of Time" by Robert Herrick is an example of **vers de société**:

> GATHER ye rose-buds while ye may,
> Old Time is still a-flying;
> And this same flower that smiles to-day,
> To-morrow will be dying.
>
> The glorious lamp of heaven, the Sun,
> The higher he's a getting,
> The sooner will his race be run,
> And nearer he's to setting.
>
> That age is best, which is the first,
> When youth and blood are warmer;
> But being spent, the worse, and worst
> Times still succeed the former.
>
> Then be not coy, but use your time,
> And while you may, go marry:
> For having lost but once your prime,
> You may forever tarry.[243]

Verset
Genre
Country of Origin: unknown
Distribution: unknown
Century: 15th century

This 15th century form was derived from the verses of the Bible. It was religious or patriotic and made use of alliteration, assonance, rhyme, anaphora, rhetoric or any other poetic devices.

---

[243] Carolyn Wells: 15-16.

Versi sciolti

Form
Country of Origin: Italy
Distribution: Italian, English
Century: 16th century

This "heroic verse" form used unrhymed hendecasyllabic lines. Some sources state the principal accent should be on the tenth syllable. It was developed to translate ancient Greek and Roman poetry into Italian. It was also considered a conversational form.[244]

x x x x x x x x x **x** x *

…

* (Perhaps with principal accent on second last syllable.)

Fabio Galeota wrote *Egloga Amarilli Elpida* in **versi sciolti**:

> Lunge dal mar a piedi al gran Vesuuio;
> Là, doue il ciel nouellamente spoglia
> L'herbe a la terra, et l'ornamento al mondo;
> Staua Elpida doglioso, e'l suo cordoglio
> Non potea nascer d'altro, che di morte.[245]

> [Beside the sea at the foot of great Vesuvius, there where heaven keeps stripping the plants from the earth and beauty from the world, Elpida lived in sorrow, and his heartache could give birth to nothing other than his death.][246]

---

[244] David G. Allen and Robert A. White: 121.

[245] Christopher J. Warner: 43.

[246] Ibid.

Verso de arte mayor
(Form, Castilian)

See *arte mayor*.

Verso pareado
Form
Country of Origin: Spain
Distribution: Spanish
Century: 14th – 15th centuries

Verso pareado were rhyming couplets in hendecasyllabic lines.

x x x x x x x x x x a
x x x x x x x x x x a
x x x x x x x x x x b
x x x x x x x x x x b

Verso sdrucciolo
Device
Country of Origin: Italy
Distribution: Italian
Century: unknown

This term referred to ending a line with an accent on the antepenultimate (third last) syllable.

Verso suelto
Device
Country of Origin: Spain
Distribution: Spanish
Century: 16th – 17th centuries

A form of blank verse, **verso suelto** used hendecasyllabic lines with no rhyme.

x x x x x x x x x x x

...

Viadera
Genre
Country of Origin: Catalonia (Spain), Occitania (southern France, Monaco, Italy, Spain)
Distribution: Catalan, Occitan
Century: 13th century

A lyric genre of the troubadours; a dance song designed to lighten the mood during a long voyage or journey. It was not often used by cultivated poets and was considered low-brow and bawdy. Also known as *viadeyra* and *viandla*. Frank M. Chambers asserts that this should not be considered a genre at all[247] as it applied only to one composition by Cerverí de Girona (fl. 1259–1285):

> No ·l prenatz lo fals marit,
> Jana delgada!
>
> I No ·l prenatz lo fals jurat,
> que pec es mal enseynat,
> Yana delgada.
>
> II No'l prenatz lo fals marit,
> que pes es ez adormit,
> Yana delgada.
> III Que pec es mal enseynat,

---

[247] Frank M. Chambers 1: 196.

no sia per vos amat,
Yana delgada.

IV Que pec es ez adormit,
no jaga amb vos el lit,
Jana delgada.

V No sia per vos amat,
mes val cel c'avetz privat,
Yana delgada.

VI No jaga ab vos el lit;
mes vos y valra l'amich,
Yana delgada.[248]

Viadeyra
(Genre, Catalan, Occitan)

See *viadera*.

Viandela
(Genre, Catalan, Occitan)

See *viadera*.

Villancico
Form
Country of Origin: Iberian Peninsula (Spain)
Distribution: Iberian
Century: 15th – 18th centuries

The **villancico** (which is both the name of the form and the

---

[248] http://bojosperlalite.blogspot.ca/2011/04/nol-prenatz-lo-fals-marit.html, March 23, 2016

opening strophe of the poem) was a song opening with a **villancio**, followed by several (often six) *glosa* (strophes) with each *glosa* followed by an *estribillo*[249] (of two to four lines). Some sources call the opening the *estribillo*, the following strophes *copla* which split into *mudanza* and *vuelta* (with the last line of the *mudanza* and the *vuetla* sharing rhyme).[250] Lines were often six to eight syllables. The subject matter could be religious or vernacular and the poem was meant to be sung as a carol.

The following is the opening of a poem by Juan del Encina (1468 – 1529?) which demonstrates the *villancio* opening, a *glosa* and an *estribillo*:

No te tardes que me muero,   (*villancio*)
carcelero,
no te tardes que me muero.

   Apresura tu venida   (*glosa*)
porque no pierda la vida,
que la fe no está perdida.

   Carcelero,   (*estribillo*)
no te que me muero…[251]

[Do not be long, I am dying, gaoler; do not be long, I am dying. Come quickly, that I may not lose my life, for I have not lost faith. Goaler, do not be long, I am dying…][252]

---

[249] Arthur Terry: 4.

[250] http://www.britannica.com/art/villancico, March 23, 2016

[251] Arthur Terry: 4.

[252] Ibid.

Villanelle

Form
Country of Origin: France
Distribution: French
Century: unknown – 19th centuries

The **villanelle** was one of the *formes fixes*. Originally, the form was a simple *ballad*-like song with no fixed form, with the hard set rules not being enforced until at least the 16th century (by the poet Passerat, d. 1602[253]). By then, the *villanelle* was a 19-line form consisting of five tercets followed by a quatrain. There are two refrains and two repeating rhymes, with the first and third line of the first tercet repeated alternately until the last stanza, which includes both repeated lines. This can be expressed as: A1 b A2 / a b A1 / a b A2 / a b A1 / a b A2 / a b A1 A2. Initially, the subject matter of the **villanelle** was pastoral.

The villanelle was not used very often by English poets until the late 19th century[254].

Below is how a 17th century *villanelle* would look written in pentameter:

x x x x x x x x x A1
x x x x x x x x x b
x x x x x x x x x A2

x x x x x x x x x a
x x x x x x x x x b

---

[253] Wynne-Davis: 998.

[254] Ibid.

x x x x x x x x x A1

x x x x x x x x x a
x x x x x x x x x b
x x x x x x x x x A2

x x x x x x x x x a
x x x x x x x x x b
x x x x x x x x x A1

x x x x x x x x x a
x x x x x x x x x b
x x x x x x x x x A2

x x x x x x x x x a
x x x x x x x x x b
x x x x x x x x x A1
x x x x x x x x x A2

The first (and some argue only) poem to be written in this format before the 19th century was *"J'ay perdu ma Tourterelle"* (pub. 1606) by Jean Passerat (1534 – 1602):

> J'ay perdu ma tourterelle :
> Est-ce point celle que j'oy ?
> Je veux aller après elle.
>
> Tu regrètes ta femelle,
> Hélas ! aussi fay je moy :
> J'ay perdu ma tourterelle.
>
> Si ton amour est fidelle,
> Aussi est ferme ma foy,
> Je veux aller après elle.

Ta plaincte se renouvelle ;
Tousjours plaindre je me doy :
J'ay perdu ma tourterelle.

En ne voyant plus la belle,
Plus rien de beau je ne voy ;
Je veux aller après elle.

Mort que tant de fois j'appelle,
Pren ce qui se donne à toy :
J'ay perdu ma tourterelle,
Je veux aller après elle.[255]

[I have lost my turtledove:
Isn't that her gentle coo?
I will go and find my love.

Here you mourn your mated love;
Oh, God–I am mourning too:
I have lost my turtledove.

If you trust your faithful dove,
Trust my faith is just as true;
I will go and find my love.

Plaintively you speak your love;
All my speech is turned into
"I have lost my turtledove."

Such a beauty was my dove,
Other beauties will not do;
I will go and find my love.

[255] http://thevillanelle.blogspot.ca/2009/05/jay-perdu-ma-tourterelle.html, March 23, 2016

Death, again entreated of,
Take one who is offered you:
I have lost my turtledove;
I will go and find my love.][256]

Villanesque
(Form, French)

See *villanelle*.

Virelai
Form
Country of Origin: France
Distribution: French
Century: at least 13th – 17th centuries

One of the *formes fixes*, the **virelai** (pronounced veer-uh-lay) was often used in poetry and music (it was, in fact, one of the most common verse forms set to music from the 13th to the 15th centuries).

If a **virelai** only had one stanza it was known as a *bergerette*.

Virelai written as songs in the 14th and 15th centuries had three stanzas and a refrain that is stated before the first stanza and again after each one. Within each stanza the structure used is the *bar form*. Within this overall structure, the number of lines and the rhyme scheme varied and often involved an alternation of longer and shorter lines. The refrain and the stanzas could be three, four or five lines each, with rhyme schemes such as aba, abab, aaab, abba, aaab or aabba. Each

---

[256] http://amandafrench.net/villanelle/?page_id=45, March 23, 2016

stanza is split in three sections with the first two sections sharing a rhyme scheme and the third sharing the rhyme scheme of the refrain. Usually, all three stanzas shared the same set of rhymes (which means the whole poem could be built on just two rhymes).

Below are examples of what the refrain and stanzas would look like in tetrameter:

Version 1

x x x x x x x a   OR
x x x x x x x b
x x x x x x x a

Version 2

x x x x x x x a   OR
x x x x x x x b
x x x x x x x a
x x x x x x x b

Version 3

x x x x x x x a   OR
x x x x x x x a
x x x x x x x a
x x x x x x x b

Version 4   OR

x x x x x x x a
x x x x x x x a
x x x x x x x b
x x x x x x x b
x x x x x x x a

Version 5

x x x x x x x a
x x x x x x x b
x x x x x x x b
x x x x x x x a

Below is *"Douce Dame Jolie"* by Guilliame de Machaut. The refrain rhymes AAAB (and is shown in italics). The three sections of the stanza are shown, with the first two sections having a rhyme scheme of aab (with a shortened second line) and the third section sharing the rhyme scheme of the refrain (aaab).

Douce dame jolie,
Pour dieu ne pensés mie
Que nulle ait signorie
Seur moy fors vous seulement.

Qu'adès sans tricherie
Chierie
Vous ay et humblement

Tous les jours de ma vie
Servie
Sans villain pensement.

Helas! et je mendie
D'esperance et d'aïe;
Dont ma joie est fenie,
Se pité ne vous en prent.

Douce dame jolie,
Pour dieu ne pensés mie
Que nulle ait signorie
Seur moy fors vous seulement.[257]

[*Sweet, beautiful lady*
For God's sake, do not think
That anyone rules over me
But you alone

For endlessly, and without falsehood
I have cherished you
And humbly

All the days of my life

---

[257] http://www.medieval.org/emfaq/composers/machaut/v4.html, March 23, 2016

I have served you
With no unworthy thought

Alas! and I beg
For hope and aid
For my joy is ended
If you do not take pity

Sweet, beautiful lady
For God's sake, do not think
That anyone rules over me
But you alone][258]

In the 15th century, when the **virelai** was no longer always set to music, its structure varied widely. Two of these variants (defined in the 17th century) are detailed below.

The *virelai ancient* had no refrain. It used an interlocking rhyme scheme between the stanzas. In the first stanza the rhyme scheme is aabaabaab (with the b lines being shorter in length). In the second stanza the b rhymes are shifted to the longer lines and a new c rhyme is introduced on the shorter ones (bbcbbcbbc).

Below is an example in tetrameter and trimeter:

x x x x x x x a
x x x x x x x a
x x x x x b
x x x x x x x a
x x x x x x x a
x x x x x b

[258] http://lyricstranslate.com/en/douce-dame-jolie-sweet-beautiful-lady.html, March 23, 2016

x x x x x x x a
x x x x x x x a
x x x x x b

x x x x x x x b
x x x x x x x b
x x x x x c
x x x x x x x b
x x x x x x x b
x x x x x c
x x x x x x x b
x x x x x x x b
x x x x x c
…

The *virelai nouveau* (pronounced veer-uh-lay noov-oh) had a 2-line refrain at the beginning, with each stanza ending with a repetition of either the first or the second refrain verse in alternation, and the last stanza ending in both refrain verses in reversed order.

Below is an example in tetrameter with two quatrain stanzas:

x x x x x x x R1
x x x x x x x R2

x x x x x x x x
x x x x x x x x
x x x x x x x x
x x x x x x x R1

x x x x x x x x
x x x x x x x x
x x x x x x x x
x x x x x x x R2

x x x x x x x R2
x x x x x x x R1

Virelai ancient
(Form, French)

See *virelai*.

Virelai nouveau
(Form, French)

See *virelai*.

Visa
Form
Country of Origin: Iceland?
Distribution: Norse
Century: unknown

A verse; made up of two *vísuhelmingr*.

Vísufjórðungar
Form
Country of Origin: Iceland
Distribution: Norse
Century: unknown

A pair of lines; a couplet, the fourth of a verse.

Vísuhelmingr
Form
Country of Origin: Iceland?
Distribution: Norse

Century: unknown

A half-verse, made up of two *vísufjórðungar*.

Vuelta
Device
Country of Origin: Spain
Distribution: Spanish
Century: unknown

A **vuelta** was a repetition of one or more lines from an introductory stanza.

Wächterlied
(Genre, German)

See *tagelied.*

Wappendichtung
Genre
Country: Germany
Distribution: German
Century: 13ᵗʰ century

A **wappendichtung** was a poem that described a coat of arms and was also known as *heroldsdichtung.*

Der Schwanritter ("The Swan Knight") by Konrad von Würzburg (1220/1230 – 1287) is thought by some to be an early example of this genre.[259] It begins:

> befitzen fine hêrfchaft.
> fëht, alfus wart dô kriechaft
> dër herzog ûz dër Sahfen lant
> mit dirre frouwen alzehant
> umb ir liute und umb ir gout;
> durch finen hôhen übermuot
> beftuont ër fi mit ftrîte.[260]

---

[259] Marian E. Gibbs and Sidney M. Johnson: unnumbered page.

[260] Lines 1-7.

See also *blason*.

Z

Zagal
(Form, English)

See *zéjel*.

Zéjel
Form
Country of Origin: Spain (with Arabic roots)
Distribution: Spanish, English
Century: examples found at least by the 10th century

The **zéjel** (anglicized as *zagal*) was a poem with an introductory strophe containing the theme about to be developed in the following strophes, which were patterned as follows: a mono-rhymed tercet (called a *mudanza*), followed by a *vuelta* (repetition) of one line or more that rhymed with the introductory stanza. The simplest form is the 4-verse which rhymed aaab, cccb, etc., with the b rhyme remaining constant throughout. Multiple variations are known; octosyllabic lines are common. The **zéjel** is likely Arabic in origin and introduced during the Muslim occupation of Spain.

Below is a simple example showing the introductory strophe, and the first strophe of the body of the poem in tetrameter and with a *vuelta* of only one line:

x x x x x x x b (intro strophe)
x x x x x x x b

x x x x x x x a (*mudanza* – line 1)
x x x x x x x a (*mudanza* – line 2)
x x x x x x x a (*mudanza* – line 3)
x x x x x x x b (*vuelta*)

…

Glossary

Abesang: Part of the German *bar form*, meaning "after-song," which followed the stollen.

Alphaeresis: The loss of sound or sounds at the beginning of the word.

Anapest: A metrical foot. In classical meters it has two short syllables followed by a long one. In accentual stress meters it has two unstressed syllables followed by one stress syllable. This can be represented thusly: ˘ ˘ — The anapest foot works well in trimeter, tetrameter and hexameter.

Apocope: The loss of a sound or sounds from the end of a word, especially the loss of an unstressed vowel.

Assonance: Repetition of vowel sounds to create internal rhyming. The words cloud, proud and round are assonating words.

Aufgesang: Part of the German *bar form* consisting of two stollen.

Ballad stanza:

Beat: A syllable.

Breton: A Brittonic language brought to Amorica from Great

Britain in the early Middle Ages by migrating Britons. It is a Celtic language from Brittany.

Caesura: A complete pause in a line of poetry.

Catachresis: Using a word or phrase in an unconventional way.

Clos: The ending of the second stollen in the German *bar form*.

Cobla: Stanza.

Consonance: The repetition of the same consonant two or three times in quick succession.

Contraction: Poetic contraction is the removal of consonants to make certain words fit the meter being used. One example is "o'er" instead of "over".

Decasyllabic: Having 10-syllables.

Dialysis: An argument that divides its terms by first stating a premise, then listing reasons and ending with a conclusion.

Doggerel: Light verse of a trivial nature, usually written in an irregular style with obvious rhymes. Sometimes used as a vehicle for parody.

Elegiac: In the form of an elegy (a poem remembering the dead).

Envoi: A concluding stanza.

Epistle: A letter.

Half rhyme: Also called off-rhyme, slant rhyme, near-rhyme or lazy rhyme, half rhyme is a type of rhyme where formed by words with similar but not identical sounds.

Head-rhyme: Also called beginning rhyme, head-rhyme is a type of consonantal alliteration at the beginning of words.

Hemistich: A half-line of verse, which is followed and preceded by a caesura.

Hendecasyllable: A line of 11-syllables.

Heptameter: A type of meter with seven metrical feet.

Hiatus: When two vowel sounds occur in adjacent syllables with no intervening consonant.

Iamb: A metrical foot consisting of an unstressed syllable followed by a stressed syllable. It can be represented thusly: ⌣ — Probably the most popular iambic meter is iambic pentameter.

Jongleur: A minstrel.

Lyric: A form of poetry that expressed personal emotions and feelings and which is usually told in the first person.

Melody: Rhythm or meter.

Minnesingers: German poets and singers.

Monorhyme: A rhyme scheme where every line uses an identical rhyme.

Occitan: A language native to France, Spain, Italy and

Monaco, which has several different dialects.

Octosyllable: A line with 8-syllables.

Ouvert: The ending of the first stollen in the aufgesang of the German *bar form*.

Oxytonic: Having a stress on the last syllable.

Paranomasia: A play on words; a pun.

Pentameter: A line with 5-feet (iambs) or 10-syllables.

Perfect rhyme: Also called full rhyme, exact rhyme or true rhyme, perfect rhyme is a form of rhyme where the stressed vowel sound in both words is identical as are any subsequent sounds. Also, the articulation that precedes the vowels must differ.

Quatrain: A stanza or poem of 4-lines.

Quintain: A stanza of a poem of 5-lines.

Refrain: A section of a poem that repeats throughout, usually at the end of stanzas or the poem itself.

Respos: A refrain.

Rimes croisées: Crossed rhyme is when the word at the end of one line rhymes with a word in the middle of the preceding or following lines.

Sixain: A stanza of 6-lines.

Strophe: A structural division of a poem.

Stanza: A grouped set of lines within a poem.

Stich: A measured section of verse; a line of poetry.

Stollen: Part of the German *bar form*, the stollen are two halves of a stanza and are followed by the abesang. Collectively, the two stollen are called the aufgesang.

Syncope: The loss of one or more sounds from the interior of a word, especially an unstressed vowel.

Synizesis: When two syllabic vowels are pronounced as a single syllable with no change in writing.

Tail-rhyme: A verse rhyme in which a set of rhymes lines (such as a tercet) is followed by a tail (a line of different — usually shorter — length that does not rhyme with the preceding lines. In a tail-rhyme stanza, the tails rhyme with each other.

Tercet: A stanza of three lines.

Ternary movement: A three part musical form where the first section (A) repeats after the second section (B).

Tetrameter: A line of four metrical feet.

Trimeter: A line of three metrical feet.

Trochee: A metrical foot in formal poetry consisting of a stressed syllable followed by an unstressed one. This can be represented thusly: — ˘

Troubadour: A class of medieval poets in the 11th to 13th centuries.

Sources: On-line

Academic Dictionaries and Encyclopedias,
http://universal_lexikon.deacademic.com/

Columbia University, http://www.columbia.edu

Dictonary.com, http://dictionary.reference.com/

Encyclopedia Britannica, http://www.britannica.com/

Encyclopædia Universalis,
http://worldserver2.oleane.com/fatrazie/fatras_et_fatrasie.ht
m

Exsultemus, http://www.exsultemus.org/#!2009-2010-flecha-
ensaladas/c1lri

Kveding – A Norse Tradition with Roots Older than 1000
Years, http://folk.uio.no/jonsm/open/Old-words-to-old-
tunes/Kveding-aNorseTradition.pdf

The Language of Poetry,
http://www.scoilgaeilge.org/academics/mairead/EarlyIrish
Literature/TheLanguageofPoetry.htm

Library of Congress, http://id.loc.gov/

Literary Kicks, http://www.litkicks.com/

Medieval Irish Poetry, http://suburbanbanshee.net/irishptr/

Old Germanic Poetry,
http://www.ancientworlds.net/aw/Article/569784

Oxford Online, http://oxfordindex.oup.com/

The Pig Pen, http://www.pigpenpoetry.com/

The Poet's Garret, http://www.thepoetsgarret.com/

Poetry Base / Poetry Gnosis, http://www.poetrybase.info/

Poetry Forms, http://popularpoetryforms.blogspot.ca/

Poetry Foundation, http://www.poetryfoundation.org/

Poetry Magnum Opus,
http://www.poetrymagnumopus.com/

The Poetry of Senex Caecilius,
http://lonestar.texas.net/~robison/poetry.html

Poets Collective, http://poetscollective.org/

Representative Poetry On-line,
https://tspace.library.utoronto.ca/html/1807/4350/terminol
ogy.html

Scriobhe.ie, http://www.scriobh.ie/Default.aspx?l=2

Shadow Poetry, http://www.shadowpoetry.com/

Yeah Write, http://yeahwrite.me/writing-help-drottkvaett/

Sources: Print

Ap Gwilm, Dafydd. Dafydd ap Gwilim: the poems. Loomis, Richard Morgan, trans. Center for Medieval and Early Renassaince Studies, Binghamton, NY, 1982. https://archive.org/stream/dafyddapgwilympo00dafyuoft/dafyddapgwilympo00dafyuoft_djvu.txt, March 23, 2016

Allen, David G. and Robert A. White, eds. The Work of Dissimiltude: Essays from the Sixth Citadel Conference on Medieval and Renassaince Literature. University of Delaware Press, Newark, 1992.

Apel, Willi. Harvard Dictionary of Music. 2nd ed. The Belknap Press of Harvard University Press, Cambridge, Mass., 2000.

Arden, Heather. Fool's Plays: A Study of Satire in the Sottie. Cambridge University Press, New York, 2010.

Baldick, Chris. The Concise Oxford Dictionary of Literary Terms. Oxford University Press, New York, 1990.

Barbé, Louis. "Ulrich von Liechtenstein." The Eclectic Magazine of Foreign Literature, Science and Art, Volume 40. E. R. Pelton, New York, 1884.

Birch, Dinah, ed. The Oxford Companion to English Literature. 7th ed. Oxford University Print: Oxford, 2009.

Bleiberg, Germán, et al, eds. <u>Dictionary of the Literature of the Iberian Penninsua: A-K</u>. Greenwood Press, Westport, Conneticut, 1993.

Bleiberg, Germán, et al, eds. <u>Dictionary of the Literature of the Iberian Penninsua: L-Z</u>. Greenwood Press, Westport, Conneticut, 1993.

Boase, Alan, ed. <u>The Poetry of France, Volume 1: 1400-1600</u>. Methuen and Co, Ltd.: London, 1964.

Boccaccio, Giovanni. <u>La Treseide</u>. 2nd ed. Della Bibloteca Scelta, Milan, 1837.

Brand, Peter and Lino Pertile, eds. <u>The Cambridge History of Italian Literature. Revised edition</u>. Cambridge University Press, Cambridge, 2001.

Brittain, F. <u>The Medieval Latin and Romance Lyric: To A.D. 1350</u>. Cambridge University Press, Cambridge, 1937.

Bruch, Benjamin. <u>Cornish Verse Forms and the Evolution of Cornish Prosody, c. 1350-1611</u>. Ph.D. dissertation, Harvard University, 2005.

Burns, Jane E. <u>Courtly Love Undressed: Reading Through Clothes in Medieval French Literature</u>. University of Pennsylvania Press, Philladelphia, 2005.

Burt, Stephen and David Mikics, eds. <u>The Art of the Sonnet</u>. The Belknap Press of Harvard University Press: London, 2010.

Campbell, Jackson J. and James L. Rosier. Poems in Old English. Harper & Row: New York, 1962.

Carlquist, Erik and Peter C. Hogg, trans. The Chronicle of Duke Erik: A Verse Epic from Medieval Sweden. Nordic Academic Press, Sweden, 2012.

Cartwright, Kent, ed. A Companion to Tudor Literature. Wiley-Blackwell, Singapore, 2010.

Cayley, Emma. Debate and Dialogue: Alain Chartier in his Cultural Context. Oxford University Press, New York, 2006.

Chambers, Frank M. An Introduction to Old Provençal Versification. American Philosophical Society, Independence Square, Philadelphia, 1985.

Chambers, Frank M. Old Provençal Versification. Memoirs of the American Philosophical Society Vol. 167, Philadelphia, 1985.

Clarke, Dorothy Clotelle. "The copla de arte mayor." Hispanic Review 8.3 (Jul 1, 1940): 202.

Crétin, Guillaume. Les poesies de Guillaume Crétin. De l'Imprimerie d'Antoine-Urbain Coustelier, Imprimeur-libraire de S. A. R. Monseigneur, le Duc d'Orleans, 1723.

Cooperman, Bernard Dov, ed. In Iberia and Beyond: Hispanic Jews between Cultures. University of Delaware Press, Cambridge, 1998.

Cox, Virginia. Lyric Poetry by Women of the Italian Renassaince. The Johns Hopkins University Press, Batlimore, Maryland, 2013.

Croker, Thomas Crofton. "The Keen of the South of Ireland."

Early English Poetry, Ballads and Popular Literature of the Middle Ages: Edited from Original Manuscripts and Scare Publications. Vol. 13. Collier, J. Payne, ed. T. Richards, London, 1744.

Cropp, Glynnis M. "The Partimen between Folquet de Marseilles and Tostemps." The Interpretation of Medieval Lyric Poetry. Jackson, W. T. H., ed. Columbia University Press Limited, London, 1980.

Crotty, Patrick, ed. The Penguin Book of Irish Poetry. Penguin Books: London, 2010.

Cudden, J. A. Revised by M. A. R. Habib. A Dictonary of Literary Terms and Literary Theory. 5th ed. Wiley Blackwell, 2013.

Cushman, Stephen, ed. Princeton Encyclopedia of Poetry and Poetics, 4th edition. Princeton University Press, New Jersey, 2012.

Dance, Richard. "The Old English Language and the Alliteative Tradition." A Companion to Medieval Poetry. Saunders, Corrine, ed. Wiley-Blackwell: West Sussex, 2010.

De Berceo, Gonzalo. Richard Terry Mount and Annette Grant Cash, trans. Miracles of our Lady. The University Press of Kentucky, Lexington, Kentucky, 1997.

Deyermond, A. D. Epic Poetry and the Clergy: Studies in the "Mocedades de Rodrigo". Tamesis Books Limited, London, 1969.

Drury, John. The Poetry Dictionary. 2nd ed. Writer's Digest Books, Cincinnatti, OH, 2006.

Fenlon, Iain, ed. Early Music History. Studies in Medieval and Early Modern Music. University of Cambridge, New York, 1997.

Fladmark, J. M., ed. Heritage and Identity: Shaping the Nations of the North. Routledge, New York, 2002.

Foster, David William. Literatura española. Tomo 1: De los orígenes hasta 1700. Garland Publishing Inc., New York, 1995.

Foster, Davis William, et al, eds. Spanish Literature: A Collection of Essays. Garland Publishing Inc., New York, 2001.

Gade, Kari Ellen. The Structure of Old Norse Dróttkvætt Poetry. Cornell University Press, New York, 1995.

Gallagher, Patrick. The Life and Works of Garci Sanchez de Badajoz. Tamesis Books Limited, London, 1968.

Ganim, Russel. Renassaince Ressonance: Lyric Modality in La Ceppède's Théorèmes. Editions Rodopi B. V., The Netherlands, 1998.

Gaunt, Simon and Sarah Kay, ed. The Troubadours: An Introduction. Cambridge University Press, Cambridge, 1999.

Gibbs, Marian E. and Sidney M. Johnson, eds. Medieval German Literature: A Companion. Routledge, London, 2002.

Gilbert, Sarah. "The Secular Song of Spain: The Often Overlooked Contribution to European Renassaince Music." Term paper, Campbellsville University, undated. Web: http://www.campbellsville.edu/Websites/cu/images/Library/Campbellsville_Review/Vol._7_/Spanish_Madrigals_(2).p df, March 11, 2016

Gossett, Philip. <u>Divas and Scholars: Performing Italian Opera</u>. University of Chicago Press, Chicago, 2006.

Greene, David and Frank O'Connor, eds and trans. A Golden Treasury of Irish Poetry: AD 600 – 1200. MacMillan Company and Limited: London, 1967.

Greene, Roland, ed. <u>Princeton Encyclopedia of Poetry and Poetics</u>. 4th ed. Princeton University Press, New Jersey, 2012.

Greentree, Rosemary. <u>The Middle English Lyric and Short Poem</u>. Annotated Bibliographies of Old and Middle English Literature Vol. 7. D. S. Brewer, Cambridge, 2001.

Grismer, Raymond L., and Elizabeth Atkins. "The Book of Apollonius". *The Book of Apollonius*. NED - New edition. University of Minnesota Press, 1936. 3–113. Web: http://www.jstor.org/stable/10.5749/j.ctttv427

Groves, Peter Lewis. "Poulter's Measure". The Literary Encyclopedia. First published 04 June 2007 [http://www.litencyc.com/php/stopics.php?rec=true&UID=1760, accessed 21 March 2016.]

Gurney, Robert. <u>Bardic Heritage: A Selection of Welsh Poetry in Free English Translation</u>. Chatto and Windus: London, 1969.

Hasler, Antony J. <u>Court Poetry in Late Medieval England and Scotland</u>. Cambridge University Press, New York, 2011.

Hatto, A. T., ed. <u>Traditions of Heroic and Epic Poetry: Volume 1: Traditions</u>. The Modern Humanities Research

Assassociation, London, 1980.

Harr, James. <u>Essays on Italian Poetry and Music in the Renaissance, 1350-1600</u>. University of California Press, Berkely and Los Angeles, 1986.

Harmon, William and C. Hugh Holman. <u>A Handbook to Literature, Seventh Edition</u>. Prentice Hall, New Jersey, 1996.

Hendersen, Dave. <u>The Medieval English Begging Poem</u> (dissertation). University of Missouri-Columbia, May 2008.

Hirsch, Edward. <u>A Poet's Glossary</u>. Houghton Mifflin Publishing, New York, 2014.

Hollander, Lee M. <u>Old Norse Poems: The Most Important Non-Skaldic Verse not included in the Poetic Edda</u>. Columbia University Press, Morninside Heights, NY, 1936. Reprinted: Abela Publishing, London, 2010.

Hueffer, Francis. <u>The Troubadours: A History of Provençal Life and Literature in the Middle Ages</u>. Chatto & Windus, Piccadilly, London, 1878.

Hyde, Douglas. <u>The Story of Early Gaelic Literature</u>. T. Fisher Unwin, London, 1895.

Imbert, Barthélemy. <u>Choix de fabliaux: mis en vers</u>. Vol. 1. Chez prault, imprimeur du roi, Paris, 1788.

Kehew, Robert, ed. <u>Lark in the Morning: The Verse of the Troubadours. A Bilingual Edition.</u> The University of Chicago Press, Chaicago, 2005.

Kelly, Douglas. <u>Proceedings of the Symposium Held at the</u>

Institute for Research in Humanities, October 5-7, 1995, The Univeristy of Wisconsin-Madison. Editions Rodolpi B. V., Amsterdam, 1996.

Kennedy, Ruth and Simon Meecham-Jones, eds. Authority and Subjugation in Writing of Medieval Wales. Palgrave MacMillan, New York, 2008.

Kibler, William W. Medieval France: An Encyclopedia. Garland Publishing, Inc., New York, 1995.

Kinsley, James. The Oxford Book of Ballads. Oxford University Press: Oxford, 1969.

Kitchin, Darcy Butterworth. An Introduction to the Study of Provençal. Williams and Norgate, London, 1887.

Kirk, Alan K. The Composition of the Sayings Source: Genre, Synchrony, & Wisdom Redaction in Q. Koninklijke Brill NV, The Netherlands, 1998.

Kleinhenz, Christopher, ed. Medieval Italy: An Encyclopedia. Rutledge: New York, 2004.

Klink, Anne L., ed. Anthology of Ancient and Medieval Woman's Song. Palgrave MacMillan, New York, 2004.

Koch, John T., ed. Celtic Culture: A Historical Encyclopdia, Vol. 1. ABC-Clio, Inc., Santa Barbara, CA, 2006.

Konzett, Matthias, ed. Encyclopedia of German Literature. Fitzroy Dearborn Publishers, London, 2000.

Kroeger, A. E. The Minnesinger of Germany. The Riverside Press, Cambridge, 1873.

Kupier, Kathleen, ed. <u>Mirriam Webster's Encyclopedia of Literature</u>. Mirriam Webster, Springfield, Massachusetts, 1995.

Kupier, Kathleen, ed. <u>Poetry and Drama: Literary Terms and Concepts</u>. Britannica Educational Publishing, New York, 2012.

Lambdin, Laura Cooner and Robert Thomas Lambdin, eds. <u>A Companion to Old and Middle English Literature</u>. Greenwood Press, Westport, CT, 2002.

Lejeune, Denis. <u>The Radical Use of Chance in 20th Century Art</u>. Rodopi, Amsterdam, 2012.

Leo, Domici. <u>Images, Texts and Marginalia in a "Vows of the Peacock" Manuscript (New York, Pierpoint Morgan Library MS G24)</u>. Koninklijke Brill NV, Leiden, The Netherlands, 2013.

Lyon, Travis. <u>Forms of Poetry</u>. TeaLemon Publications, Pittsburgh, PA, 2003.

Machan, Tim William, ed. <u>Imagining Medieval English: Language Structures and Theories</u>. 500-1500. Cambridge University Press, Cambridge, 2016.

Macpherson, Richard and Ralph Penny, ed. <u>The Medieval Mind: Hispanic Studies in Honour of Alan Deyermond</u>. Tamesis, London, 1999.

Malcolm, Andrew and Ronald Waldron. <u>The Poems of the Pearl Manuscript</u>. York Medieval Texts, second series. University of California Press, Los Angeles, 1978.

Mancing, Howard. <u>The Cervantes Encyclopedia. Vol. 2: L-Z</u>. Greenwood Press, Westport, CT, 2004.

Marenbon, John, ed. <u>Poetry & Philsophy in the Middle Ages:</u> <u>A Festschrift for Peter Dronke</u>. Koninklijke Brill NV, Leiden, The Netherlands, 2001.

Marrone, Gaetan, ed. <u>Encyclopedia of Italian Literary Studies:</u> <u>Vol. 1: A-J</u>. Routledge, New York, 2007.

Marsh, George B. <u>A Compendious Grammar of the Old-</u> <u>Northern or Icelandic Language: Compiles and Translated</u> <u>from the Grammars of Rask</u>. Hiram Johnson & Co., Burlington, 1838.

McGinley, Kevin J. and Nicola Royan, eds. <u>The Apparelling of</u> <u>Truth: Literature and Literary Culture in the Reign of James</u> <u>VI: A Festschrift for Roderick J. Lyall</u>. Cambridge Scholars Publishing, 2010.

Metcalfe, Rev. Frederick. <u>History of German Literature: Based</u> <u>on the German Work of Vilmar</u>. Longman, Browne, Green, Longmans, & Roberts, London, 1858.

Murray, Christopher John. <u>Encyclopedia of the Romantic Era,</u> <u>1760-1850. Vol. 2: L-Z</u>. Fitzroy Dearborn, New York, 2004.

Myers, Jack and Don Wukasch. <u>Dictionary of Poetic Terms</u>. University of North Texas, Denton, Texas, 2003.

Neijmann, Daisy, ed. <u>A History of Icelandic Literature</u>. Vol. 5 of Histories of Scandinavian Literature. University of Nebraska Press, Lincoln, Nebraska, 2006.

Norberg, Dag. Ziolkowski, Jan, ed. Roti, Grant C. and Jacqueline de la Chapelle Skubly, trans. <u>An Introduction to the</u> <u>Study of Medieval Latin Versification</u>. The Catholic University of America Press, Washington, DC, 2004.

Newman, Barbara. <u>Frauenlob's Song of Songs: A Medieval German Poet and His Masterpiece</u>. Pennsylvania State University Press, University Park, PA, 2006.

O'Brien, John. <u>Focalóir gaoidhilge-sax-bhéarla: or, An Irish-English dictionary</u>. No publication information.

O'Donovan, John. <u>A Grammar of the Irish Language: Published for the use of the senior classes in the Colege of St. Columbia</u>. Hodges and Smith, Dubin, 1845.

Paden, William, D., ed. <u>Medieval Lyric: Genres in Historical Context</u>. University of Illinois Press, Chicago, 2000.

Paden, William D. and Frances Freeman Paden, trans. <u>Troubadour Poems from the South of France</u>. D. S. Brewer, Cambridge, 2007.

Paden, William D., et al, eds. <u>The Poems of the Troubadour Bertran de Born</u>. University of California Press, London, 1986.

Parini, Jay. <u>The Oxford Encyclopedia of American Literature. Vol. 1</u>. Oxford University Press, 2004.

Pedrick, Daniel Harvey. "Poetic Lisence: Lyrical Forms and Syncretic Fusion in al-Andalus." Academic paper, December 1999. Web: **http://carriagehousebandb.ca/poetic-license.html** Accessed: March 23, 2016

Peraino, Judith A. <u>Giving Voice to Love: Song and Self-Expression from the Troubadours to Guillaume de Machaut</u>. Oxford University Press, New York, 2011.

Parrish, Carl, ed. <u>A Treasury of Early Music: Masterworks of the Middle Ages, Renaissance, and the Baroque Era</u>. Dover Publications, Inc. Mineola, NY, 2000.

Parsons, James, ed. <u>The Cambridge Companion to the Lied</u>. Cambridge University Press, Cambridge, 2004.

Petrarch. <u>The Sonnets, Triumphs, and other Poems of Petrarch</u>. George Bell and Sons, London, 1875.

Poets World-wide. <u>Practical Poetic Anthology: A Genuine Glossary of Great Poems: Styles, Forms and Pageanted Portrayals</u>. Passion for Publishing Publishers: 2009.

Potts, Debbie. "Skaldic Poetry: A Short Introduction". Undated academic paper.

Preminger, Alex, ed. <u>Princeton Encyclopedia of Poetry and Poetics</u>. Princeton University Press, New Jersey, 1974.

Quiller-Cuch, Arthur, ed. <u>The Oxford Book of English Verse: 1250–1900</u>. Oxford University Press, 1919.

Quiller-Couch, Arthur, ed. <u>The Oxford Book of English Verse: 1250–1918</u>. Oxford University Press, 1984.

Rask, Erasmus. <u>A Grammar of the Anglo-Saxon Tongue, With a Praxis</u>. Thorpe, B., trans. S. L. Meller, Copenhagen, 1830.

Rasmussen, Ann Marie. "Gendered Knowledge and Eavesdropping in the Late-Medieval *Minnerede*." 2002.

Reichl, Karl. <u>Medieval Oral Literature</u>. Walter de Gruyter GmbH & Co. HG, Berlin, 2012.

Reichl, Karl. Singing the Past: Turkic and Medieval Heroic Poetry. Cornell University Press, Itaca, NY, 2000.

Race, William H. The Classical Priamel from Homer to Boethius. E. J. Brill, Leiden, The Netherlands, 1982.

Riccio, Ottone M. and Ellen Beth Siegel. Unlocking the Poem. iUniverse Inc., New York, 2009.

Rogers, Pat, ed. The Oxford Illustrated History of English Literature. Oxford University Press: Oxford, 1987.

Rosenberg, Samuel N., et al, eds. Songs of the Troubadours and Trouvères: An Anthology of Pems and Melodies. Garland Publishing, Inc., New York, 1998.

Rowland, Jenny, ed. A Selection of Early Welsh Saga Poems. The Modern Humanities Research Association, London, 2014.

Sayce, Olive. Exemplary Comparison from Homer to Petrarch. D. S. Brewer, Cambridge, 2008.

Scattergood, John. "The Jongleur, the Copyist, and the Printer: The Traditions of Chaucer's Wordes unto Adam, His Own Scriveyn." Keith Busby and Erik Kooper, eds. Courtly Literature: Culture and Contex: Selected Papers from the 5th Triennial Congress of the International Courtly Literature Society, Dalfsen, The Netherlands, 9-16 August, 1986. John Benjamins Publishing Company, Philadelphia, PA, 1990.

Schwyzer, Philip. Literature, Nationalism and Memory in Early Modern England and Wales. Cambridge Univeristy Press, New York, 2004.

Sfetcu, Nicolae. Poetry Kaledioscope. CreateSpace

Independent Publishing Platform, 2014.

Sisam, Celia, ed. <u>The Oxford Book of Medieval Verse</u>. Oxford University Press: Oxford, 1970.

Skelton, John. "The Tunnyng of Elynour Rummyng." <u>The Poetical Works of John Skelton. Vol I.</u> Rev. Alexander Dyce, ed. Boston: Little, Brown, and Company, 1866. 109-131.

Sharman, Ruth Verity. <u>The cancos and sirventes of Girault de Borneil: A Critical Edition</u>. Cambridge University Press, Cambridge, 1989.

Shaw, Mary Lewis. <u>The Cambridge Introduction to French Poetry</u>. Cambridge University Press: Cambridge, 2003.

Small, John. <u>The Poems of William Dunbar. Vol. 1: Introduction</u>. The Scottish Text Society. William Blackwood and Sons, Edinburgh, 1893.

Solling, Gustav. <u>Dintiska: An Historical and Critical Survey of the Literature of Germany, from the Earliest Period to the Death of Göethe</u>. Trübner and Co., London, 1863.

Soranzo, Matteo. <u>Poetry and Identity in Quattrocento Naples</u>. Ashgate, Surrey, England, 2014.

Stein, W. J. <u>The Ninth Century and the Holy Grail</u>. Temple Lodge Publishing, England, 2009.

Strachan, John and Richard Terry. <u>Poetry: An Introduction</u>. New York University Press, New York, 2000.

Suzuki, Seiichi. <u>The Meter of Old Norse Eddic Poetry: Common Germanic Inheritance and North Germanic</u>

<u>Innovation</u>. Walter de Gruyter GmgH, Berlin, 2014.

Talbot, Michael, ed. <u>Aspects of the Secular Cantata in Late Baroque Italy</u>. Ashgate, Surrey, England, 2009.

Terry, Arthur. <u>Seventeenth-century Spanish Poetry: The Power of Artifice</u>. Cambridge University Press, Cambridge, 1993.

Turco, Lewis. <u>The Book of Forms: A Handbook of Poetics</u>. 3rd ed. UPNE, 2000.

Von Eschenbach, Wolfram. Weston, Jessie L., trans. <u>Parzival: A Knightly Epic. Vol. 1</u>. G. E. Stechert & Co., New York, 1912.

Uitti, Karl D. <u>Story, Myth and Celebration in Old French Literature, 1050-1200</u>. Princeton University Press, Princeton, NJ, 1973.

Vidal, Peire. <u>The Songs of Peire Vidal</u>. Fraser, Veronica M., trans. Peter Lang, Germany, 2006.

Voretzsch, Karl. <u>Introduction to the Study of Old French Literature</u>. Slatkine Reprints, Genève, 1976.

Warner, Christopher J. <u>The Making and Marketing of Tottel's Miscellany, 1557: Songs and Sonnets in the Summer of the Martyrs' Fires</u>. Routledge, New York, 2013.

Wekerlin, J. B., ed. <u>Bergerettes: Romances and Songs of the Eighteenth Century</u>. Oliver Ditson Co., Boston, 1913.

Wells, Carolyn, ed. <u>A vers de société anthology</u>. Charles Scribner's Sons, New York, 1907.

Williams, Gym, trans. and ed. <u>Welsh Poems: Sixth Century to 1600</u>. University of California Press, Berkely and Los Angeles, 1974.

Woodring, Carl, ed. <u>The Columbia History of British Poetry</u>. Columbia University Press, New York, 1994.

Würzburg, Konrad von. <u>Der Schwanritter: Eine Erzählung</u>. Roth, Dr. Franz, ed. Gedruckt in C. Naumann's Druckerei, Frankfurt, 1861.

Wynne-Davies, Marion, ed. <u>Penguin Guide to English Literature: The New Authority on English Literature</u>. Viking: London, 1989.

Yandell, Cathy M. <u>Carpe Corpus: Time and Gender in Early Modern France</u>. Associated University Press, Cranberry, NJ, 2000.

Zwartjes, Otto. "Love Songs from al-Andalus: History, Structure & Meaning of the Kharja". <u>Medieval Iberian Penninsula Texts and Studies, Vol. XI: Love Songs from al-Andalus</u>. Rachel Arié and Angus MacKay, ed. Koninkklijke Brill, Leiden, the Netherlands, 1997.

INDICES

By Region

CASTILLE

CATALONIA

FRANCE

IBERIAN PENNINSULA

MONACO

THE NETHERLANDS

OCCITANIA

PORTUGAL

By Century

9th CENTURY

10th CENTURY

11th CENTURY

12th CENTURY

13th CENTURY

14th CENTURY

16th CENTURY

17th CENTURY

About the Author

Todd H. C. Fischer is a graduate of York University in Canada, with a double honours BA in English and Creative Writing, where he studied many different forms of literature and poetry. He has published 17 books on various subjects though Stonebunny Press, as well as a monograph published by *The Compleat Anachronist* (a medievalist journal). As well, Todd has had work appear in several small press publications around the world. Todd has been a member of the Society for Creative Anachronism (a medieval re-enactment group) for over a decade and a half, and has been recognized with several awards for his research into, and reproduction of, medieval writing (including poetry). You can read more about Todd on his website: **todd-fischer.com**

Manufactured by Amazon.ca
Bolton, ON

28880325R00245